MISSOURI
OUR HOME

Gibbs Smith, Publisher
Salt Lake City

This book is dedicated to my family, whose life-long support made this project possible. My grandparents and parents instilled in me a love of history and a love for Missouri. My wife, Susie, and my children, Becky and Micah, have always been proud that I am a teacher. Their love makes me the person I am.

—Jeff Gall

Published by
Gibbs Smith, Publisher
P.O. Box 667
Layton, UT 84041
800-748-5439
www.gibbs-smith.com/textbooks

Managing Editor: Susan A. Myers
Editorial Assistants: Jennifer Petersen, Courtney Thomas, Carrie Gibson
Cover and Book Design: Alan Connell
Maps and Graphs: Alan Connell

Cover Painting Credit:
Painting "Westward Travelers at Miller's Landing, 1843" by Gary R. Lucy. Courtesy of the Gary R. Lucy Gallery, Inc. Washington, Missouri – www.garylucy.com

The painting is a depiction of life as it was in a small Missouri River port in 1843. There were many landings along the river where travelers would stop for a rest or perhaps do some trading of goods. Today the site is known as New Haven, Missouri.

Background map: Library of Congress

Printed and bound in China.

ISBN 10 : 1-58685-428-3

ISBN 13 : 978-1-58685-428-3

12 11 10 09 10 9 8 7 6 5 4 3

ABOUT THE AUTHOR

Jeffrey Gall is a life-long Missourian. Born in Kansas City and raised in Independence, he taught high school history for 14 years in Lee's Summit. He received his Ph.D. in American history from the University of Missouri and since 1997 has taught U.S. and Missouri history at Truman State University. He also trains future high school history teachers.

As a public school teacher, Jeff Gall was a finalist for Missouri State Teacher of the Year, received the Milken National Educator Award, and in 1994 was named the Nation's Outstanding Teacher of American History. He believes successful teaching of history begins with a teacher who has a passion for the subject and loves working with young people. He knows that history is first a great story that can engage all children if they see an excitement for that story in the eyes of their teacher.

Jeff is an avid sports fan who teaches a course on the history of baseball at Truman State. He and his wife, Susie, enjoy small-town life in Kirksville. They have two grown children.

REVIEWERS

W. Raymond Wood earned B.A. and M.A. degrees at the University of Nebraska and a Ph.D. at the University of Oregon. He has taught anthropology at the University of Missouri since 1963. During that time he's been involved in archaeological and historical work in Missouri and in each of the states through which the Missouri River passes. He has extensively studied the Native Americans who lived along the Missouri River. One of his published books is *Prologue to Lewis and Clark*, published in 2002.

Charlene Chaffin is a fourth-grade teacher at Greenwood Elementary. As this book goes to press, Mrs. Chaffin is in her 24th year of teaching at the school that she attended as a child. She earned B.S.E. and M.S.E. degrees from Central Missouri State University. She lives on a farm in Cleveland, Missouri, with her husband and 10-year-old daughter.

Maria Bradshaw has taught in the Kirksville School District for over 22 years, including 16 years as a fourth-grade teacher. She has worked on various curriculum writing committees and is presently teaching night classes on computers at Moberly Area Community College. She is the Technology Educator/Webmaster at Kirksville High School. Mrs. Bradshaw received a B.S.E. from Northeast Missouri State University (now Truman State University) and an M.S.E. from Northwest Missouri State University. Mrs. Bradshaw lives outside of Kirksville on 120 acres with her husband and family.

Christine Crites teaches at East Carter R-II School. She earned a B.S. degree from Southeast Missouri University and is currently pursuing a master's degree. She lives on a farm in southeast Missouri with her husband and four children.

Contents

Chapter 1 History Close to Home 2
Chapter 2 Missouri's Place in the World 14
Chapter 3 The First People 46
Chapter 4 French and Spanish Missouri 68
Chapter 5 Missouri Becomes a State 96
Chapter 6 Gateway to the West 114
Chapter 7 Frontier Life 144
Chapter 8 The Civil War 170
Chapter 9 Reconstruction and Growth 190
Chapter 10 Into a New Century 208
Chapter 11 Modern Missouri 234
Chapter 12 Government for Missouri 248
Chapter 13 Making a Living in Missouri 266

Maps 282
Glossary 286
Index 290
Credits 294

Maps

Missouri, Our State 16
Where in the World Are We? 19
Missouri Map Skills 23
Ice Age Glaciers 25
Major Rivers and Lakes 26
Missouri Land Regions 29
Tornado Alley 39
Native People Used Natural Resources 51
Jolliet and Marquette's Route 74
North America After the American Revolution, 1783 91
The Louisiana Purchase 99
Lewis and Clark's Journey 102
The Missouri Compromise 110
The Santa Fe Trail 126
The Oregon Trail 128
Trails to the West 133
Choosing Sides, 1860 178
Missouri Counties and County Seats 259
From Missouri to the World 275
The United States of America 282
The World 284

Activities & Skills

Read a Timeline 5
Use a Table of Contents, Glossary, and Index 6
Use Reference Books 7
Examine a Current Document 9
Identify and Interpret Artifacts 10
Different Points of View 11
Calendar Time 13
Make a Mental Map 18
Longitude and Latitude 20
Missouri on the Map 22
Information on the Move 37
Your Hometown 45
What Is Your Global Address? 45
Indian Names 58
What Can We Use From Legends? 65
What Changed, and What Stayed the Same? 67
Cities and Rivers 79
A Primary Source: Big Soldier 107
Who Lived Here? Population Graph 112
Missouri's Borders 113
Record Information on a Chart 143
Child's Play 153
Make a Book: People on the Frontier 168
Use a Dictionary: Corn Clues 169
Answer With Art 169
Hardly Worth Eating 189
Write a Poem About Your Town 199
Trends Help Us Learn From Numbers 207
Meeting Our Needs 233
The Census: It Counts! 247
Write to Your Representatives 254
Volunteer in Your Community 263
Your Fair Share of Taxes 264
Local Laws 264
Make a Book About Government 265
The Pledge of Allegiance 265
How Much Does It Cost? 272
Make a Product Chart 273
Where Do Missourians Work? 274
Big Business 280
Technology Changes Agriculture 280
Understand a Budget 281
Make a Map of Places to Visit 281

Portraits

Auguste Chouteau 78

Daniel Boone 92

Mary Easton Sibley................... 106

James Beckwourth 120

Father Jean de Smet.................. 129

John Berry Meachum 166

William Wells Brown 166

Martha Jane Tolton................... 183

Susan Elizabeth Blow................. 193

Jesse James 194

Tom Bass 199

Mark Twain 202

Laura Ingalls Wilder............... 204

Scott Joplin 205

John "Blind" Boone............ 206

George Washington Carver 214

J.C. Penney 217

John J. Pershing 221

Harry S. Truman 222

Walt Disney 224

Yogi Berra 228

Helen Stephens 229

Thomas Hart Benton 230

Omar Bradley 237

Cool off in the water at Oceans of Fun in Kansas City.

MISSOURI State Symbols

State Tree:
Flowering Dogwood

State Mineral:
Galena (lead)

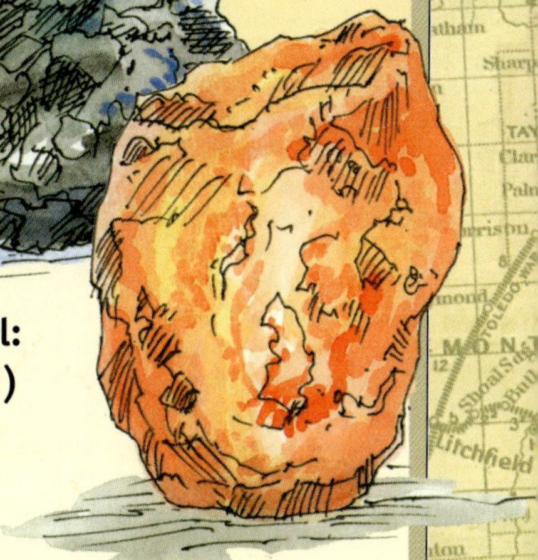

State Rock:
Mozarkite

State American
Folk Dance:
Square Dance

State Grape:
Norton/Cynthiana Grape

State Insect: Honeybee

State Flower:
White Hawthorn Blossom

Our State Flag

The Missouri state flag has one red, one white, and one blue stripe. The red stripe stands for valor (bravery). The white stripe stands for purity (goodness). The blue stripe stands for justice (fairness). The flag has the Missouri State Seal in the middle.

The original flag, made by Marie Elizabeth Oliver, can be seen at the Secretary of State's office in Jefferson City.

Our State Song

Missouri Waltz

Music by John Valentine Eppel as arranged by Frederick Knight Logan

Hush-a-bye, ma baby, slumber time is comin' soon;
Rest yo' head upon my breast, while mommy hums a tune;
The sandman is callin', where shadows are fallin',
While the soft breezes sigh as in days long gone by.

Way down in Missouri where I heard this melody,
When I was a little child on my mommy's knee;
The old folks were hummin', their banjos were strummin'
So sweet and low.

Strum, strum, strum, strum, strum,
Seems I hear those banjos playin' once again,
Hum, hum, hum, hum, hum,
That same old plaintive strain.
Hum, hum, hum, hum, hum,
That same old plaintive strain.

Hear that mournful melody,
It just haunts you the whole day long,
And you wander in dreams, back to Dixie, it seems,
When you hear that old song.

Hush a-bye, my baby, go to sleep on Mommy's knee,
Journey back to Dixieland in dreams again with me;
It seems like your Mommy is there again,
And the old folks were strummin' that old refrain.

Way down in Missouri where I learned this lullaby,
When the stars were blinkin' and the moon was climbin' high,
Seems I hear voices low, as in days long ago
Singin' hush a-bye.

"The only thing new in the world is the history you don't know."

— Harry S. Truman

History Close to Home

Chapter 1

Learning about history is kind of like going on a journey to the past. You can find new friends who lived long before you were born. You can get courage by seeing how they did what was right even if they were shy or afraid. You can learn that people everywhere have had hard times and good times.

LESSON 1

WORDS TO UNDERSTAND

glossary
index
reference books
table of contents

How to Use This Book

Welcome to *Missouri, Our Home*. You live in a state with an amazing past. In this book you will learn that Missouri is part of our country and our world. You will learn how people in Missouri lived many years ago and how they live today. You will think about things you can do to make Missouri a better place now and in the future.

This book has some special features that will help you learn about Missouri. Watch for them as you read.

Chapters: The Big Picture

This book is divided into chapters. Every chapter starts with a big picture. Look at what the picture is showing. It will give you clues about what you will read in the chapter. Pretend you can "step into" the picture. What do you see? What do you hear? What do you smell? What do you feel?

Timelines

At the beginning of most chapters, you will see a timeline. It shows the dates when things happened. If you study the timeline before you begin reading the chapter, you will get an idea of how long ago things happened. You will also learn which events came first and which came later.

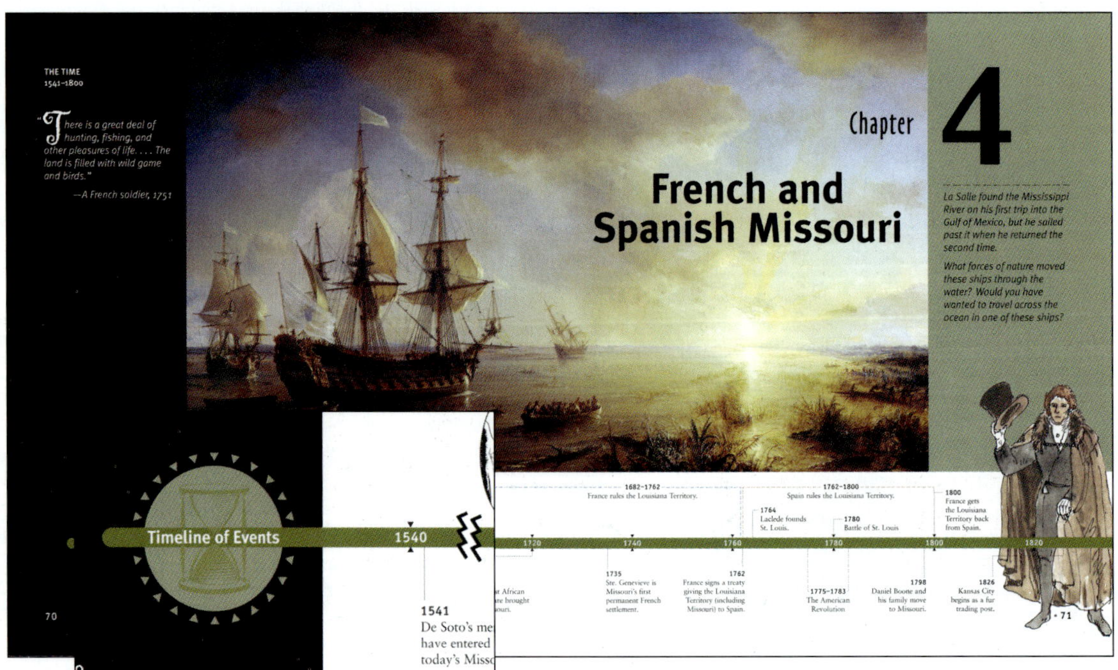

Activity

Read a Timeline

One way to learn about history is to use a timeline. A timeline helps us see the order in which things happened.

We read a timeline from left to right. The first events are usually on the left side. Look at the timeline below. What year does it start? What year does it end? In between, the time is divided into equal parts. There might be a mark every year, every 5 years, every 10 years, or every 50 years.

Jamal has written down some things that happened in his life. Use his timeline to answer the questions below.

1. What year was Jamal's baby sister born? How old was Jamal?
2. How long has Jamal had his dog?
3. Which happened later, Jamal earned his Bear Badge, or the family moved to St. Louis?
4. In 2004, Jamal got his own bedroom. Where would you place that event on the timeline?
5. Make a timeline of your own life. Decide what year to start and end your timeline. Put at least five events in the order in which they happened. Make sure the marks in between show equal amounts of time.

Lessons: Learning More

Each chapter is divided into lessons. Each lesson has some important lists.

- Can you read the names of the **People to Know**? They are people you will read about in the chapter.
- With your class, find the **Places to Locate** on a map. Are any of them near your city or town?
- Read the **Words to Understand** out loud with your class. Talk together about what the words mean. You can find each word in the back of this book in the Glossary.

What Do You Think?

Many questions have no right or wrong answer. In this book, "What do you think?" questions help you think about things you have read. They help you think about what you would have done if you had been in the story.

Linking the Past to the Present

So many events around us today have ties to the past. Because pioneer settlers cleared trees and rocks to make a path for their wagons, you might have a road today.

Portraits

Our state's history was made by people who had both hard times and good times. They worked and made mistakes. They helped others. In this book, you will find short biographies called portraits. They tell a little bit about a person's life.

Memory Master

At the end of each lesson you will find a few questions about what you have read. Test your memory and review what you learned.

Activities

In this book, activities are not like going outside to play soccer or ride a bicycle. They are ways to learn about history. They are fun to do alone or with a friend. Sometimes you will pretend you lived long ago. Sometimes you will draw a picture, write a poem or a story, or make a model with twigs, dirt, and rocks. You will read, research, and report in different ways.

Activity

Use a Table of Contents, Glossary, and Index

There are other tools to help you on your journey through this book. At the beginning of the book there is a ***Table of Contents.*** It tells you what pages the chapters start on. It also tells you where the maps and activities are. Go to the Table of Contents and read the title of each chapter.

At the end of the book, there is a Glossary and an Index. The ***Glossary*** explains the meaning of all the Words to Understand in the lesson. The ***Index*** lists the page numbers where you'll find important subjects, people, and places. Can you find the Glossary and Index pages?

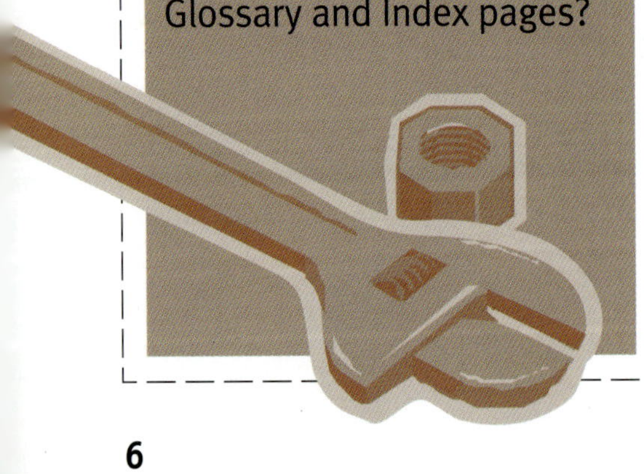

Activity

Use Reference Books

Before we study our state's history, it is fun to know some basic facts. Where can you find them? You can look up facts in ***reference books.*** They have many kinds of useful information. You might use an atlas, encyclopedia, or almanac. These are all reference books. You can also find information on the Internet.

- An **atlas** is a book of maps.
- An **encyclopedia** has information on many different topics. They are listed in alphabetical order so you can find facts quickly.
- An **almanac** is like a record book. It has all kinds of information, such as how many people live in a country, how much rain a city gets, or who the fifth president of our country was.

On a piece of paper, write your answers to the questions below. Choose which kind of reference book you would use to find the information.

1. If you wanted to learn about foxes, you could look in a(n) __________ or a(n) __________.
2. If you looked under "S" in a(n) __________, you would find topics like snakes, stars, and John Smith.
3. If you wanted to find the countries next to Mexico, you would look in a(n) ______________.
4. To find out how many days of rain people in Missouri get, you could look in a(n) _________.
5. What kind of reference book would you use to learn how far it is from your town to Jefferson City? ______________.

1 MEMORY MASTER

1. How can timelines help you learn about the past?
2. How can a Table of Contents help you use a book?
3. Do questions always have right and wrong answers? Explain.
4. In this book, another word for a biography is a ________.
5. What can you learn from a Glossary?
6. How can an Index help you learn about history?

LESSON 2

WORDS TO UNDERSTAND

document
fact
fiction
historian
opinion
oral history
primary source
secondary source

What Is History?

Look at the coins in your pocket. Which has the earliest date? Do you have a coin from the 1950s? The 1960s? Those coins were first carried by someone many years ago. Was she a student too? What was his school like? Have you heard your grandparents talk about life when they were young? All of these things have to do with the past.

History is the story of the past. It is the story of people and events. It is the story of what people thought, how they lived, and the choices they made.

For example, women, Native Americans, and African Americans were not allowed to vote for many years. Only some of their children went to school. Other children were not allowed in schools.

Then people made choices to change things because they believed there was a better way. Finally, leaders changed our government. Now almost all adults can vote. All children can go to school.

What do you think?

What if leaders had made different choices? How would our lives be different?

Learning from the Past

History was not always peaceful. Sometimes people worked well together to build homes and roads and make laws. Other times people fought over land, religion, and who should do the work. People often did not treat each other very well.

We can look back and see what mistakes people made. We can also see what good things people did. We can see how men and women were brave, honest, and worked very hard. We can see how they showed courage. By studying history, we begin to understand who we are.

What do you think?

- How can learning about the past help us today?
- What choices will you make today that might affect the future?

Think Like a Historian!

People who study history are called ***historians.*** In many ways, historians are like detectives. A detective tries to figure out who committed a crime. A historian tries to figure out what happened in the past. You can be a detective by asking questions such as:

- **What** happened?
- **Where** did it happen?
- **When** did it happen?
- **Who** took part in it?
- **Why** did it happen?
- **How** did it change things?

A historian uses clues from different sources to learn about the past.

Primary Sources

Diaries or journals, photographs, paintings, speeches, and old objects were made by people who lived at the time. These items are called ***primary sources.***

Pretend that your great–great–grandmother lived on a farm long ago. She wrote in a diary every day. Her diary would tell us what it was like to live in a time with no electricity and no cars. Her diary would be a primary source.

A Native American stone tool is another primary source. By looking at the stone tool, you might learn what materials the people found in nature.

Papers, letters, and official forms are called ***documents.*** A letter from a soldier is a document. A birth certificate is another kind of document. So is the first copy of the Constitution. Documents are also primary sources because they were made at the time.

Suppose your grandpa was remembering a time when he was a young soldier in the army. Then you used a tape recorder to record his voice as he was talking. If you could write down the words fast enough, you could also write down his words as he said them.

This kind of history is called ***oral history.*** Oral history is history that someone tells you out loud. We can learn a lot by listening to people's stories of the past. Oral histories are other forms of primary sources.

Activity

Examine a Current Document

Ask your parents to show you your birth certificate.

1. What does it tell you about your birth?
2. If a historian looked at your birth certificate 100 years from now, what could he or she learn about you?
3. What wouldn't this document tell a historian?

Photographs can be primary sources. This one shows the Vasquez family. They came to the United States from Spain. What clues do you see in the picture that tell what life was like for this family?

Can You Tell the Difference?

Compare the two images below. Can you tell why the photograph of Lincoln is a primary source and the statue is a secondary source?

This is a photo of Abraham Lincoln. It is a ***primary source.***

This statue was made long after Lincoln died. An artist created it to honor Lincoln. The artist used pictures and paintings of Lincoln to make it look like him. It is a ***secondary source.***

Activity

Identify and Interpret Artifacts

1. Do these items tell us anything about people of the past?
2. Choose one artifact. Write about why you think someone might have had it. What was it used for? How does it compare to something similar today?

Photo by Jean Crossman, Courtesy of the Amherst History Museum ◄

Secondary Sources

A ***secondary source*** is something written, said, or made by someone who was NOT involved in the event at all. A historian gathers primary sources from an earlier time or place. Then the historian, who was not even there at the time, writes a book or paints a picture about what happened.

For example, a book written today about steamboats in early Missouri is a secondary source. The author of the book gathers a lot of stories and pictures and puts them together in the book. But the author was not there to watch steamboats go up and down the river.

Stories and paintings are often secondary sources. What can you learn from a secondary source?

Use Many Sources to Learn More

Because there are many points of view, it is important to look at many primary and secondary sources to learn what really happened.

Amber loves to read. She went to the library and checked out an exciting story of a pioneer boy who moved to Missouri. Then she visited a museum and saw an old covered wagon and a pioneer boy's wrinkled shirt and straw hat.

Later, Amber's teacher showed her a faded map of old wagon roads. Then Amber's class read a diary of a red-haired 11-year-old boy who helped drive the oxen that pulled his family's wagon. The boy's father had drowned crossing a raging river.

What if the boy's mother had written the diary? What if the diary had been written by an African American boy who came to Missouri at the same time? Can you see how using many sources helps us learn about history?

Point of View

A primary source does not always tell what life was like for everyone at the time. What if your older brother remembers a trip to the zoo one way. He loved watching the furry apes with long arms, and then he wrote about them in his journal. You remember the zoo another way because you had a hard time leaving the huge elephant mother and her baby. You wrote about that in your journal.

A long time ago there were battles between settlers and Native Americans. A settler might say that they had to kill buffalo so the trains could go across the prairie. A Native American might say that no one should kill buffalo unless they needed the meat and the fur. As you read this book, think about different points of view.

What do you think?

- How can different points of view help you better understand why people did what they did?
- Why is it important to consider another person's point of view?

Activity

Different Points of View

Pretend teachers are talking about giving students more homework. Three students tell their points of view. Read what each student says, then answer the questions below.

Juan: I want to play, but it will be good for us to do more homework. We can learn more and maybe get into a better college when we grow up.

Sarah: I help baby-sit my brother after school. Then I have soccer practice. I don't have time to do more homework.

Keisha: They should just give us more time to do work in school. Then we wouldn't have to do it at home. We could do it instead of story time, or while we are waiting for lunch.

1. In your own words, what is each person's point of view?
2. Ask your classmates what they think about having more homework. Now how many points of view are there?
3. Do any of the students share the same point of view?

Fact or Opinion?

In history there are facts, and there are opinions. A ***fact*** is something you can prove. Here are some facts:

- Groups of Native Americans lived in today's Missouri before white settlers came.
- Lewis and Clark started exploring the West near St. Louis.
- The capital city of Missouri is Jefferson City.

An ***opinion*** is something someone thinks or believes, such as, "Strawberry ice cream is better than vanilla." Opinions often have words like "better," "best," "I think," "right," and "wrong" in them. They express a point of view.

It is important to know the difference between facts and opinions. Why? Because if something is a fact, we can trust that it is true. If something is an opinion, we need to look at some facts or other opinions to get a better idea of the truth.

Fact or Fiction?

Stories that people make up are called ***fiction.*** Some of your favorite stories are probably fiction. Writers imagined these stories. They didn't really happen. The people were not real.

Folklore is kind of like fiction. It is the stories we hand down to each other over time. Sometimes the stories get stretched. They may or may not be true. For example, Mike Fink was a real riverboat man, but people tell many stories that make him seem larger than life. "I can outrun, outjump, out-shoot, and out-brag any man on both sides of the river." Did Mike Fink really say that? No one knows for sure.

2 MEMORY MASTER

1. What is history?
2. Give an example of a primary source.
3. Give an example of a secondary source.
4. How can you learn more by using more than one source of history?
5. Why is it important to consider point of view?
6. What is the difference between fact and opinion?

Chapter 1 Review

From There to Here

On what day were you born? What has happened in your life so far?

At home, find some primary sources that tell about you, and bring them to class. You could bring a baby picture or one of your favorite toys from when you were younger. Maybe you could bring a copy of your birth certificate or one of your report cards.

What do these primary sources tell about you?

Activity

Calendar Time

When we learn about history, we often use dates. What do you do when you want to know what today's date is or how many months there are until your birthday? You probably look at a calendar. A calendar is a good tool for dividing up the time in each year. It shows us the months, weeks, and days in a year.

Find a calendar at home or in your classroom. Use the calendar to answer these questions:

1. How many months are in one year?
2. What month is it now?
3. What is your favorite month?
4. How many weeks are there in your favorite month?
5. How many days are in each week?

Make a Calendar

Make your own calendar on a piece of poster board. Show your favorite month. Use a ruler to draw the lines and make the boxes for all the days in that month. Draw a scene that shows something you love about the month. Leave some space at the bottom to tell why it is your favorite.

"For those who have seen the earth from space, . . . the experience most certainly changes the way we look at things. The things that we share in our world are far more valuable than those that divide us."

—Donald Williams, astronaut

Chapter 2

As seen from space, the earth looks like a big blue marble in a black sea. The shape of Missouri is not clear from so far away. To understand Missouri, we must look closer. We must find our place on our continent, our country, and our state.

Missouri's Place in the World

Missouri, Our State

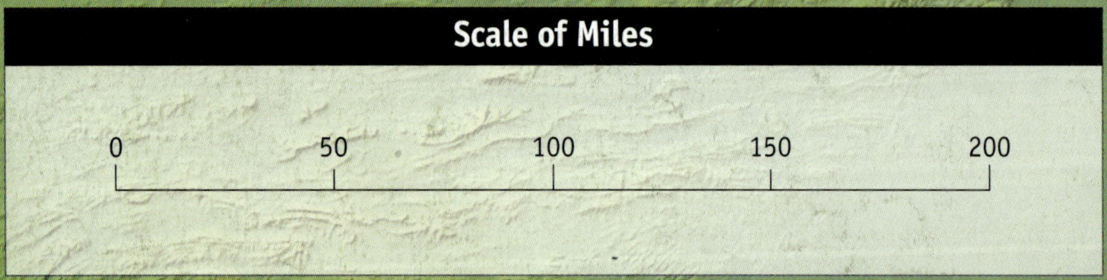

Legend

- ✪ Capital
- ◉ Large city
- ○ Medium city
- • Small city or town
- -·-·- State boundary
- ~ River

A Place Called Missouri

Long ago, when the first white explorers came here, they named the great river that runs through our state the Missouri River. It meant "People of the Big Canoe." This was the name of the American Indian people who lived along the river. Later, our state was called Missouri. People say the name in two ways. Some say "Missour-AH." Others say "Missour-EE." How do you say our state name?

Missouri seems very large, but it is just one small part of the world. Because we live in Missouri, it is important to us. It is our home. People all over the world live in places that are important to them.

WORDS TO UNDERSTAND

cardinal directions
geography
hemisphere
intermediate directions
latitude
longitude

Geography Makes a Difference

In this chapter, we will begin to learn about Missouri by studying its geography. ***Geography*** is the study of the land, water, plants, animals, and people of a place. We will examine where Missouri is located in the world. We will study Missouri's land and waterways. We will learn about the plants and animals that live in the state.

Many people in Missouri live in towns and cities on flat land near a river or a lake. Large boats carry products and people up and down our rivers. People swim, boat, and fish in lakes. Our land and water are very important to us.

Get up early in the morning and watch the sun rise in the East. It is a beautiful way to start the day.

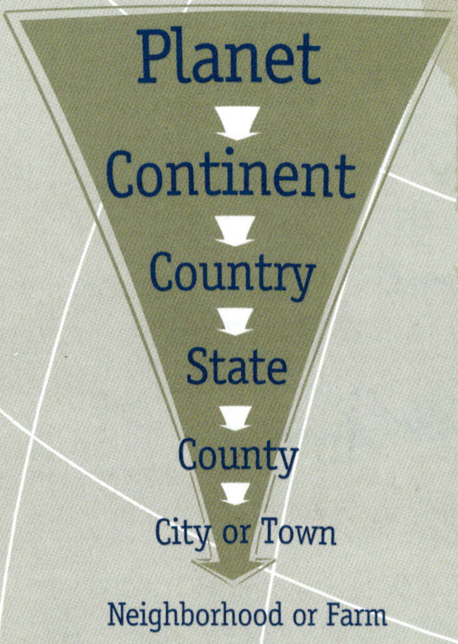

Where in the World Is Missouri?

We live on the planet Earth. But just where on the planet is Missouri located?

On a globe or world map, we see seven large land areas. They are called **continents.** Can you find and name them all? Missouri is on the continent of North America.

There are four very large oceans around the continents. Oceans are the earth's largest bodies of water. Can you find and name the four oceans? What oceans touch the borders of North America?

North America is divided into **countries.** A country is a land area with its own government. Our country is the United States of America. The country south of us is Mexico. Which country is north of us?

Our country has 50 **states.** Missouri is one of them. Eight states surround Missouri. What are they?

Counties, Cities, Towns, and Farms

States are divided into **counties.** Within counties there are cities, towns, villages, neighborhoods, and farms.

Do you live in a **town** or **city**? If you do, many other people live there, too. A city is usually larger than a town. Your neighborhood is a small part of your town. Maybe a friend lives nearby.

Do you live on a farm? If you do, your friends may live farther away. Your farm may be close to a city or far away.

Activity

Make a Mental Map

Study the shape of our state. Why do you think people call part of our state the "boot heel"? Now close this book. Can you draw Missouri from memory?

Now try it a second time. Was your second map better?

Where in the World Are We?

1. Our world is the **planet** Earth.

2. Our **continent** is North America.

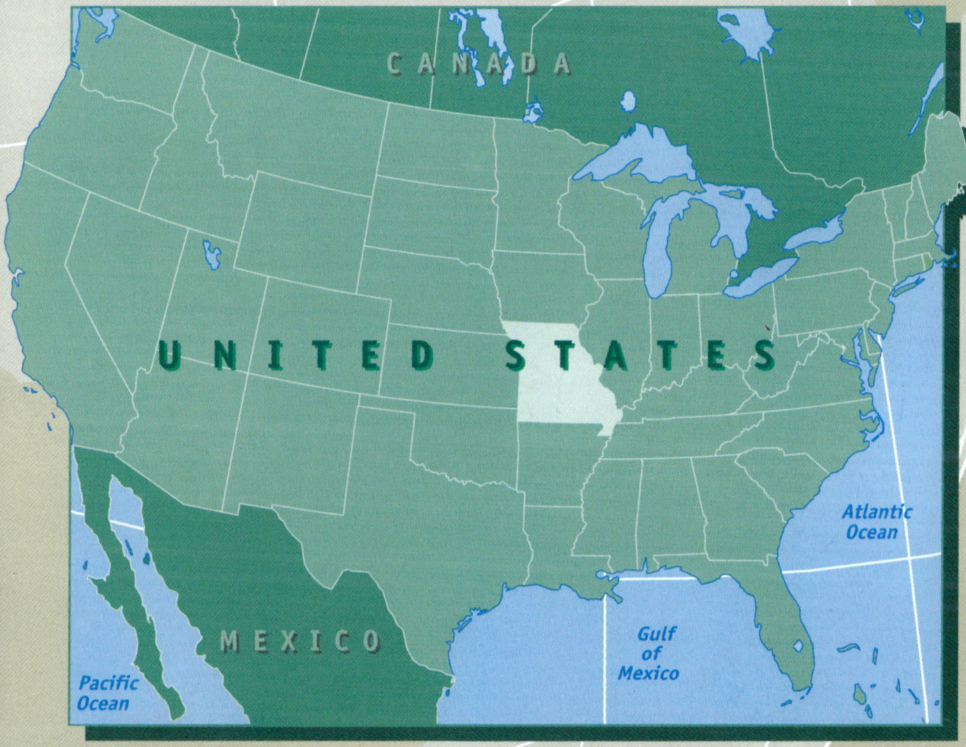

3. Our **country** is the United States of America.

4. Our **state** is Missouri.

Activity

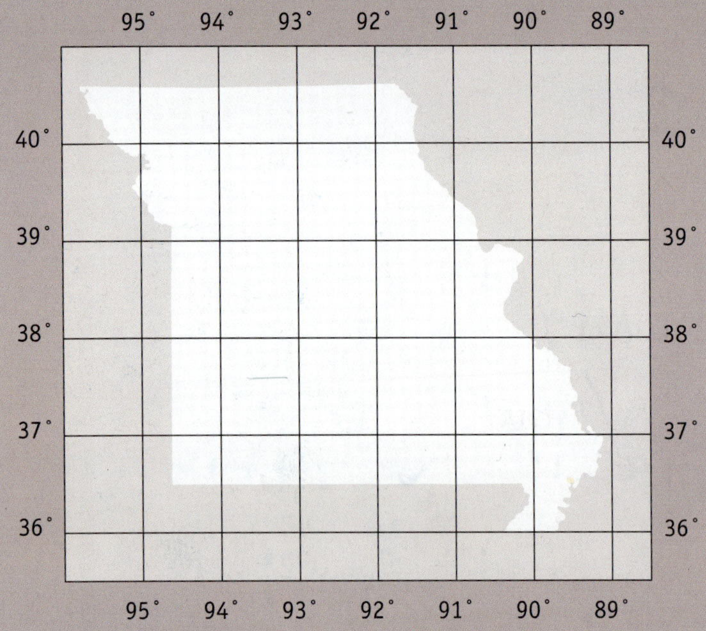

Longitude and Latitude

On this map, find Missouri's latitude (side to side) and longitude (up and down) lines. Use a globe in your classroom to trace these lines all the way around the world.

1. Which longitude line is nearest to the western border of our state?
2. Locate your town on the map. What latitude and longitude lines are nearest to you?

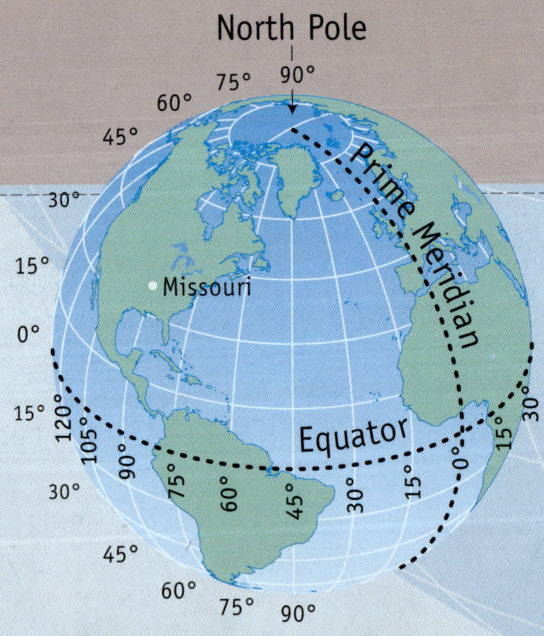

How Do We Locate a Place?

Pretend you meet some people from a different country and they want to visit your home. How would you tell them where to find it? There are two ways we can describe a location.

Relative location tells us where a place is in relation to other places or things. For example, Missouri is between Iowa and Arkansas. It is next to Illinois. You could tell someone you live near Table Rock Lake. Or your house might be near a college or a bank. What is the relative location of your school?

You often hear the words north, south, east, and west. You could say you live in southern Missouri, north of St. Louis, or on the west side of the Mississippi River. These would also be relative locations.

Absolute location is the exact spot where a place is located. An address is an absolute location. No other house is in the same place as yours. What is the address of your home or apartment? Your city is also in an absolute location. Every place on the earth has an absolute location.

Latitude and Longitude

We can use ***latitude*** and ***longitude*** lines to find an absolute location. These are the imaginary lines that you see on a globe or map. You could walk forever and never see a longitude line on the ground. They aren't real. If you were to step from Missouri into Iowa, you wouldn't see any line, either. The lines are only on maps and globes.

Look at the globe. Find the equator. It is the imaginary line that runs around the middle of the globe. The equator is a latitude line.

Now find the prime meridian. It is the imaginary line that runs from the North Pole to the South Pole through England. It is far across the Atlantic Ocean. The prime meridian is a longitude line.

Other latitude and longitude lines go north, south, east, and west of the equator and prime meridian. On a map, the lines cross each other to make a grid. Once you have the latitude and longitude of a place, you can use the grid to find an exact or absolute location of any place on the earth.

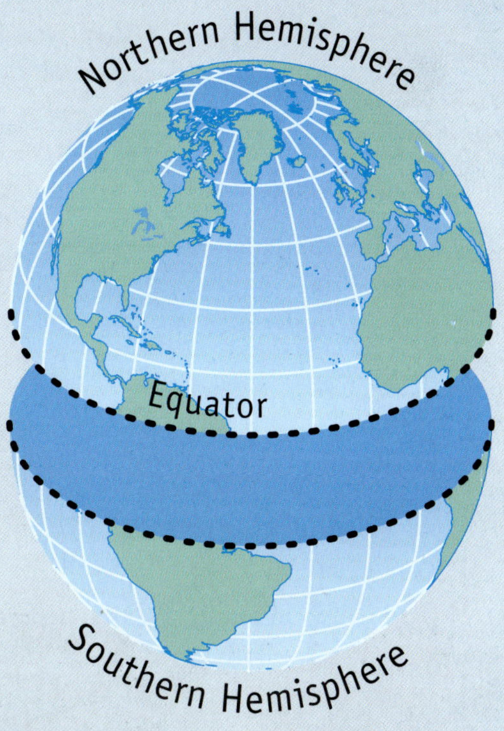

Hemispheres

There is another way we divide the earth. We pretend it is cut into two equal pieces. We call each half a ***hemisphere.***

Look at the drawings. Find the equator. Find the hemisphere north of the equator. Since north is nearly always "up" on a map, it is not hard to guess that the hemisphere north of the equator is the Northern Hemisphere. Find the hemisphere south of the equator. What is the hemisphere south of the equator called?

We can also divide the earth another way. We can cut it from the North Pole to the South Pole. We can make the cut directly down the prime meridian. Then we would have two different kinds of hemispheres. We would have a Western Hemisphere and an Eastern Hemisphere.

- Is Missouri in the Northern or Southern Hemisphere?
- Is Missouri in the Eastern or Western Hemisphere?

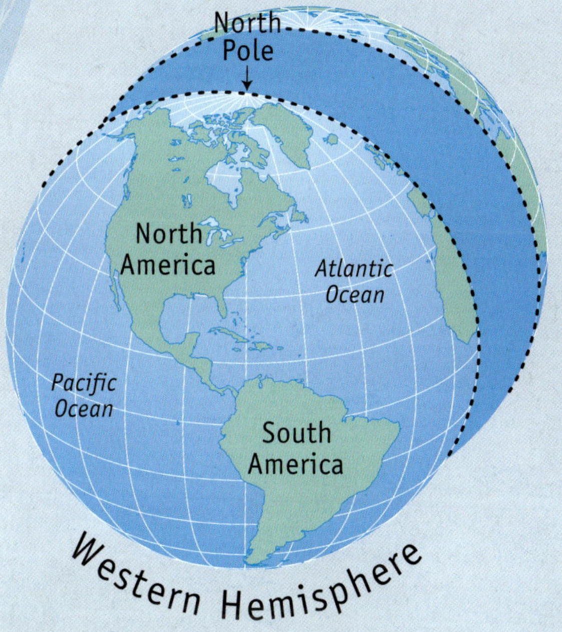

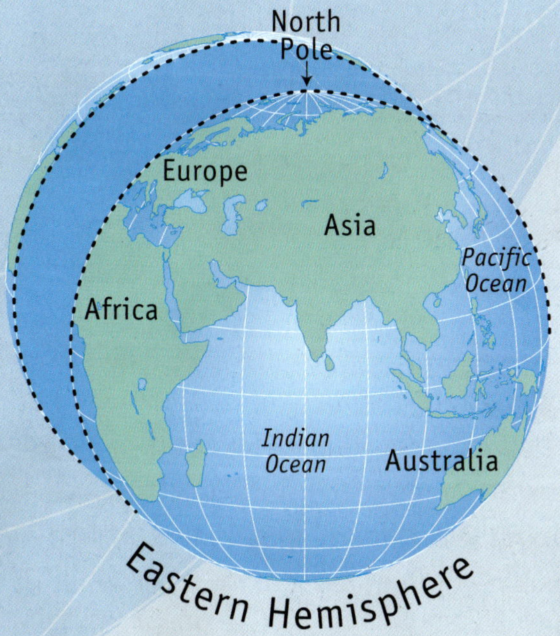

Reading a Map

There are many kinds of maps. Can you think of some? Maybe you thought of a treasure map! Maybe you thought of the road maps your parents use on trips.

Maps help us know where we are. They help us get where we want to go. Look at this map of Missouri. The colored boxes point to tools that help us read a map.

Activity

Missouri on the Map

Use the map to answer the questions:

1. What is the title of this map?
2. What symbols are shown on the map?
3. If you wanted to go from Springfield to Carthage, what direction would you go?
4. If you wanted to go from Jefferson City to St. Louis, what direction would you go?
5. About how many miles is it from Kansas City to Columbia?

Cardinal Directions:

Maps show the directions north, south, east, and west. We call these ***cardinal directions.*** You will find them on a compass.

Halfway between north and east is northeast, or NE. Halfway between south and east is southeast, or SE. These are called ***intermediate directions.***

Map Grid:

Latitude and longitude lines are one type of map grid. Sometimes grids use letters and numbers. On this map, numbers run across the top of the grid. Letters run along the sides. The location of a place can be described by where it is on a grid.

Scale of Miles:

To show us how far apart things are, map makers use a scale of miles. This helps us measure the distance between places.

One inch on a map might stand for 50 miles on real land. Or one inch might mean 100 miles or even more.

1 MEMORY MASTER

1. What is geography?
2. Give an example of a relative location.
3. Give an example of an absolute location.
4. What are the two kinds of imaginary lines on a map?
5. Where would you look on a map to see what the symbols stand for?

Title:

The first thing to look for is the title. It is usually at the top. It tells you what kind of information the map shows.

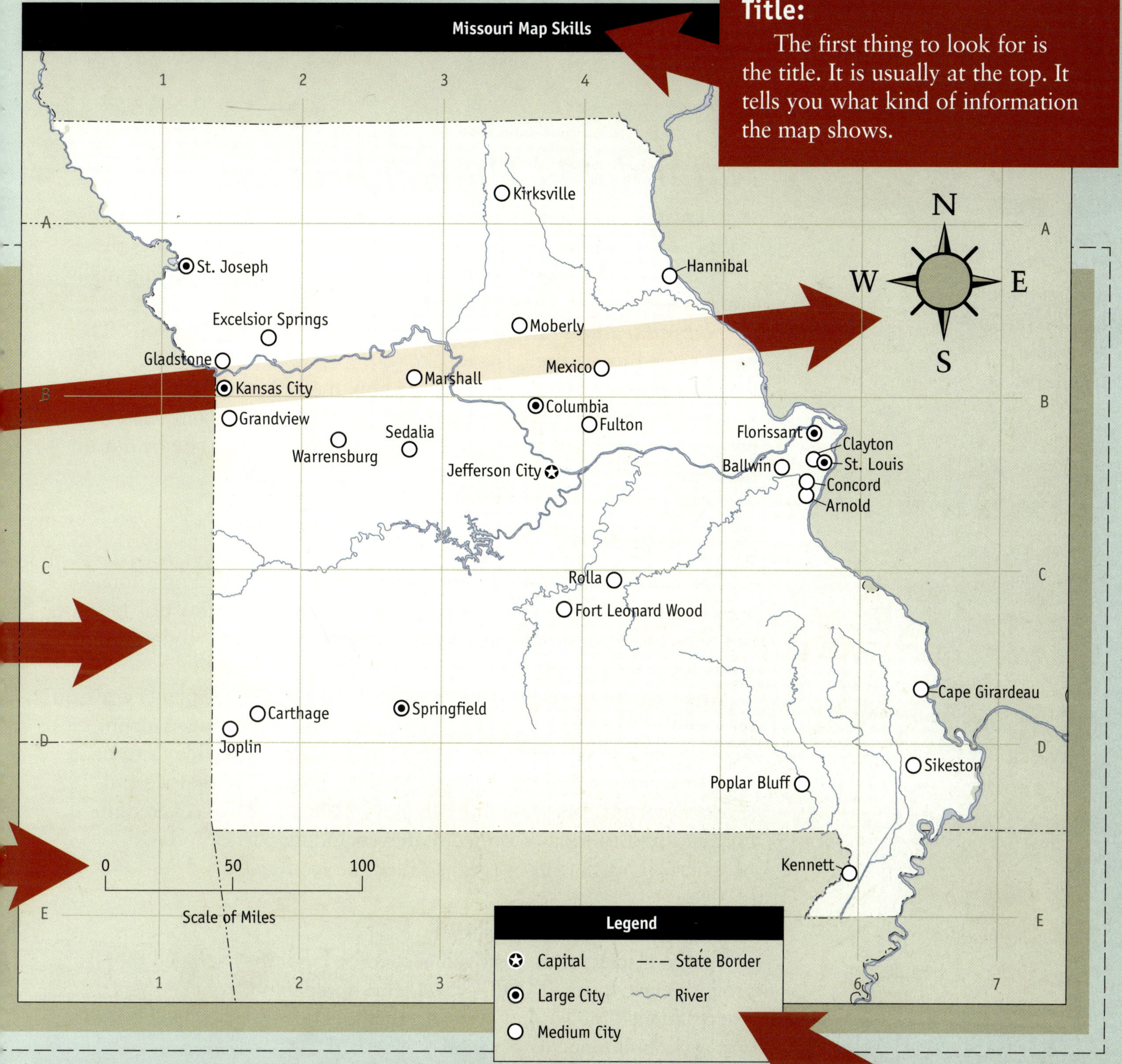

Legend or Key:

Map makers use symbols so they don't have to print words all over the map. The symbols stand for cities, rivers, and other things. The legend or key explains what the symbols mean.

LESSON 2

WORDS TO UNDERSTAND

fossil
glacier
human feature
natural feature
reservoir
tributary

Natural and Human Features

All places have certain features that make them different from other places. They also have features that make them similar to other places.

Places have ***human features*** such as houses, barns, shopping malls, bridges, and roads. They were made by people.

Natural features are hills, mountains, rivers, rocks, and soil. They were formed by nature.

The next time you go outside, see how many natural and human features you see. How would the place be different if it only had natural features? Do you see more human features in a city or out in the country?

An Ancient Land

The land you live on was not always like it is today. Long, long ago, Missouri was covered with sea water. Scientists know this because tiny shells of sea animals sank to the bottom of the sea. Today these shells form the limestone we use for buildings.

After the sea dried up, many kinds of trees and other plants grew on the swampy land. More time passed, and the earth changed again. The climate got much colder. A large ***glacier*** covered today's Canada and slowly moved south. Glaciers are very heavy sheets of ice and snow. Some glaciers were more than a mile high. They covered the northern part of today's United States, including part of today's Missouri. This time in history is called the Ice Age.

Glaciers Changed the Land

As the glaciers slowly moved across the land, they scraped the ground. They pushed sand, gravel, and boulders in front of them. They flattened the land underneath them. They even scooped out dirt and rocks and made low places.

Later, when the glaciers melted, some of the water ran into these lower places and formed lakes and rivers. The Great Lakes, the Mississippi River, and the Missouri River were formed by Ice Age glaciers. Sand, gravel, and soil carried by the glaciers were left behind as hills.

Ice Age Glaciers

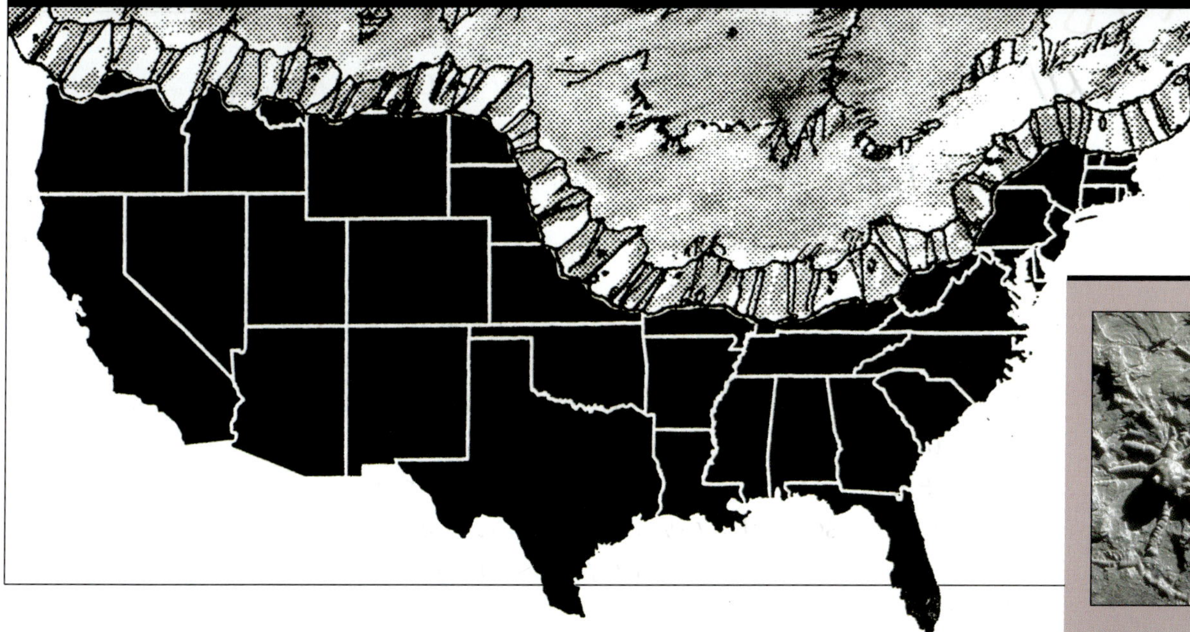

The earth warmed and cooled over and over again. Each time, Ice Age glaciers covered parts of the land. Over time, the climate slowly warmed.

Our State Fossil

An ancient sea animal called a crinoid is our state fossil. A crinoid is similar to a starfish that lived when an ancient ocean covered the land millions of years ago.

Ancient Animals

During the Ice Age, animals either died or moved to a warmer place. Then giant bears, giant beavers, and mastodons roamed the land. Mastodons looked like large elephants with tusks.

How do we know about animals that lived so long ago? We know about them because *fossils* have been found in the ground. A fossil is an imprint or the remains of a plant or animal in a rock.

Mastodon fossils have been found in caves and on hillsides. Mastodon bones have been found in a place we now call Mastodon State Park near St. Louis. Some of the bones had spear points near them. That tells us that early hunters killed the animals for food.

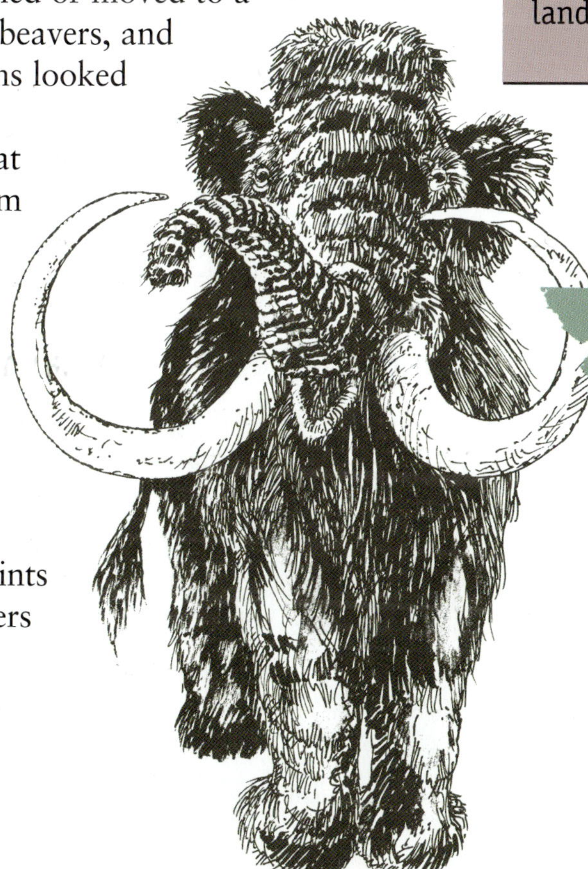

Major Rivers and Lakes

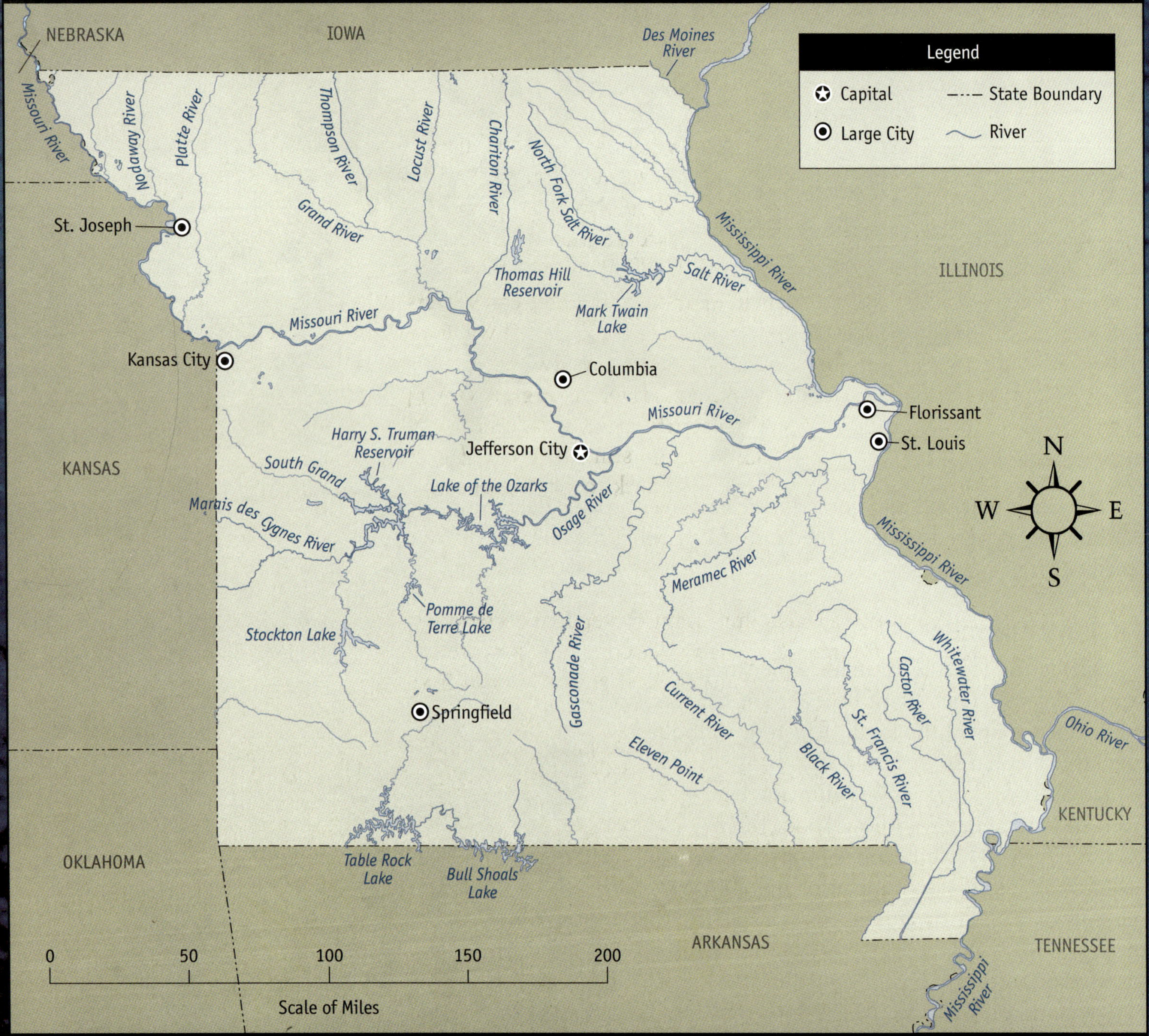

- *What rivers are closest to where you live?*
- *What rivers form some of our state boundaries?*
- *What river flows all the way across the state?*
- *Find the place near St. Louis where the Missouri River flows into the Mississippi River. Where will the Mississippi River flow from there?*

Missouri's Rivers and Lakes

Some people call Missouri the "Heart of America." Here the Ohio River flows into the Mississippi River. Farther north, the Missouri River also flows into the Mississippi River.

Rivers were important to Native Americans who once lived here. They used the rivers like great highways. They traveled on the rivers in canoes. They fished and hunted along the waters. Native Americans called the Mississippi River the "Father of Waters" because it is very wide and long and flows all the way to the Gulf of Mexico.

The rivers brought the first French, Spanish, and American settlers. The settlers built towns along the rivers because they needed water for washing and cooking. They also used the rivers as highways.

The Missouri River is the country's longest river. It begins way up in the mountains of Montana. As it crosses the land, it picks up mud and dirt, giving it a muddy color. Many people still call it the "Big Muddy." Old farmers used to say, "It is too thick to drink and too thin to plow."

Other Rivers

Other rivers in Missouri are also important. Several rivers feed into the Missouri River. The Grand, Osage, and Gasconade Rivers are called ***tributaries.*** A tributary flows into a larger river. Can you find these rivers on the map on page 26?

Some of our smaller rivers, such as the Current, Jack's Fork, and Eleven Point, flow through beautiful scenery. Each summer people come from faraway places to float down the rivers in canoes or rubber boats. People camp along the rivers and spend time with their families.

What a ride! What an adventure! Paddle a canoe down the Current River to see nature in a fresh new way.

Rivers at Work

Rivers do more than provide water for people, plants, and animals. They do some real work!

In the past, rushing water was used to turn large wheels. The moving wheels moved heavy stones that ground grain. Other wheels moved saws back and forth to cut logs into boards. Water power moved machines in factories that made things to sell.

Barges carry products up and down rivers. A barge can carry a lot more than a truck or train.

Then Missourians shipped the things they made down the rivers on boats. The ships traveled to distant places where people bought things made in Missouri.

Today, you can see barges traveling up and down the Missouri and Mississippi Rivers. The goods will be sold all over the world.

Lakes and Reservoirs

Our largest lakes are made by people. This means that workers built a large dam to block the flow of a river. Behind the dam, the water had no where to go, so it rose higher and higher and formed a lake, or ***reservoir.*** Some of the water was released to flow out of the dam and continue downstream.

The moving water going through the dam also turns parts in machines that produce electricity. Then the electricity is carried by wires to cities and farms.

The Lake of the Ozarks, Stockton Lake, Truman Reservoir, and Table Rock Lake are all reservoirs. People from all over the country come to water ski, fish, and camp at the reservoirs.

High above the water, cars drove over Bagnell Dam at Lake of the Ozarks.

2 MEMORY MASTER

1. Give some examples of natural and human features.
2. How did Ice Age glaciers change the land?
3. How do we know ancient animals once lived here?
4. How did Native Americans and explorers use rivers?
5. What work do rivers do?
6. What is a reservoir?

Many Kinds of Regions

WORDS TO UNDERSTAND

landform
plains
region
rural
urban

Geographers divide large areas of the world into smaller parts. We call these parts ***regions.*** A region is a place that has things that are alike in some way. Maybe everyone in a region speaks the same language. Maybe everyone in the region has the same type of government. Maybe all of the farmers in the region grow the same crop.

A region can be large or small. In fact, an entire continent can be a region. A state is one kind of region. So is your neighborhood. You can live in many regions at the same time. Missouri has ***urban*** (city) regions, and ***rural*** (farm) regions.

In the urban regions, such as St. Louis and Kansas City, houses are close together. Streets and highways are often crowded with traffic. There are many businesses, factories, and stores.

In rural regions, many people live on farms. When they need to shop for clothes or food, they travel to small towns nearby. They might not have as many stores to choose from, but people in rural areas enjoy places that are more peaceful than crowded cities.

The land around the Lake of the Ozarks is a natural region where families come to camp, hike, ride mountain bikes, swim, and go boating.

Land Regions

Some regions are land regions. Each land region has mostly one type of ***landform.*** Landforms are natural features such as mountains, hills, valleys, and plains. Even rivers and lakes are landforms. If you live in a river valley, your life might be different than if you lived in the mountains.

Missouri has four land regions. Each region has a lot of the same kind of landforms.

Missouri Land Regions

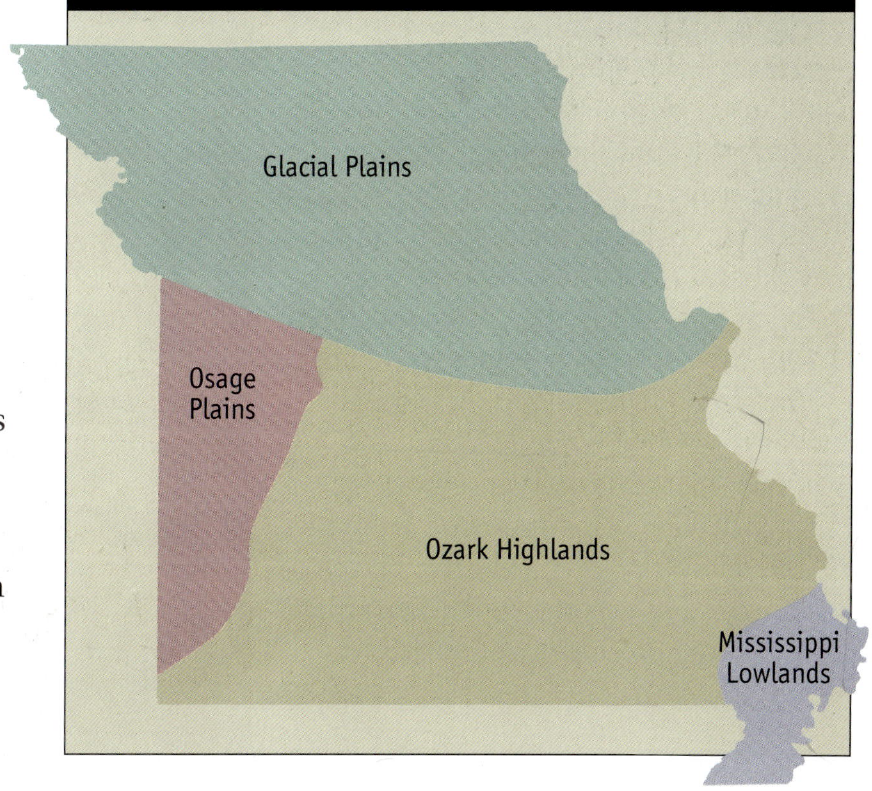

Glacial Plains

During the Ice Age, glaciers covered the land north of the Missouri River. When they melted, they left land that is mostly level, with rolling hills and small valleys.

This region has some of the best land in the state for growing crops. Farmers in northern Missouri grow large crops of corn, wheat, fruit, vegetables, and soybeans. Farmers also raise cattle and hogs and the food that makes them grow.

Communities

Each region has interesting communities. A community is a group of people living together. Towns and cities are communities.

Towns and cities in the Glacial Plains region include Columbia, St. Joseph, Kirksville, and Hannibal. Kansas City, Jefferson City, and Independence are on the border of the region. St. Louis is considered to be part of this region as well, but because it is along the Mississippi River, the land there is different in some ways.

Hannibal was the boyhood home of Missouri's greatest writer, Mark Twain. He wrote *The Adventures of Tom Sawyer* and *The Adventures of Huckleberry Finn*. People from all over the world come to visit the home where Mark Twain grew up.

Kirksville is the home of Truman State University, named after Harry Truman. He was the only Missourian to become president of the United States.

It is time to cut and bale the golden hay on the Glacial Plains. The hay will feed cattle in the winter.

Osage Plains

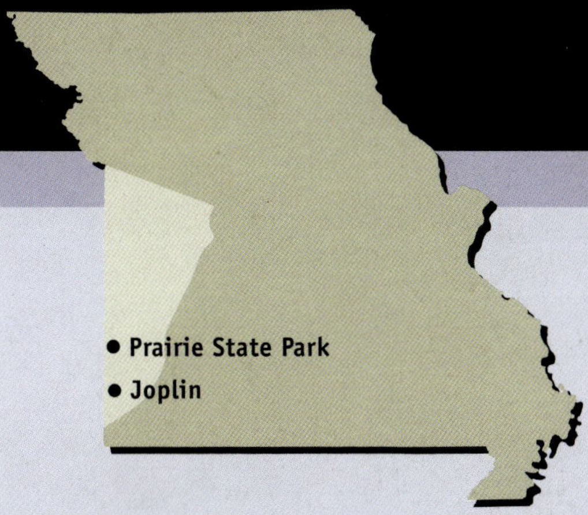

The Osage Plains are named after an important Indian tribe that used to live in the region. ***Plains*** are a landform that is mostly flat. The Osage Plains extend into the Great Plains of Kansas and Colorado.

Before farmers came to the region and cleared the land, many types of grasses covered the land. The grasses had grown on the plains for thousands of years. In the summer, when the wind blew, the plains looked like the waves of the ocean. Many farmers still let grass grow on their land to feed grazing cattle. Farmers also grow wheat and hay.

Look at the shaggy hair on buffalo at Prairie State Park.

Communities

Joplin is the fourth largest city in Missouri. It started around lead mines over 100 years ago. Joplin is near a place where Missouri, Kansas, and Oklahoma meet, so many visitors travel through the town. People who live in Joplin say it is one of the best places in the country to live, work, and raise a family.

Prairie State Park

Missouri's largest remaining tallgrass prairie landscape is part of this region. Prairie State Park contains hundreds of kinds of plants and birds. Bison and elk herds roam free. Visitors like to wander along the nature trails and study the natural prairie.

The Current River wanders through the Ozark Highlands past springs, caves, and forests. What a place!

Ozark Highlands

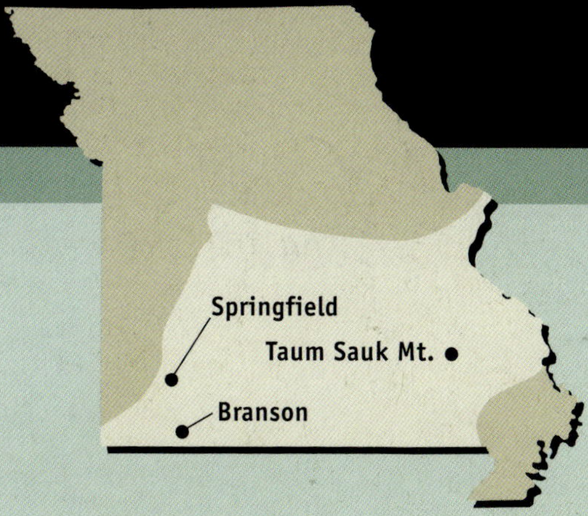

Since Ice Age glaciers did not push this far south, the Ozarks look different than the glacial plains. The land is very hilly, with deep valleys and steep cliffs. The region has a lot of zinc, iron, sand, clay, limestone, and gravel. When you travel through the region you will see forests. Many wild animals still live in the region. Since the land is rocky, much of it is not good for growing crops. Many small farmers still raise cattle in the region.

Because of the beauty of the Ozarks in this region, many tourists take vacations here. Have you ever skied in the Ozarks? Have you fished in the streams there?

Beautiful clear rivers such as the Niangua, White, and Current Rivers run through the Ozark valleys. Many of the rivers are fed by freshwater springs. Springs bubble up from beneath the ground. Big Spring pumps over 800 million gallons of water a day! There are also many salt springs. Early settlers boiled the water from these springs to get salt for their food.

The highest point in the state is in the Ozarks. Taum Sauk Mountain is 1,772 feet high.

Communities

Towns and cities in this region include Springfield and Branson. Branson draws over 6 million visitors a year. They come to enjoy all the country music shows. Near Branson, tourists visit Silver Dollar City. It is an amusement park, but it also tries to preserve Missouri's past. People demonstrate the way settlers used to make quilts and tools. Other people play guitars, banjos, and fiddles.

Leave the city behind and explore a forest in the Ozarks. Don't be surprised if you see deer and chipmunks at home in the woods.

Mississippi Lowlands

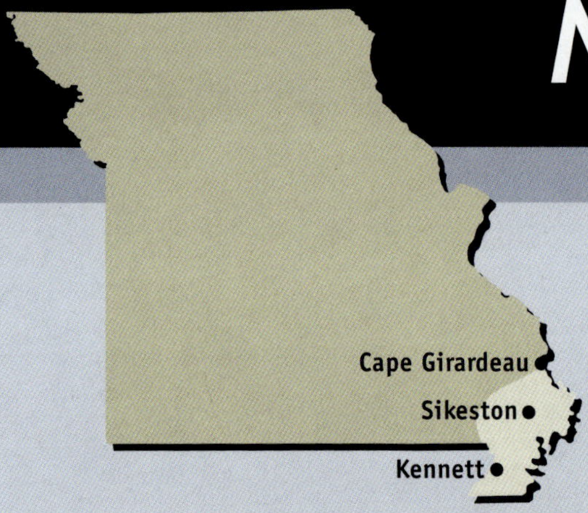

Can you tell from looking at the map why this region is called the boot heel? The boot heel region is also known as the Mississippi Lowlands. The Mississippi River flows along one side, and the St. Francis River flows along the other side.

Until 100 years ago, forests and swamps covered the region, but farmers cleared the land and built ditches to drain the swamps. The land now is very flat, and the soil is very fertile. Farmers grow corn, wheat, soybeans, rice, and cotton.

Communities

For over 100 years, farmers have brought their cotton to Kennett to be "ginned." That means putting the cotton through machines that take out the cottonseeds, so the cotton can be made into cloth.

Sikeston is the largest town in the region. Cape Girardeau is a river town on the border of the region.

Missouri soybeans are sold to make soymilk, energy bars, tofu, and other healthy foods.

Earthquake!

Under the region is a fault, or crack in the earth's crust. The fault has caused earthquakes. In 1811 the New Madrid Earthquake struck the region. It was probably the most powerful earthquake in American history. Large areas sank into the earth, new lakes were formed, and forests were destroyed. "Houses, gardens, and fields were swallowed up," wrote one man who lived in the town.

Scientists believe an earthquake could strike the region again. No one knows for sure.

The Gateway Arch says, "Welcome to St. Louis."

Union Station is a well-known landmark in Kansas City.

Urban Regions

You have already read about some of Missouri's many towns and cities. Our two largest cities are St. Louis and Kansas City. Other important cities are St. Joseph, Jefferson City, Columbia, and Springfield. Each is home to factories, businesses, schools, and colleges. Find these cities on the map on page 16.

St. Louis was Missouri's first great city. It began as a place where Indians and French settlers traded furs. Later, it was a port for steamboats that traveled up and down the Mississippi River. St. Louis became the "Gateway to the West" for Americans leaving the East. The famous Gateway Arch helps us remember this today. St. Louis is a place where many things people need, like shoes and furniture, are made. Banks and businesses have their main offices in St. Louis.

Kansas City began as a fur trading village along the Missouri River. It grew into Missouri's second major city. Over the years, Kansas City has been an important place for farmers to bring hogs and cattle to market. It was also a place where farmers brought wheat to be ground into flour and baked into bread. Today, Kansas City has thriving businesses that employ many people.

Freeways make traveling fast. There are no stoplights and no intersections to slow drivers down. Cars carry people from place to place. Trucks carry clothes, food, books, and many other things to stores across the country. These freeways in Kansas City cross the Missouri River.

People on the Move

People have always moved from region to region and place to place. Long ago, American Indians moved around seeking food and water. They traveled great distances to trade tools and other things with different groups of people. As people moved, they exchanged not only things, but ideas. They learned new ways of doing things.

People from all over the world come to Missouri each year. Many of them come for vacations. Missouri has lakes, beautiful state parks, campgrounds, and museums to visit. Some people come to visit relatives and friends. Other people come to Missouri for business. Some people come to Missouri to live.

Missourians also travel to other states and countries. What other places have you visited? Have you lived in another place?

Things on the Move

People in our state send lumber, farm products, manufactured items, and other things to places in the United States and around the world.

These things move in and out of Missouri by land on our highways, by water along our rivers, and by air on planes.

Other people in the world ship their products to Missouri and sell them to us. What things in your home come from another place?

People carry information with them when they travel. Information also moves by mail, telephone, fax, and the Internet. We also get ideas and information from books, newspapers, television, radio, movies, and teachers.

People Depend on Each Other

People in different regions depend on each other. In Missouri, a farm family goes to town to buy things, visit a zoo, or watch a ballgame. A family in an urban region might pack up their tent and sleeping bags and drive to a forest with hiking trails and a campground.

All people shop in stores and buy food that comes from other regions. They wear clothes from other places. Where do your books and games come from? Where did the wood, brick, and glass for your home or apartment come from? Where did your clothes come from?

What do you think?

Today, it is easy for us to make trips between different regions. Many years ago it was much harder. What has made travel so much easier?

Activity

Information on the Move

Think of two different ways you have given information to someone today. What two ways have you received information?

Talk about these ideas with your class and your family:

- Do you think it is important to exchange ideas? Why?
- What kinds of movement do you see in your school and your home?

3 MEMORY MASTER

1. In what land region do you live?
2. Which region has most of Missouri's largest cities?
3. Which region is mostly forests and mountains?
4. Which region is part of the Great Plains?
5. What region once had a huge earthquake?
6. In what ways do people, products, and ideas move?

LESSON 4

WORDS TO UNDERSTAND

climate
ecosystem
natural resources
pollution
precipitation
refuge
renewable

What is the difference between climate and weather? ***Climate*** is the weather of a place year after year. Weather is what we get each day. You can live in a mild climate, but still have cold, snowy weather on some days.

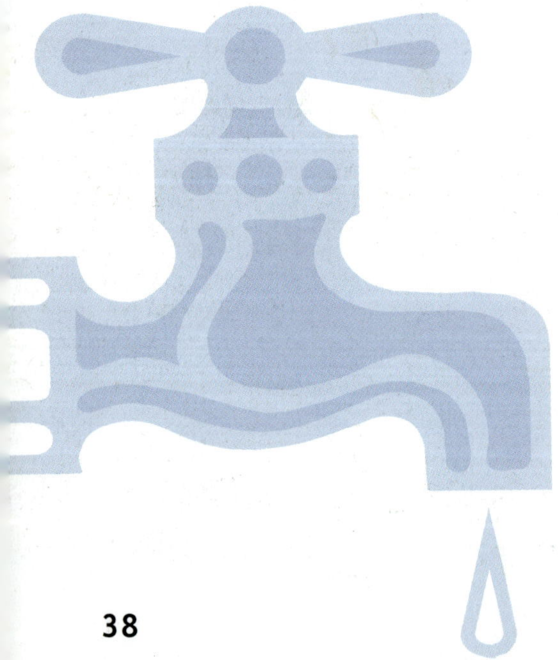

Our Climate

Can you imagine living in a place where the weather was the same all year long? What if it never rained or snowed? Climate is important to the animals, plants, and people that live in a place. It is a part of our environment.

Missouri can be very hot or very cold. Summer days in July and August can be over 100 degrees. In the winter, it can be freezing cold.

What causes these great changes in the weather? Look at Missouri's location on a globe. The state is in the middle of North America. It is not very close to the North or South Poles, where it is cold all year. It is not near the equator, where it is very hot all year.

Warm air comes to Missouri all the way from the Gulf of Mexico. Cold air comes from Canada. When these two masses of warm and cool air collide, they sometimes cause large storms.

Amazing Seasons

People in Missouri enjoy all four seasons: spring, summer, fall, and winter. In spring, the grass in our yards begins to grow again. Green buds pop out on trees. Summers can be very hot and humid. There is a lot of water in the air. This makes the air feel even hotter.

In the fall, the weather cools, and the trees turn brilliant gold, orange, and red. In winter, our towns and farms are covered in a beautiful blanket of snow.

Water for People and Plants

Water in the form of rain, snow, sleet, or hail is called ***precipitation.*** Do you like to walk in the rain? Do you like to look out your window to see hail bouncing on the ground? Do you like to slide down a snowy hill on a sled?

We get more rain in the spring and fall than we do in the summer. Every few years it is too dry in the summer. This can lead to a drought. A drought is a very dry time. If a drought lasts too long, animals and farmers' crops can die.

Some years there is too much rain. This can cause floods. Floods can wash away crops and roads. Sometimes families have to leave their homes until the water goes down.

Tornadoes

High winds are common in Missouri, and they can be very sudden. They can dry up lakes, and blow soil away.

One kind of windstorm is called a tornado. Sometimes you can see a tornado-shaped cloud in the sky. The spinning air can also move over the ground. Tornadoes can reach speeds of hundreds of miles per hour. Some are so strong they can push straw through a tree trunk! Tornadoes can even knock a train off its track, pick a house up off the ground, or blow a car through the air.

Because tornadoes can be very dangerous, scientists watch the weather and report danger. Have you seen a tornado warning on television? Does your school have a tornado safety plan?

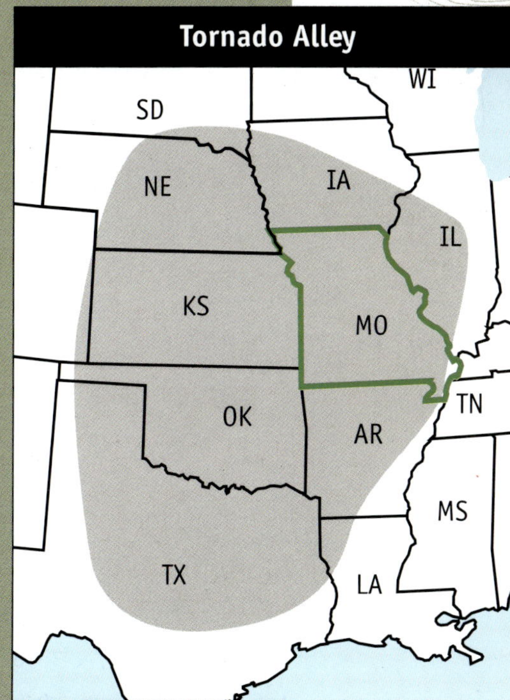

The shaded region on the map shows where tornadoes occur. Can you find Missouri?

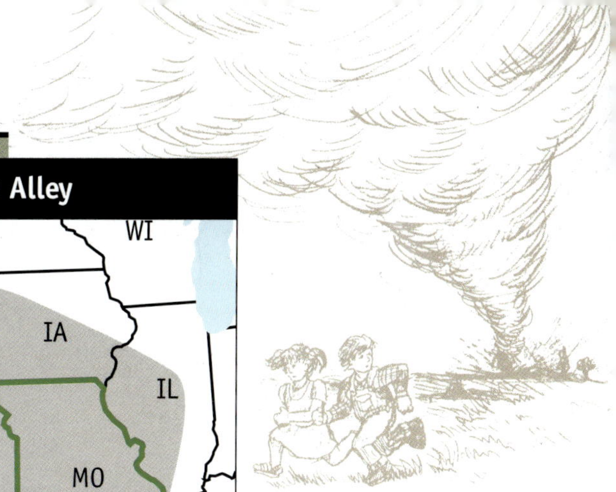

Plants and Animals

No matter where in the world you live, your environment is important. The land, the water, the air, and living things are part of your environment. So are the language you speak, the games you play, the neighborhood you live in, and the school you go to.

Animals and plants all live on the land. They could not live without each other. Missouri is covered with grasses and shrubs. Pine, oak, maple, ash, cottonwood, birch, and hickory trees provide wood, give shade, and provide homes for birds and other animals.

In the spring, dogwood trees break out with beautiful flowers. The flowering dogwood is our state tree. What plants do you see near your home and your school?

Many animals live in the wild. Deer and wild turkeys live in many places. Coyotes, raccoons, foxes, and skunks also live in our wooded areas. If you see a skunk, don't go near it!

Bald eagles nest along the Missouri and Mississippi Rivers. In the fall, millions of ducks and geese come through the state, and many stay all winter. Owls, hawks, and buzzards live here. Beautiful songbirds, such as the cardinal and the bluebird, also live in Missouri. The bluebird is our state bird.

You and Your Environment

People, animals, and plants all live on the land. Geographers study how the land, people, animals, and plants affect each other.

Ecosystems

An ***ecosystem*** is a community. It includes the animals, plants, soil, water, and air that interact with each other. Every living creature is part of an ecosystem. Human beings, animals, and plants get everything they need from their ecosystem. They also put things back into the ecosystem.

An ecosystem contains many kinds of life. Each does its own special job. Some animals eat smaller animals. Some animals eat only plants. Plants depend on soil that has been made richer by dead plants and animals. Plants need this rich soil to grow.

All parts of nature work together in an ecosystem.

Missouri's Natural Ecosystems

Forest near Jefferson City

Forests

Forests cover large regions of Missouri. Many trees and other plants grow in the forests. Forests are also home to many animals and insects. Missouri sets aside some land as state forests. In a state forest, the land is preserved for its beauty. It also gives people a place to hike, fish, and see wildlife.

Castor River

Freshwater

Rivers, streams, lakes, and ponds all belong to the freshwater ecosystem. Drinking water often comes from lakes and reservoirs. A reservoir is a lake that was made by people to store water. When people pollute water or bring in animals and plants from other regions, they can harm the freshwater ecosystem.

Fantastic Caverns near Springfield

Caves and Caverns

Some people call Missouri "The Cave State." There are nearly 5,300 natural caves in Missouri. What kinds of animals like the damp, cool caves? Millipedes, flatworms, beetles, spiders, and salamanders do. These animals can't see very well because it is always dark where they live. Bats visit caves and live in them during some parts of the year but not all the time. Sometimes they raise their babies there in the summer.

Missouri wetlands

Wetlands

Wetlands include marshes, swamps, and shallow ponds. They are home to many plants and animals. One of the largest wetlands in the state is the Squaw Creek National Refuge. Thousands of ducks and geese spend time there every fall and spring as they migrate south or north. Missouri has only a small amount of wetlands. Before modern settlement, there were over 2 million acres of wetlands in the boot heel. Now there is much less. But wetlands are important for the state. When there is heavy rain or melting snow, the soil holds water and helps prevent flooding.

People Use and Change the Land

People have always found ways to live in their environment. They have also changed it. Long ago, people ate wild animals, fish, nuts, roots, berries, and grasses for food. They used animal skins for clothing. They cut trees and moved earth and rocks to build shelters. Later, people cleared the land to plant crops.

People still use the land. In Missouri, we raise crops and farm animals on the land. We cut timber for wood to build houses and make other products. We make bricks out of clay taken from the earth. We take coal from the ground. We build roads, dams, malls, houses, and barns. When we use cars, trucks, factories, and fertilizers, we change the air, water, and soil.

Trash Can Hurt Animals

Do you know that a balloon or an old plastic bag can harm turtles, deer, and other animals? They might eat the plastic, thinking it is a yummy snack. The animals may die because the plastic sticks in their stomachs.

- What do you think we should do with our trash?
- Do you think sending balloons into the air is a good or bad idea? Why?

Our Natural Resources

Missouri is rich in ***natural resources.*** They are things found in nature that are useful to people. As you study the history of Missouri, you will see that natural resources and our environment are important to all of us. You will learn that some changes have been very good. Others have not been as good.

Water
Water is one of our most important natural resources. We need to drink it. We cook with it and bathe in it. Our crops must have water to grow. Animals must have it to live. We use water power to make electricity. Water is also a wonderful resource for fishing, swimming, boating, rafting, and water skiing.

Fertile Soil
Farmers raise grain, vegetables, hay, tobacco, and fruits in different parts of the state. Farmers also raise cattle and grow feed for them. There are pastures where cows can graze. Our Glacial Plains Region has the richest soil in the state.

Minerals
Missouri mines produce a lot of minerals. Lead is used in car batteries, televisions, and computers. Zinc is used to cover road signs and cars to keep them from rusting. Copper is used in electrical wires. Missouri also mines crushed limestone for cement. Sand is used to make glass.

Timber
Missouri has many natural forests and trees that have been planted by growers. Together they provide timber. Our Ozark Highlands Region is covered with forests.

Using Natural Resources

What natural resources do you see outside? Now look around your classroom. What things were made from natural resources?

Natural resources have many uses. One of them is to make energy. It takes energy, or power, to run machines and provide heat and light. Coal, oil, gas, the sun, and moving water and wind all provide energy.

Renewable and Non-Renewable Resources

Some resources are **renewable**. That means they will probably come back again. If a forest is cut down or burned in a fire, new trees will grow back. The wind is a renewable resource. So is water.

Other resources will never come back. These are non-renewable resources. All we have is what is here now. Coal is an example. Missouri used to have lots of coal mines, but now we have only a few. Most of our coal has already been used.

Taking Care of the Land

If Missouri is to remain a healthy and beautiful place, we must take care of the land, air, and water. Groups of people have set aside certain places so they can protect these resources.

- Wildlife ***refuges*** are places where animals can live without being hunted or harmed.
- Rare plants and many kinds of trees can grow and be protected in special gardens.
- State and national parks and other places are protected. People can enjoy these places, but they cannot change them.

People have made laws that protect the environment from ***pollution.*** Factories and mines have to be careful to keep our land and water clean and safe. People who drive cars, trucks, and buses have to make sure they do not put too many harmful fumes into the air.

What do you think?

- What can we do to make sure we have enough resources for the future?
- Why are some people wasteful of natural resources?

The bald eagle is our national bird. For many years the eagles were dying out. Now they are protected. It is against the law to capture, buy, or sell the majestic birds.

4 MEMORY MASTER

1. How does Missouri's location affect our climate?
2. What is an ecosystem?
3. List three natural resources and tell what each is used for.
4. How can we help protect our environment?

Chapter 2 Review

From There to Here

Pretend a helicopter is dropping you down right in the middle of the Glacial Plains region. Look all around you. What has changed during the years since the last Ice Age? Is the climate the same? Are the plants and animals the same? Has the land changed?

Now imagine that you are dropped in the middle of the Ozark Highlands. What has changed there? How about the Osage Plains region? Has it changed much since the Ice Age? How?

Activity

Your Hometown

At the top of a piece of plain paper, write the words: **My Kind of Place**

- In the center of the paper, draw your house or apartment building.
- Then, around your home, draw a circle. Under the circle, write the name of your town or city.
- Anywhere on the page, draw and label pictures of things that show what kind of place your town is. Include both natural and human features. Include pictures of different kinds of weather. Include places you like to visit.
- If you have room, add pictures of what people are doing for work and to have fun.

Activity

What Is Your Global Address?

Pretend you have spent the last week on a planet far away. Now you are ready for the return trip to Earth. As you settle into your seat on the spaceship, your new friend Jorp comes running up to say goodbye.

"Hey!" he says, "What's your address? Mom says I can visit you next month."
You tell him you live at 513 Becker Street.
"I will need to know more than that to find your house!" says Jorp.

Jorp also needs to know your planet, continent, country, state, county, and city. On a piece of paper, write down your global address for Jorp.

THE TIME
12,000 B.C.–A.D. 1825

The First People

When you arise in the morning,
Give thanks for the morning light,
Give thanks for your life and strength,
And give thanks for the joy of living.

—Osage prayer

Timeline of Events

12,000 B.C.–8000 B.C.
Paleo Indians move across America.

12,000 B.C. | 10,000 B.C. | 8000 B.C. | 1000 B.C.

10,000 B.C.
The Paleo Indians enter the land we call Missouri.

8000 B.C.–500 B.C.
The Archaic Indians live a more advanced lifestyle.

Chapter 3

American Indians lived here long, long ago, before any explorers came from Europe. They used natural resources to make their homes, clothes, and tools. They raised families near rivers and streams. The people planted crops and harvested them so they would have food for the cold winters. They used spears, then bows and arrows to hunt animals.

900
The Woodland Indians enter the Missouri region, farm, and make pottery.

900–1500
The Mound builders build Cahokia and smaller towns up and down the Mississippi and Missouri Rivers.

1500–1800
The Missouri and Osage tribes live and hunt in Missouri.

1600s
French and Spanish explorers and traders come to Missouri.

1800s
Europeans begin to settle Missouri.

1808
The Osage sell some of their land to settlers.

1825
The Osage sell the rest of their land and move to Kansas and Oklahoma.

0 — A.D. 1000 — A.D. 1500 — A.D. 1600 — A.D. 1800 — A.D. 1900

LESSON 1

WORDS TO UNDERSTAND

adobe
archaeologist
artifact
atlatl
culture
extinct
hunter-gatherer
ruins

Paleo Indians

Many thousands of years ago, the first people made their way into what is now Missouri. Scientists call them Paleo Indians. Paleo means ancient, or very old.

Missouri was much colder then, and Ice Age glaciers still covered part of the land. These early people may have walked on the land where you live. They may have camped and hunted on land where your school sits.

The people traveled in family groups. They slowly moved south across North America. No one knows for sure, but scientists believe they made it to today's Missouri about 12,000 years ago.

These first people probably followed large animals. They went where the animal herds went. They were always moving from place to place.

These people are also called ***hunter-gatherers*** because they hunted and gathered everything they needed to live. They gathered wild berries, roots, and nuts to eat. They ate the food fresh and dried some of it to eat during the winter.

The animals they hunted would amaze us today. The hunters killed huge mastodons, large buffalo, giant sloths, and other animals with sharp spears. The people needed these large animals for food. They ate the meat. They also scraped fur off the animal skins with tools made from bones and stones. Then they used the skins for clothing.

To hunt such large animals, the people had to work together. They sometimes ran the animals over a cliff. Other times they surrounded a large animal that was stuck in a marsh.

Linking the Past to the Present

How do people in your community work together to get important jobs done?

Women and children gathered roots, seeds, and nuts from wild plants.

Mastodons provided food and fur. To kill such large animals, the men thrust spears into them.

Archaic Indians

As time passed, the climate of North America began to change. It became warmer and drier. Glaciers began to melt. The melting water formed new rivers and lakes. More trees began to grow.

This climate change may be the reason many of the big animals disappeared, or became ***extinct.*** They also may have died because of disease. Or, the early hunters may have killed too many of the animals. Scientists don't know for sure. It may have been all of these things.

When the climate changed, the early people had to change, too. They had to adapt, or change the way they lived. This happened slowly.

Instead of mastodons, the hunters killed deer and smaller animals. They also began to move less and settled in one place. They might live in caves, or in other shelters.

The people used bone, stone, and wood to make spear points, knives, fishhooks, and scrapers. Bone needles helped them make clothes from animal skins that fit better and kept them warmer.

The people got more and more skilled at making hunting tools. An important tool was the ***atlatl*** (at LATL). The *atlatl* helped hunters throw their spears farther and faster than throwing them alone.

Linking the Past to the Present

What are some new tools or inventions that have made your life easier in the past few years?

Graham Cave State Park

Inside Graham Cave, archaeologists uncovered artifacts that showed that people had used the cave 10,000 years ago. They found bone needles, small bags, and nets. The people may have used the nets to trap rabbits or other small animals. What might the people have put in the bags?

Today, you and your friends can peek inside the cave. You and your family can walk on trails in the forest, ride a boat on the Loutre River, have a picnic, or camp in a place where ancient people and animals once lived.

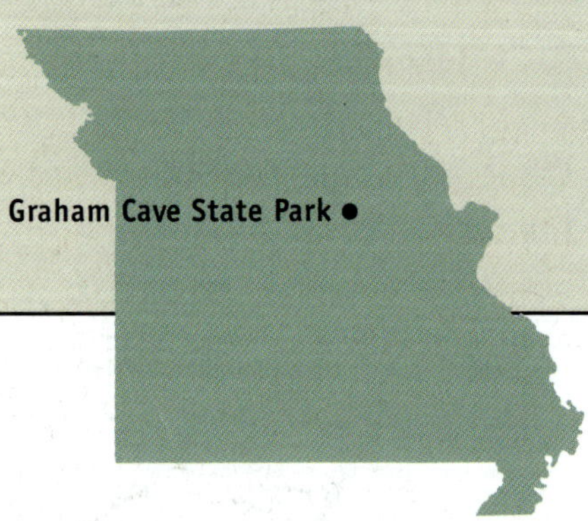

How Do We Know?

How do we know about the ways the early people lived? No one living today saw these people or places. We have no written records from the people.

The people did leave important clues behind. The clues tell us some things about how the people lived. ***Archaeologists*** are scientists who learn about people of the past. The archaeologists study ***ruins*** and ***artifacts.*** Ruins are part of homes and other buildings the people once made and lived in. Artifacts are the things people used and left behind. A very old knife, a sandal, and arrowheads are artifacts.

Archaeologists often dig carefully into the earth and find bones, fire pits, burial sites, and trash piles. They examine artifacts such as broken pieces of pottery, tools, weapons, and musical instruments.

Archaeologists put these clues together to tell a story. Like detectives and historians, they work to tell us what happened in the past.

What do you think?

- Do you think archaeologists can learn everything about people just by studying artifacts and ruins?
- What things about life long ago might the artifacts not tell?
- What might the things in your house and your town tell about you in the future?

American Indians

Over thousands of years, the people who lived in different regions of North America developed their own ***culture,*** or way of living. Their culture had a lot to do with what natural resources they had. All the people hunted and gathered food. In later times, they learned to grow corn and beans. If the people lived near water, they ate a lot of fish. If a group lived in the desert, they made ***adobe*** bricks of mud and dried them in the sun. If the people lived near a forest, they made homes of wood and tree bark. On the plains, the people made homes of brush and buffalo skins.

Native People Used Natural Resources

Native people are the people who were already living here when the white people came from Europe. Why are Indians also called Native Americans and American Indians?

American Indians living on the Northwest Coast carved totem poles and canoes from tall tree trunks. They decorated them with symbols of animals.

American Indians living on the Great Plains used buffalo skins and furs to make clothing and tepees. Bead designs were mostly geometric.

American Indians living next to the Great Lakes used birch bark from trees to make canoes, boxes, baskets, and to cover their homes. Porcupine quill designs of flowers and leaves decorated clothes and other items.

American Indians living in the Great Basin and California made tightly woven baskets out of grasses.

American Indians living in the Southwest built houses of stone and adobe. They made pottery from clay and painted it.

American Indians living in the Southeast wove baskets of cypress and cane that grew in the swamplands. Zigzag patterns decorated their baskets and clothes.

Woodland Indians

Over hundreds of years, people kept making changes in the way they lived. A big change came about 3,000 years ago when Native Americans began to plant gardens. They still hunted animals and gathered fruits and nuts, but they grew much of their own food. They stored part of the food for the winter.

Some of the Native Americans are called Woodland Indians. Different groups of Woodland Indians lived in many places all the way from the Great Lakes to the Atlantic Ocean.

Because they grew crops, the people no longer had to travel so far to find wild animals to hunt. People could settle down in one place. They settled in villages. Each village was part of a larger group called a tribe. Some tribes joined with each other and formed an Indian nation. They helped protect each other from other tribes.

Members of a tribe and a nation all spoke the same language. They shared a common culture. Language, religion, and customs are all part of culture.

The people planted three crops together. Tall corn stalks provided a "pole" for bean vines to crawl up. Pumpkins or squash spread out along the ground and kept the weeds out and the soil moist. These crops have been called the "three sisters."

Pottery

The people learned how to make things that made life easier. They dug clay to make pottery. After the pots were shaped, the people baked them to make them hard and strong. Pots helped the people store food for long periods of time. A strong pot kept out insects and mice!

Bows and Arrows

The bow and arrow was an important new hunting tool. Bows were carefully made from wooden branches. Arrowheads were carved from stone and sharpened. With practice, a hunter could kill an animal with a fast arrow.

1 MEMORY MASTER

1. How did the Archaic Indians adapt to changes in nature?
2. How do archaeologists help us learn about the past?
3. In what ways did the Woodland Indians get food?
4. What new things did the Woodland Indians learn to make?

The Hopewell People

WORDS TO UNDERSTAND

stockade

One group of Woodland Indians are now called the Hopewell people. No one knows what they called themselves. The Hopewell lived all up and down the Mississippi River valleys from the Great Lakes to the Gulf of Mexico. Their way of life spread along the Missouri River in the western part of today's Missouri.

The Hopewell built high mounds and walls of earth. The mounds were sometimes in the shape of circles, squares, and animals.

The people grew corn in fields around the mounds. They used some of the corn to trade for things they wanted from other tribes. They used copper and seashells from faraway places to make jewelry and other items.

The Hopewell buried their loved ones in large hills of earth. As more people died, they were buried in higher layers and covered with earth. This made the mounds higher and higher. Sometimes things that were important to the dead person were buried with him or her. Seashells, blankets, arrowheads, clothing, and jewelry have been found in burial mounds.

The Hopewell people pressed thin sheets of copper onto clay figures.

Mississippian Mound Builders

About 1,000 years ago, the Native Americans made even more changes in the way they lived. They built one of the most amazing cultures ever seen in North America. These Indians are called Mississippians because thousands of them lived along the great river. The people are also call mound builders because, like the Hopewell, they built amazing hills of earth.

Instead of many smaller villages, the people built large cities. The cities were built up and down the Mississippi River and south toward the Gulf of Mexico. Smaller towns were built near where Kansas City now stands.

Why did the people build the mounds? No one knows for sure, but palaces for leaders, government buildings, and temples for religious leaders were built high on some mounds. People were buried inside other mounds. Modern scientists have dug up many mounds. They have found the bones of people who died long ago.

When white settlers first came to St. Louis, the land was covered with mounds. An early nickname of St. Louis was Mound City. Settlers leveled off many of the mounds so they could build homes and other buildings.

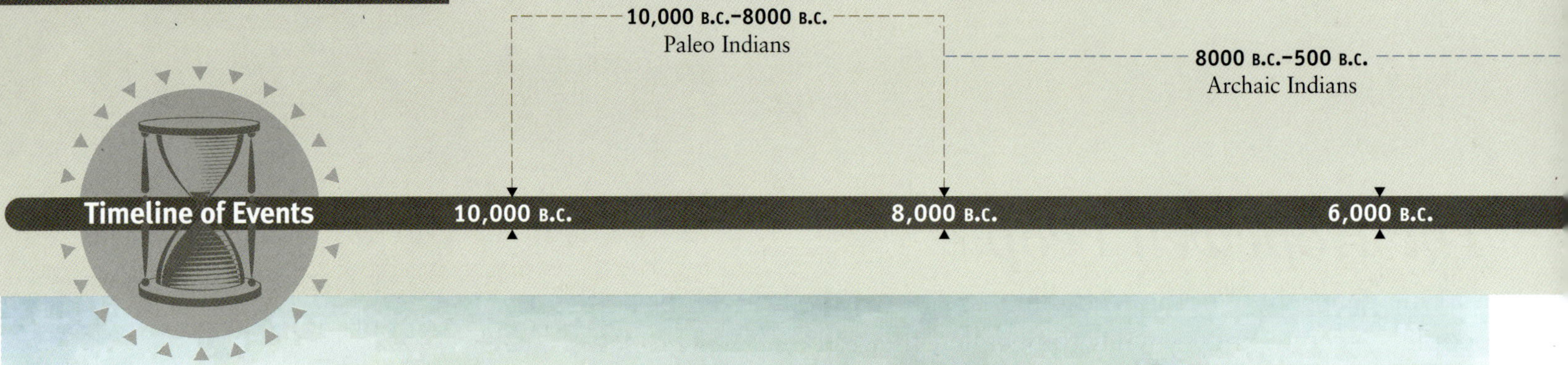

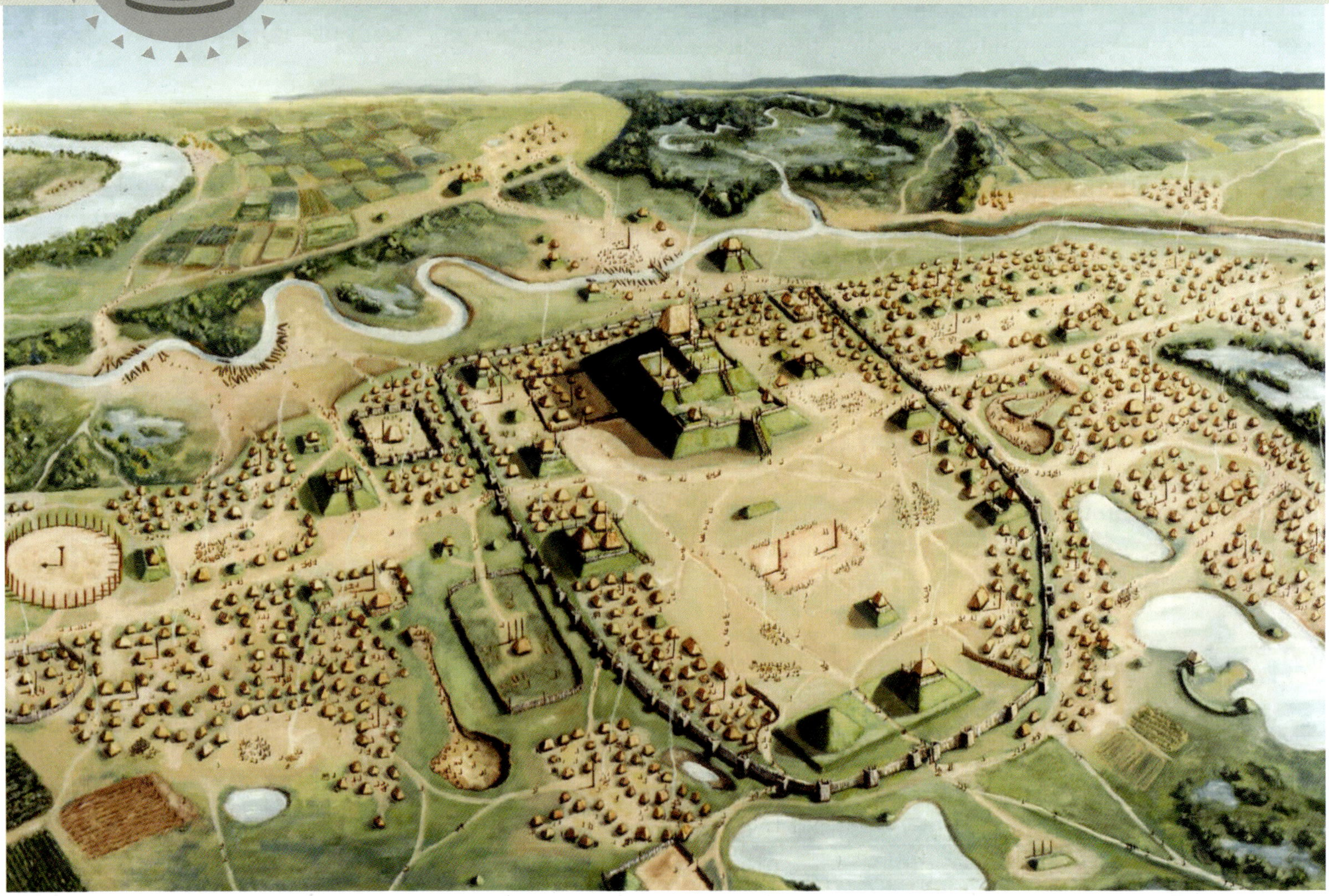

This artist's drawing shows Cahokia around 1150. What can you learn about Cahokia from the painting?

Cahokia, an Ancient City

One major city, now called Cahokia, was once on both sides of the Mississippi River. Part of it was where St. Louis is now, and part was in today's Illinois. Many people lived and worked on both sides. Cahokia became one of the largest cities in the world.

What did Cahokia look like? You can imagine what the area looked like when 20,000 people lived around the tallest mounds. The city had different neighborhoods with different types of craftsmen. People traded in a marketplace. A tall log fence called a ***stockade*** circled the center of the city. The stockade protected the leaders and

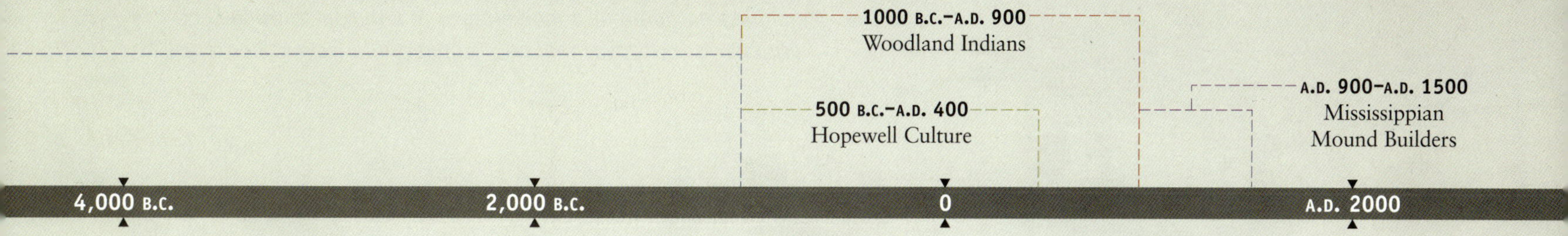

the other important people who lived inside.

The biggest mound at Cahokia today is called Monk's Mound. It was about as large as your whole school yard. Think about how many people it took to build this mound of earth. Today, you can stand on top of Monk's Mound and see for miles.

Around Monk's Mound were thousands of small houses. Most were big enough for one family. The people built them by making a pole frame from small trees. Then they covered the frame with mats made of cattails or reeds from the nearby river.

In the winter, people built fires to stay warm in their small houses. With so many people living in one place, the smoke from the fires polluted the air. This was harmful to the health of the people who lived in Cahokia.

What do you think?

What are the major causes of pollution in our cities today? What is being done to stop the pollution?

The River of Life

Life revolved around the rivers that ran beside the towns. Children drank water from the river. Women washed clothes in the river. The people built their houses from reeds that grew along the river. They ate fish and mussels they got from the river. They hunted animals that came to the river to drink. They also hunted ducks and geese.

The people also used the rivers for travel. They made dugout canoes from trees and floated up and down the rivers to visit other towns. The rivers were the center of life.

Cahokia had burial mounds and flat mounds that once had buildings on top of them. Steep stairs went up to the buildings.

Merchants gathered at a marketplace in Cahokia to trade shell ornaments, pottery, flint tools, copper, and woven fabrics.

Daily Life

The Mississippians were skilled at growing food. Unlike earlier Indians, they grew more food than they hunted or gathered. They grew corn, squash, beans, pumpkins, sunflowers, and many other crops. Corn was the most important crop. Women dried it and then ground it into cornmeal with heavy stones.

Since they grew so much food, most of the people did not have to travel and hunt. They could live in the city. They had time to do other things. They played music. They played games. Many were skilled craftsmen. They wove cloth and made it into clothing. They made clay bottles and jars and painted designs on them. The jars were used to store food and water and keep insects out. The people also made pottery shaped like animals.

Trading in Distant Places

The Mississippians traded with other people in distant places. They got mica (a rock that can be peeled off in thin sheets) from the Appalachian Mountains, seashells from the Gulf of Mexico, and copper from the Great Lakes region. They used these items to make beautiful jewelry and tools.

Trips to the faraway places would have taken many weeks by boat or on foot. Other people from faraway places probably came to the mound builder cities to trade. There were noisy market-places where people could bring the things they had made and traded for other things they needed, just like in many cities of the world today.

Work and Play

In the towns, everyone worked. Men built houses and buildings, hunted, fished, and made

This bowl in the shape of a duck is like those found in the mounds.

tools. Women watched the children, did most of the gardening, made clothing from animal skins, cooked meals, and made pottery. Children helped their mothers, but they still had time to run in the streets of the city and play games with their friends.

The Mississippians loved to play games. What is our most popular game today? Baseball? Football? Soccer? For the Mississippians, it was a game called chunkey. Two players threw spears in front of a round, rolling stone called a chunkey stone. Each player tried to get his spear to land closest to where the stone would stop rolling. Chunkey was played by all ages, from children to adults.

A History Mystery

After a few hundred years, the people left Cahokia and other Mississippian towns and cities. Why this happened is a mystery. The people may have hurt their environment and had to leave. They may have cut down all of the trees to build houses and stockades. With no trees, the animals may have left. With no trees and tree roots to hold back water when it rained, the muddy water could have flooded the cities.

Some people believe the people died in battle or from disease. No one knows for sure what happened to the mound builders.

2 MEMORY MASTER

1. Why did the people build cities next to rivers?
2. What was the nickname of St. Louis?
3. Describe some of the ways the mound builders lived.

LESSON 3

WORDS TO UNDERSTAND

impressive
longhouse
robust
sinew
tattoo
warrior
wigwam

The Plains Indians

When white traders and settlers first came to what is now Missouri, there were several Native American groups living in the region. The two largest groups were the Missouri and the Osage.

Over the years, many other tribes lived here for a short time. Most of them were pushed from the East as new white settlers moved there. Among those tribes who lived in or moved through Missouri were the Iowa, Delaware, Shawnee, Cherokee, Sac and Fox, Miami, Oto, and Kickapoo.

The Missouri Indians

When the first French explorers came to this area, they named the great river that runs through our state the Missouri River. This was the name of the native people who lived along it. Later, our state was called Missouri.

The Missouri's main village was once a busy place. The men hunted buffalo and other wild animals to feed their families. The women and children grew corn and squash. The people gathered seeds, nuts, and berries to eat.

By the time the first white traders and settlers came, the Missouri had lost many people in wars with other tribes. Many of the people got sick from diseases the white people brought. The Missouri families joined with other tribes and moved west.

Linking the Past to the Present

Today, you can visit Van Meter State Park at the Great Bend of the Missouri River and see the beautiful place where the Missouri Indians used to live.

Activity

Indian Names

We remember the Native Americans by all of the names they left behind. Our state and a great river are named after the Missouri tribe. Look at a map of Missouri. Can you name other places in our state that have Indian names?

Can you find the cities of Neosho, Miami, Wyaconda, and Kansas City? Their names come from Indian words.

Can you find the Missouri, Mississippi, Meramec, Niangua, and Osage Rivers on a map? These rivers also have Indian names.

The Osage Indians

When white settlers began to arrive in what is now Missouri, the largest tribe was the Osage. Most of the Osage lived in western Missouri. About 200 years ago, over 6,000 Osage lived there.

The Osage were an ***impressive*** people. One early explorer said they were a "tall, robust, broad shouldered people who looked like giants." ***Robust*** means strong and healthy.

Most Osage men were over 6 feet tall, which was very tall for that day. There were stories of Osage men being able to run 60 miles in a single day and being strong enough to throw a spear all the way through a buffalo! The stories may or may not be true, but they tell us that the settlers thought the Osage were very strong.

Osage men ***tattooed*** their bodies with designs. They wore bracelets and ear ornaments. They shaved their eyebrows and most of the hair on their heads, but they left one strip of black hair down the back. They often painted their heads as well. When the Osage first met white men, they thought men with so much hair on their heads and faces looked horrible!

Osage women wore their hair long down their backs. Like the men, they wore bracelets and ear ornaments. They also tattooed their bodies. Women and girls painted part of their hair red each morning. The red paint showed the path of the sun across the sky. They believed the paint would help them face the day bravely.

Bravery in Battle

Although the Osage were at peace with nature, they often took part in wars with other tribes. Osage boys grew up wanting to be ***warriors.*** The highest honor for an Osage man was to show bravery in battle. Stealing horses and killing enemies brought a warrior honor. But the bravest thing a warrior could do was touch an enemy warrior in battle or just after he died. This act would earn a warrior a feather reward.

Chief White Hair

The Osage were tall people. Chief White Hair was said to be 6 feet, 8 inches tall. One story says that one day, when White Hair was in battle, he grabbed the hair of a white man, and the man's wig came off in the chief's hand! It was the custom at the time for white men to wear white wigs to special events.

The chief put on the wig and wore it to special events from then on. He wore the wig when he sat to have his picture taken and when he met important people.

In 1804 White Hair was one of the Osage chiefs who went to Washington, D.C., to meet with President Jefferson. People in Washington, New York City, and Philadelphia were fascinated by the tall Osage leaders who traveled through their cities on the special trip.

The Yearly Cycle

Life for the Osage moved between two of Missouri's land regions—the Osage Plains and the Ozark Highlands. Their lives followed the seasons.

Spring began when the men traveled to the Ozark hills to hunt for bear, deer, and elk. While the men were away, women planted corn, beans, squash, and pumpkins in the family garden.

In the summer, the Osage men, women, and children traveled to the plains to hunt buffalo. A few older people stayed behind to tend the gardens. Buffalo were very important. The people ate the meat. They used the hides for clothing and robes to keep them warm in the winter.

In the fall, the tribe returned to their villages to harvest the crops and gather berries, roots, and nuts. Women did most of the work in the gardens. Children helped their mothers with this job. The men went on one last hunt. They had to make sure they had enough meat to get through a long, cold winter.

During the winter, the children stayed warm by small fires in their houses. They slept under thick robes of animal skins.

Making Things From Buffalo

At one time over 40 million buffalo roamed North America. Buffalo provided food, shelter, and clothing. The people used all parts of the buffalo.

- Meat was eaten.
- Skins were made into blankets, tepee covers, drums, shields, saddles, and clothing.
- Hair was used to make rope.
- Horns were used for spoons, bowls, and cups.
- Bones were made into tools, knives, and needles.
- Fat was made into soap.
- Tongues were made into hairbrushes.

Longhouses and Wigwams

Osage families sometimes lived in large homes called **longhouses.** To build a longhouse, the people made a framework of wooden poles. Then the women wove mats of long grass and covered the framework with the mats. Some tribes covered their longhouses with large pieces of bark. Animal skins were also used to keep out the rain and keep in the heat from indoor fires.

The roof had openings where smoke from fires could escape. The door to the house was on the east side, facing the rising sun.

Sometimes the people lived in smaller round homes called **wigwams.** Wigwams were built about the same way as the longhouses. The families often lived in wigwams during the cold winters. It was easier to keep wigwams warm with a small fire. People also lived in wigwam villages when they went on hunting trips to the Ozarks. Year after year, the group came back to the same wigwam village to hunt.

Linking the Past to the Present

- What are some of the different jobs you and your family do in each of the four seasons?
- How does your home compare to the homes of the Osage?

A longhouse was home to several families. Your family might live with your grandparents, aunts, uncles, and cousins!

Riding Horseback

For thousands of years, there were no horses in North America. Then, during the 1500s, explorers came on wooden sailing ships from Spain, a country far across the ocean. They brought horses on the ships. Those explorers never came close to where we live now, so it was a long time before people in Missouri saw horses.

When French traders came to Missouri, they saw that the Osage had horses. Years before, the Osage got the horses from other tribes. The Osage rode horses to travel farther to hunt buffalo, bear, and other large animals. They also rode horses in battle. From a horse, a hunter could shoot arrows and ride away quickly.

Osage children grew up riding horses. They became expert riders and learned how to take care of the horses.

This drawing on animal skin shows that horses were important to the Plains Indians. They rode the animals during battles and while hunting.

Making Things From Nature

Today, we buy clothes, food, furniture, tools, and toys at a store. Because of this, we sometimes forget where things really come from. Everything has to begin with something natural. Wooden tables and chairs begin as trees. So does paper. Many of our clothes begin as a plant, such as cotton. What natural supplies were used to build your home? What plants provide much of your food?

Native Americans knew where all the things they used came from because they made their houses, clothes, and tools themselves. They grew some of their food, hunted and fished for food, and gathered roots, berries, and nuts. They built their houses from materials found in nature. Their clothes were made of animal skins.

Clothes

To make clothes, women took the hide of a deer or bear and scraped off the fur. Then they wet and stretched the skins to make them smooth and light. They used bone needles and ***sinews,*** or animal tendons, to sew dresses, leggings, shirts, robes, and shoes called moccasins. No part of an animal was wasted.

Just like today, the people wore warmer clothes in the winter. They wore little in the hot summer months. Compare these clothes to clothes adult men wear today.

3 MEMORY MASTER

1. Why was our state called "Missouri" by the explorers?
2. Describe how the Osage people looked.
3. What kind of homes did the Osage live in?
4. How did the American Indians get horses?

LESSON 4

WORDS TO UNDERSTAND

ancestor
elders
legend

The Osage View of the World

When Osage children asked where their ancestors came from, their elders told of how they were children of Grandfather Sun. The story said they fell to the earth in three groups. The People of the Water fell first. Then came the People of the Land. Finally, the People of the Sky came to complete the earth.

The Osage worshiped *Wah-Kon-Tah*. *Wah-Kon-Tah* was a force that tied all of nature—the sun, the wind, the rain, and lightning—together. Because they lived outdoors much of the time, the people saw themselves as part of nature. *Wah-Kon-Tah* gave them everything they needed to live. They gave thanks for all they received.

Legends and Myths

We can learn about the lives of the Osage and other Native Americans from myths and legends. A ***legend*** is a story that explains how something came to be. Legends answer questions about nature, such as why the owl stays up at night, why the fox is sly, or how the land was created. Some legends taught the children about what was right and wrong. Others told the history of the people.

Elders were respected older people. They told legends out loud from memory. The stories were passed from one generation to the next, all the way to modern times.

Animal Legends

The Osage lived in clans. A clan was a large family group. Each clan had one or more animal symbols. A clan might be called a turkey clan or a bear clan.

The Osage had many legends about animals. They believed animals could teach them lessons about how to live. This is the story of how one Osage clan took the spider for its symbol.

The Legend of the Spider Symbol

One day, an Osage chief was hunting in the forest. He came upon the tracks of a huge deer. He became excited and began to talk to the deer. "Deer, please let me find you. You will be a symbol of great strength to my people."

The chief began to follow the deer tracks. His eyes were on the ground as he ran faster and faster, trying to catch the deer. Suddenly, he ran right into a spider's web that had been strung between two trees across the path. The web was very sticky, and this made the chief angry. He tried to kill the spider that was sitting on the edge of the web. The spider jumped away just in time.

The spider began to talk to the chief. "Why are you running through the woods with your eyes on the ground?" the spider asked. "Because I am trying to catch a great deer that will be a symbol of strength to my people," the chief answered.

"I can be a symbol of strength for your people," said the spider. The chief laughed and said, "How can you be a symbol of strength? You are so small, I didn't even see you as I ran by looking for the great deer."

"Look at me," answered the spider. "I am patient. I watch and I wait. All things I need come to me. If your people learn this, they will be strong indeed."

The chief understood, and the spider became a symbol of his people.

—Adapted from an Osage legend

Activity

What Can We Learn From Legends?

1. What lesson did the spider teach the Osage chief?
2. What does this legend tell us about the way the Osage lived?
3. What can people today learn from this legend?

With your class, think about what it would be like to sit on the ground around a fire at night and listen to your elders tell you a story about how things came to be. Talk about how this way of learning is different from the ways you learn about nature and how to live.

The Osage Leave Missouri

After 1800, white settlers moved to Missouri in large numbers. This caused trouble between the settlers, who wanted to farm and fence the land, and the Osage, who wanted to be free to hunt everywhere.

The Osage knew there would always be conflict with the settlers. The tribe sold almost all of its land in Missouri to the United States. About 20 years later, the Osage sold the rest. Then they moved to Kansas and Oklahoma.

Native Americans Today

Many Native Americans live in our state today. Some have ***ancestors*** who lived here long ago. Others moved to Missouri in recent years.

Many Native Americans learn the stories of their ancestors. They talk to older people about their lives. They collect legends and write them down. They make baskets, pots, and tools as they used to be made. They work with the government to protect important Indian sites. Indian men, women, and children are proud of their history. They work to keep their customs and traditions.

Native Americans today hold feasts and powwows where there is singing and dancing and a lot of good food.

4 MEMORY MASTER

1. Wah-Kon-Tah was an important force that tied __________ together.
2. What is a legend?
3. What were some reasons the Osage left Missouri?
4. How do modern Native Americans preserve their history?

Chapter 3 Review

From There to Here

When this chapter began, people were hunting mastodons and giant bison. They were making weapons from stone and wood. They were traveling most of the time, living in caves and small shelters. Then the people figured out how to make spear throwers so they could hunt better. Later groups learned to make pottery and bows and arrows. They planted crops and saved part of the harvest for winter.

Mound builders built huge cities and large earth mounds and traded with people in faraway places. By the end of the chapter, the Osage lived in wigwams, went on long hunts into the Ozarks, and rode horses. Then they gave up their land to settlers and moved away.

Today, Native Americans live in large cities, small towns, and on farms. Adults work in many jobs and children go to school. They try to keep their history and heritage alive. Have you ever been to an Indian powwow or other celebration?

Activity

What Changed, and What Stayed the Same?

Look at the chart below. Charts help us organize and compare information. On a piece of paper or on the chalkboard, copy the chart. Fill in the blank spaces to compare the different groups of people. The first one is done for you. What things changed over time, and what things stayed the same?

	Paleo Indians	Archaic Indians	Woodland Indians	People Today
Homes	Caves and shelters made of rock or brush	Caves and shelters made of rock or brush	Wigwams or longhouses	
Food				
Tools				
Trade/Travel				
Work				

THE TIME
1541–1800

"There is a great deal of hunting, fishing, and other pleasures of life. . . . The land is filled with wild game and birds."

—A French soldier, 1751

1673
Marquette and Jolliet float down the Mississippi River.

1540 | 1660 | 1680 | 172

1541
De Soto's men may have entered today's Missouri.

1682
La Salle sails down the Mississippi to the Gulf of Mexico and claims all of the Louisiana Territory for France.

1720
The first African slaves are brought to Missouri.

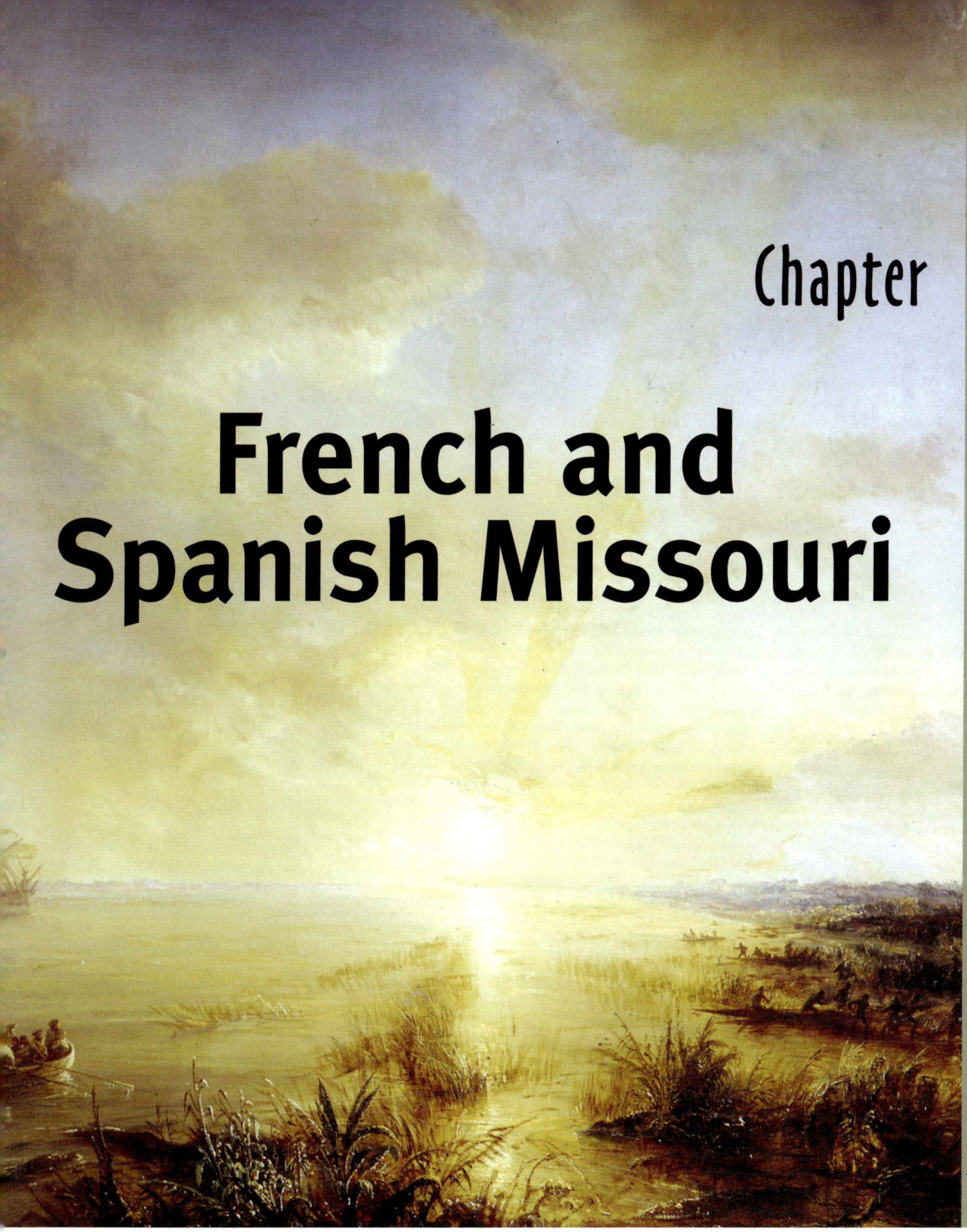

Chapter 4

French and Spanish Missouri

La Salle found the Mississippi River on his first trip into the Gulf of Mexico, but he sailed past it when he returned the second time.

What forces of nature moved these ships through the water? Would you have wanted to travel across the ocean in one of these ships?

1682–1762
France rules the Louisiana Territory.

1735
Ste. Genevieve is Missouri's first permanent French settlement.

1762
France signs a treaty giving the Louisiana Territory (including Missouri) to Spain.

1762–1800
Spain rules the Louisiana Territory.

1764
Laclede founds St. Louis.

1775–1783
The American Revolution

1780
Battle of St. Louis

1798
Daniel Boone and his family move to Missouri.

1800
France gets the Louisiana Territory back from Spain.

1826
Kansas City begins as a fur trading post.

1740 — 1760 — 1780 — 1800 — 1820

LESSON 1

PEOPLE TO KNOW

Christopher Columbus
Louis Jolliet
Father Jacques Marquette
Robert La Salle
Hernando De Soto

PLACES TO LOCATE

Canada
Europe
North America
Spain
France
Florida
Arkansas
Atlantic Ocean

WORDS TO UNDERSTAND

convert
disease

Two Worlds Meet

In Europe, people were talking about the new land across the Atlantic Ocean. They told each other stories of the beautiful land that was good for farming. They thought there was a lot of gold in the New World. They wanted to trade with the Indians for thick animal furs. They also wanted to bring their Christian religion to the Indians.

Traders and Catholic priests sailed in wooden ships to North America. The first meetings between the Europeans and the Native Americans brought great changes to the lives of the native people.

In this chapter you will read that the white traders and settlers brought some things that were good for the Indian people. They brought metal weapons and pots. The Indians liked the glass beads and mirrors they had never seen before.

Soon, however, there were problems between the Indians and the white men. They had different spiritual beliefs. They each had their own ways of thinking about how the earth was made and how to ask for blessings from a god or gods.

The American Indians also had different ideas about owning land. The Indians didn't believe land was something that could be owned by one person. Like air, it was to be shared by the whole group. The white explorers wanted to claim the land for their own country. Later, the white settlers wanted to own land, fence it, and farm it. They did not want the Indians on their land. This caused problems and conflict.

Disease Kills Native Americans

Another problem was ***disease,*** or sickness, brought to the Indians by traders and settlers. Smallpox, whooping cough, and measles spread quickly from person to person across the country.

The Indians had lived here for thousands of years. They had never had smallpox or measles before, so their bodies could not fight off the illness. The old and the young had the hardest time. Many Indians got well, but thousands died. In some places, entire villages died.

De Soto and the Spanish

In the 1500s, about 50 years after Christopher Columbus had found the New World, explorers came across the Atlantic Ocean in wooden boats. They started exploring places in North America. The first Europeans to see Missouri may have been the Spanish.

Spanish explorer Hernando De Soto explored America from Florida all the way to Arkansas. He was the first European to see the Mississippi River. He crossed that great river into Arkansas. He learned from Indians that there was "yellow metal" in the north.

De Soto hoped the yellow metal might be gold. He sent two of his men to check out the story, but they returned with just bits of copper. Did they find the copper in Missouri? If they did, they would have been the first Europeans in Missouri.

Was this story true? If so, who were the men? History is full of mysteries. There were many people who did important things, but no one today knows who they were or what they did.

What do you think?

Should we only study famous people who did famous things? Why or why not?

The first major European expedition to the Mississippi Valley was led by Hernando De Soto.

French Explorers

The first Europeans to come to Missouri to stay were the French. In North America, the French lived in Canada, but the French king wanted to control more land in North America.

French explorers moved down the Canadian waterways and through the Great Lakes. They dreamed of finding an easy water route all the way to the Pacific Ocean, but they never found one.

The Fur Trade

The French explorers did find something else of great value. They found fur. Fur was an important trade item in early America. The hides of deer, bear, elk, otter, and many other animals were used to make shoes, clothing, and other useful products. Indians often trapped and killed animals and traded the fur for things the Europeans had. But the French also had their own trappers, called *couriers de bois*. The name meant "men of the woods."

Trappers and skilled boatmen called *voyageurs* paddled canoes across lakes and down rivers toward Missouri. Along the way they trapped and traded with Indians.

On many of the trading trips, Catholic priests traveled with the fur trappers and explorers. The priests tried to ***convert*** the Indians to the Catholic religion.

Beaver Hats and Buffalo Robes

Europeans wanted animal fur from raccoons, foxes, deer, muskrats, river otters, and bears. But beaver fur was the gold of the plains. Beaver hats were the fashion in Europe. Hat makers could hardly keep up with all the hats people wanted. A felt hat made from beaver fur was the best hat a person could buy.

Indians and fur trappers found many beavers in Nebraska's rivers and in the mountains farther west. But it didn't take too long before men had trapped almost all the beavers living here. So people needed something else to trade. Buffalo hides became very popular. Fur traders especially wanted hides from buffalo killed in the winter. Those hides were thick with fur and made good warm robes.

How To Catch a Beaver

To catch a beaver, a person used a strong steel trap with a long chain. He placed the trap in shallow water. Then he poured an oil that smelled like beaver on a twig above the trap. When the beaver tried to smell the twig, it was caught in the trap and drowned. The trapper then cut off the fur and dried it. A fur skin, or pelt, weighed up to two pounds. Trappers pressed pelts in bundles and tied them together.

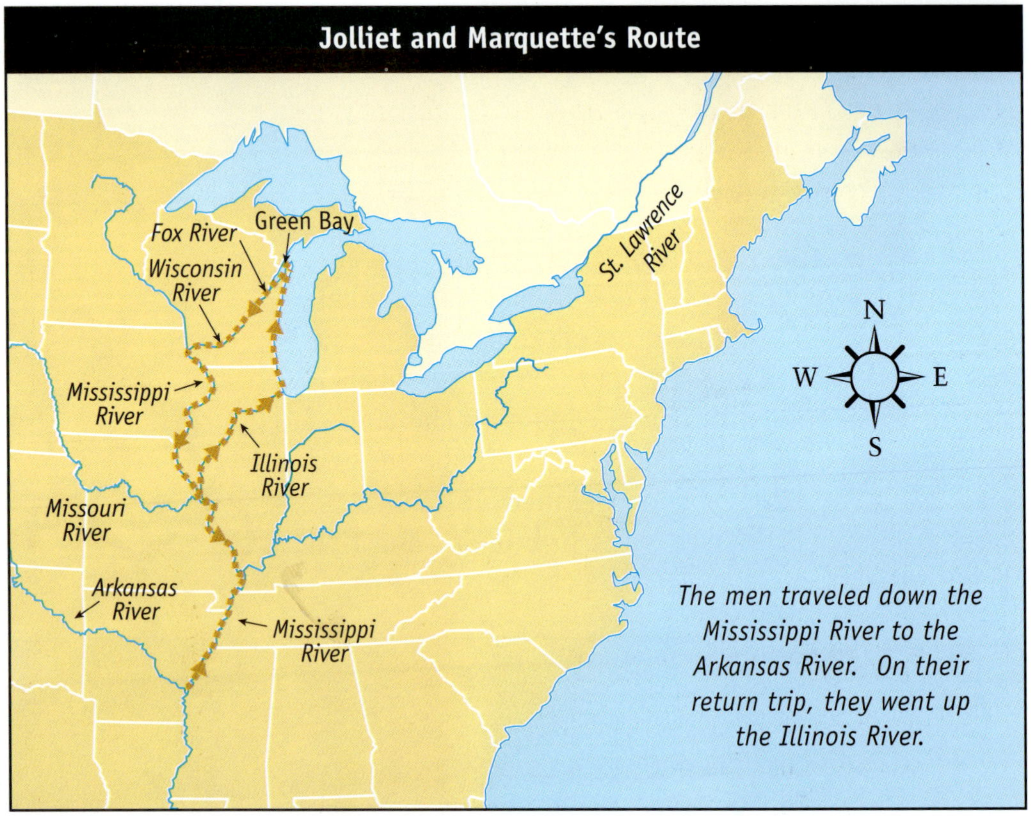

"Would that I be ordered to set out for foreign lands. This has been the object of my thoughts since my earliest childhood."
—Marquette, age 17, France

Marquette and Jolliet

The first Frenchmen to see the riverbanks of today's Missouri were a *voyageur* named Louis Jolliet (joh le ET) and a Catholic priest named Father Jacques Marquette (mar KET). Marquette and Jolliet floated in boats down the Mississippi River from the north. As they traveled down the river, Father Marquette made a map of the trip.

As the men came toward today's Missouri they saw some amazing things. They saw catfish so big they thought the fish might destroy their canoes. They saw Indians watching them from the shore.

At one point the men in the boats were terrified when they saw what Marquette called "black and red monsters" glaring at them from the riverbank. He said they had horns, red eyes, and beards. He said they were covered in scales like a fish. It turned out the monsters were Indian paintings on large rocks. Marquette and Jolliet were amazed at the art.

The most amazing sight the men saw as they floated past today's Missouri was something they first heard. They heard noisy rapids. Then they saw a large new river entering the Mississippi on their right. The huge river was moving so fast that the raging water was spitting out entire trees, branches, and even pieces of land. The river was the muddiest they had ever seen.

This river was the Missouri River. It was the second great river to impact the history of our state. Where the two great rivers met, Father Marquette put on his map an Indian village he called *Ou-Missouri.* Frenchmen then gave the name "Missouri" to both the river and to the Indians who lived there. American settlers later gave the name to their new state.

Marquette and Jolliet did not complete their trip all the way down to the Gulf of Mexico. Instead, they traveled past the land that is now Missouri and down to the Arkansas River. Then they turned around and returned north to the Great Lakes.

La Salle traveled down the Mississippi River all the way to the Gulf of Mexico. He claimed the whole river and the land next to it for France.

La Salle

Another important French explorer came down the Mississippi and floated right by today's Missouri. He was Robert de La Salle. He floated down the river all the way to the Gulf of Mexico. When he got there, he claimed the land around the Mississippi River and all of the rivers and streams that run into it for Louis, the king of France. He named the land Louisiana in the king's honor.

The Louisiana Territory included the land that is now Missouri and most of the middle part of what is now the United States. This is why Missouri would be French for many years.

1 MEMORY MASTER

1. What did the French explorers find that brought them much wealth?
2. Louis Jolliet and Father Jacques Marquette came down the ___________ River from the north.
3. La Salle claimed all the land around the Mississippi River for France and called it ____________________.

LESSON 2

PEOPLE TO KNOW

Auguste Chouteau
Francois Chouteau
Madame Therese Chouteau
Pierre Laclede
King Louis IX
Valle family

PLACES TO LOCATE

Haiti
Kansas City
New Orleans
St. Louis
Ste. Genevieve
Kansas River
Missouri River
Mississippi River

WORDS TO UNDERSTAND

frontier
merchant
tragic

Life on the ***frontier*** was hard. The frontier towns were far away from places in the East. The frontier was thought of as wild country.

Children today learn about the past at Ste. Genevieve.

Ste. Genevieve, the First French Town

French fur traders came in and out of Missouri for the next few years. But the first permanent French town in Missouri was Ste. Genevieve. It was a small town along the Mississippi River where settlers came to trap fur, mine lead, and make salt.

Salt and lead were very important. There were large amounts of salt and lead near Ste. Genevieve. Lead miners dug lead from underneath the ground.

- Lead was used for bullets, in roofs, and in windows.
- Salt was important to flavor food and to keep meat from rotting.

The settlers made salt by taking the water from very salty springs that bubbled up from under the ground. They boiled the salty water in large kettles. After the water boiled away, salt was left behind. It was something every family needed.

Linking the Past to the Present

Do you know of a business in your community that uses minerals found in the ground? How are lead and salt used today?

An Important Family

The Valle family in Ste. Genevieve had 14 children! Sadly, 7 of the children died when they were young. Children often died of diseases that doctors did not know how to cure. Small towns had no doctors at all.

The Valle family were leaders in the town. Even though many of her own children died, Marie Valle helped other mothers take care of their sick children. Francois Valle II, her husband, was a ***merchant.*** He bought and sold goods from faraway places like New Orleans. The goods were moved on boats up and down the Mississippi River. A lot of the goods came all the way from Europe.

The Valle family and their workers also farmed. They owned mills that sawed logs into boards and ground grain into flour. To help with the work, the Valles bought many slaves. You will read the hard story of slavery later in this chapter.

You can visit Ste. Genevieve today and learn how the people lived in Missouri long ago.

MISSOURI PORTRAIT

Auguste Chouteau
1749–1829

Young Auguste Chouteau came with his mother and step-father to the Missouri frontier and helped to build St. Louis on the great Mississippi River. Chouteau worked hard as he grew up. He learned how to trade with the Indians for fur. He earned their respect by treating them well.

When he grew up, Chouteau and his wife, Therese, lived with their many children in a large rock home in St. Louis. The two-story house had a porch that went all around the top floor. The family often invited important guests into their home and served fancy dinners on special dishes from France. The guests were surprised that so fine a home existed way out in the unsettled land by the Mississippi River. They were also surprised by the hundreds of beautiful books in the home. At that time, few people could afford books.

Chouteau made a lot of money in the fur trade. He sold furs to countries in Europe and to people in the United States and Canada. The family was able to buy a lot of land in Missouri. Chouteau helped start the first bank in St. Louis. Because he knew the Indians well, he helped government leaders make treaties with the Indians. He also served in the government.

St. Louis

The second permanent French settlement in today's Missouri was St. Louis. The great city we know today began as a few houses, a trading post, and a church.

The city was started by a Frenchman from New Orleans named Pierre Laclede. He made the long, hard trip up the Mississippi to come to Missouri and trade with the Indians. He brought his wife, Madame Therese Chouteau. Her son from an earlier marriage also made the trip. His name was Auguste Chouteau. Auguste was 13 years old.

It took three months for the family and their workers to make it up the river. They brought guns, tools, knives, cloth, and blankets from New Orleans to trade with the Indians. Going upstream with so much weight was terribly hard.

By the time the group made it to Missouri, winter was coming on. It was too late to build their trading post. They spent the winter on the Illinois side of the Mississippi at a French settlement called Fort Chartres.

A New Trading Post

In December, Laclede and young Auguste crossed the river for a few days and looked for a site on the Missouri side to build their settlement. They found a spot 18 miles below the mouth of the Missouri River. It was flat, so it would be easy to unload supplies. They marked trees where they would begin building the next year. Laclede said he believed this site might one day be the location of one of the greatest cities in America.

Then Laclede and Auguste went back across the river. In February, ice on the frozen Mississippi River began to break up. Laclede sent young Auguste back across the river and put him in charge of 30 workers. They built cabins and a stone building for a trading post. Auguste, now only 14 years old, finished this very important task.

Laclede came across the river in April and joined the work. He named the new settlement St. Louis in honor of an earlier French king, Louis IX. It would be a fur trading center and a gateway to the West.

A frontier trading post was like a store. People could trade what they had for what they needed. Indians brought in furs to trade for guns, food, and tools.

Activity

Cities and Rivers

Missouri's two largest cities are located along large rivers. Is this true for major cities in other states?

- On a map of the United States, can you find five cities next to rivers?
- Draw a map of Missouri. Add at least two rivers and three cities next to the rivers.
- Talk with your class about why towns and cities were often started along rivers.

Remember that in earlier times, it was faster and easier to travel in boats on rivers than to clear paths over the land and travel with horses and wagons. Remember that people can't live anywhere without water.

The Future Kansas City

Missouri's second largest city also has French roots. More than 60 years after people were living in St. Louis, Francois Chouteau (the grandson of Pierre Laclede and Madame Chouteau) and his wife, Bernice, left their home. They traveled a long way through the wilderness to a place in western Missouri.

There, near the great bend of the Missouri River, they opened a fur trading post. The place became known as Chouteau's Landing. The trading post and settlement around it remained very small for many years. The small settlement, however, would one day become today's Kansas City.

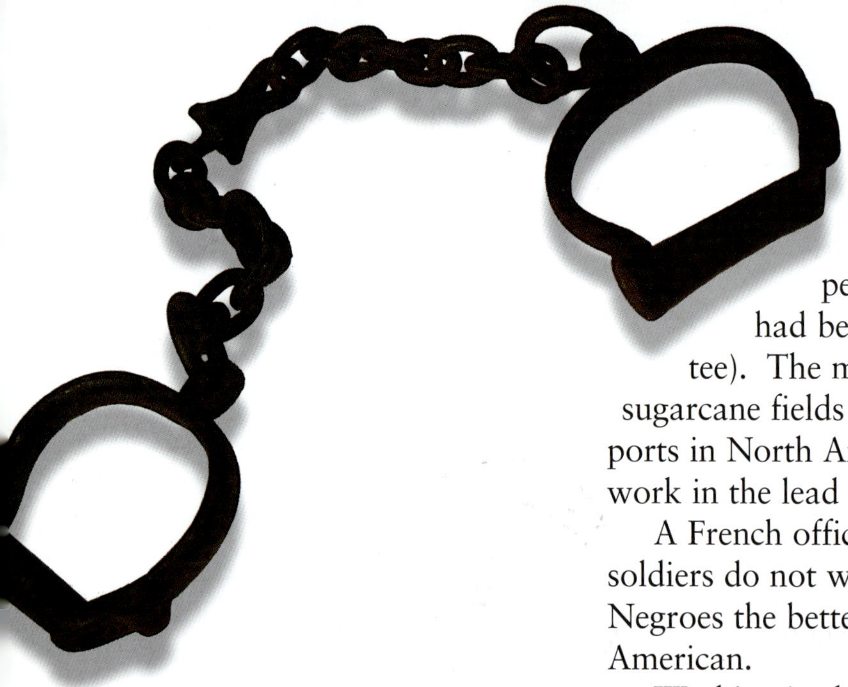

Slavery Comes to Missouri

The need for workers in the lead mines led to a *tragic* tradition in Missouri. The first enslaved people had been taken by force from Africa. Then they had been moved by ship to the French island of Haiti (HAY tee). The men and women worked out in the sun in the sugarcane fields there. Then the Africans were taken by ship to sea ports in North America. From there, some were taken to Missouri to work in the lead mines.

A French official in Ste. Genevieve wrote: "You can imagine that soldiers do not work in the mines, therefore the sooner we shall get Negroes the better it will be." Negro is another name for African American.

Working in the mines meant lots of digging. It was hard, sweaty work. French men bought slaves to do the hardest work. Sadly, there would be slaves in Missouri for 145 years.

The French treated slaves a little better than most other slave owners did. One of the

Men and women were brought from the continent of Africa on wooden sailing ships. When they arrived in America they were sold to different masters. Slaves worked for masters for the rest of their lives.

worst parts of slavery was that children were taken from their parents and sold. The king of France made laws that stopped this on French land.

About 40 percent of the people in Ste. Genevieve were slaves. Most French families who owned slaves had three or four. Many houses in Ste. Genevieve and St. Louis had a slave cabin behind the main house. The slave family lived in the cabin. Sometimes the slaves were treated very poorly. They had little food and no comforts. Other slaves were treated better. However, living under the control of another person was a horrible way to live.

Free Blacks

Most of the African Americans in Missouri were enslaved. Some, however, were free. One free black woman in St. Louis was Jeanette Fourchet. She had four children and lived in her own house. The family had some cows and grew vegetables. After her first husband died, Jeanette married Valentine, a free black man. He made money by hunting, trapping, and selling furs.

Different Cultures Meet

People of different cultures met in the Missouri region. They had different lifestyles and beliefs about the land they shared. How did their lives affect each other?

2 MEMORY MASTER

1. The first permanent French town in Missouri was ______.
2. The second permanent French settlement was _______.
3. Describe three important things Auguste Chouteau did in Missouri.
4. Kansas City started as a place to buy and sell ________.
5. What work did the first slaves in Missouri do?

LESSON 3

PLACES TO LOCATE

France
Canada
Montreal, Canada
New Orleans

WORDS TO UNDERSTAND

buckskin
calico
isolated
portage
voyageur

American Indians and French settlers enjoy a celebration. What instrument made the music?

Linking the Past to the Present

Would you rather live on an isolated farm or in a village? In a small village or a big city? Why?

Village Life

French settlers made places like St. Louis and Ste. Genevieve very different from English settlements on the other side of the Mississippi River. Most French settlers in Missouri were not actually from France, but from French Canada.

English frontier families usually lived on ***isolated*** farms, far away from each other. The French in Missouri did not live this way. They lived in villages like they had in Canada or France.

A village was better in many ways. People in a village could more easily defend themselves against Indian attacks. People could work together to farm. The French were very faithful to their Catholic Church, and by living closer together, each family could help support a priest and a church.

There was another important reason the French liked village life. English visitors often remarked on how much the French loved to hold dances and dinners. Many families owned fiddles, and the French even brought pianos to Missouri. They loved to hold festivals.

You can still see early French houses in Ste. Genevieve.

French settlers were called "habitants."

Land and Houses

In the village, the small houses were usually made of heavy logs with white plaster on the outside. Plaster gave the houses a fresh, clean look.

The houses often had a living area, a bedroom, and a fireplace in between. Most houses were one story with a steep roof.

Each house had large a porch that sometimes went around all four sides of the house. The porch was called a gallery. It protected the family inside from sun and rain. It also allowed the house to be opened up in the summer to take in cool breezes. People could sit and work outside on the porch and stay up off the dirt. Porches were a good place for children to play.

French Clothes

The French settlers dressed in colorful clothes. They combined European-style clothes with other styles from the Indians. The French did not weave their own cloth. Instead, they bought it from traders who brought it across the ocean from France.

A French man might wear a bright ***calico*** (printed cotton) shirt with ***buckskin*** (leather) pants and moccasins. Women wore long calico skirts and blouses. Both men and women tied colorful cloths over their hair. In the winter, all the people wore warm capes, jackets, hats, and mittens made of fur or wool.

For special days the people wore nicer clothes made of special silk and satin from France. The women decorated their clothes with ribbons and lace.

Feeding the Family

French settlers raised chickens, pigs, and cattle to provide meat, milk, and eggs. The people also loved to hunt and fish to feed their families. There were still buffalo along the Mississippi River when the French arrived. Wild bears, deer, turkeys, ducks, and geese lived in many places and were hunted for food. Fathers and sons did most of the hunting and fishing.

Early visitors to Ste. Genevieve reported that the French did not take good care of their farms. Why? Because they were often away hunting and fishing!

The Great Field

Outside the village were very large fields. There were fields called the commons where everyone could collect firewood and let their pigs and cattle roam. There was also a large field next to a river where the entire village, including men, women, and children, raised their crops of wheat, oats, and barley. It was called the grand champ, or great field. There was a fence around the grand champ, and everyone helped keep it repaired.

In the great field, every family got one long strip of land from the French king. This way, almost all families had part of their land touch the river. Since travel was much easier on the river than on the land, this made it easier to send their crops to market.

Families also had a small garden next to their homes. They grew fresh potatoes, pumpkins, corn, cabbages, peas, carrots, and melons. They grew apple, peach, and plum trees. They grew grapes to make into wine. They also collected wild fruits.

Cooking

Mothers and daughters ran the house and did most of the cooking. Even the poorest French families took cooking very seriously. Rather than frying or roasting meats over the fire as English or American settlers did, the French spent hours slowly cooking their meat in rich gravy. A favorite dish was buffalo tongue!

Linking the Past to the Present

Children in French Missouri helped their families with many chores. What chores do you do for your family?

Today, you can learn about how women made butter at Ste. Genevieve.

Voyageurs worked hard. They moved goods and people from river to river and place to place. Who is riding in this long birch bark canoe?

The French Fur Trade

Many French men preferred taking part in the fur trade to farming. They believed they could make more money that way. They were also drawn to the adventure of the fur trade. In fact, the fur trade was the most important way people made money.

Many single men, and even married men, left Ste. Genevieve or St. Louis and went up the Missouri River to trap animals and trade with Indians for furs. They were gone for months. The men were called ***voyageurs.*** Voyageurs loaded furs on boats and took them up and down the rivers to trading posts. The men learned many things about living in the wilderness from the Indians. They dressed a lot like Indians. Single men far away from their Missouri settlement often married Indian women.

French traders built small forts for fur trading up and down the Mississippi and Missouri Rivers. The Indians came to the forts and traded furs for tools, weapons, and blankets. The voyageurs then took the furs to St. Louis. Then the piles of fur were taken on a long journey to New Orleans or Montreal, Canada. From there the furs were often shipped to Europe. Missouri was at the heart of a vast trade network that covered thousands of miles.

River Travel

It took weeks to go by boat from St. Louis to New Orleans. The trip to Montreal took even longer because the men often had to leave their boats and carry all of their equipment and the valuable furs on foot. This was called a ***portage.***

The Indians taught the French to make birch bark canoes and buffalo boats. A buffalo boat was a round willow frame covered by buffalo skins.

The French also built *pirogues*. A *pirogue* was a hollowed-out log that looked like a canoe. Planks were added between the sides of the boat.

For large shipments of fur, the trappers used long keelboats. A keelboat had a wooden wedge called a keel along the bottom of the boat and a sail that pushed the boat along in the wind. The trip upriver was very hard. Men on the boat stuck long poles in the river and pushed the boat upstream. Men on the bank pulled ropes tied to the boat to force it upstream, inches at a time.

What do you think?

Why did French traders want to go into the wilderness for months or years at a time?

Native American Life Changes

The French were known for treating the Indians with respect. Some French fur traders, however, were not honest and cheated the Indians. Some traders also traded alcohol with the Indians. This brought misery to many Indians because their culture was not used to such strong drink.

The French borrowed many ideas from the Indians, including boats, moccasins, snowshoes, and ways of farming. The French and the Indians were partners in the fur trade. They cooperated with each other. Since the French never came to Missouri in large numbers, they did not kill too many wild animals or use too much Indian land.

But still, the French fur trade changed the lifestyle of the Native Americans. The Indians traded for French axes, hammers, and metal pots. Once they began to trade furs for these things, the Indians stopped making many of their own tools. Year after year, the Indians lost the ability to make everything they needed.

The Missouri Princess

Trappers and explorers changed the lives of some of the native people by marrying Indian women. In the early 1700s, the French explorer Bourgmont married the daughter of a Missouri chief.

Later, he took her on a very long trip across the ocean to Paris, where she met the king of France. The people of Paris called her the Missouri Princess.

No More Buffalo or Beavers

The fur trade also changed how the Indians lived with their environment. Since both Indian and French trappers had to trap and kill more animals than ever before, there were fewer and fewer animals. Buffalo were driven from Missouri. Streams that once had hundreds of beaver had none.

Each tribe wanted more furs to trade with the French. At times there were terrible wars between the tribes. They fought over hunting grounds. Where could they find more wild animals?

3 MEMORY MASTER

1. What were three reasons the French settlers lived near each other in villages?
2. How were the great fields used?
3. Why were furs important to the French?
4. Name at least two ways the Indians helped the French.
5. How did trading with the French settlers affect the Native Americans?

LESSON 4

The Spanish Gain Control of Missouri

When the French ruled part of North America, Missouri was part of a large territory called Louisiana. It included a huge region of land down the middle of what is now the United States. At that time, France, Spain, and England (the British), ruled most of North America.

Later, France gave Spain all of Louisiana. For two years, the French people in Missouri did not even know that Spain controlled the region. That is how slowly news spread in those days. When Pierre Laclede founded St. Louis as a French village, he did not even know he was in Spanish territory!

Then England took over Canada and the land between the Appalachian Mountains and the Mississippi River. When French people in Illinois and Indiana heard about this, many of them moved to Missouri. They decided they would rather live there under the Spanish king, who was Catholic, than under an English king, who was not. Religion was very important to the people.

The Spanish ruled the Louisiana Territory (and Missouri) until 1800. During that time, however, only a handful of Spanish settlers ever came to Missouri. The Spanish sent a few government leaders and a few soldiers to St. Louis, but most of the people here were still French. They spoke French and lived like they had before.

New French Towns

During the Spanish period, more new French settlements sprang up in Missouri. A French hunter and trader, Louis Blanchette, founded St. Charles. It was a small trading village up the Missouri River from St. Louis.

Florissant was another new French village north of St. Louis. Cape Girardeau was founded by French fur traders south of St. Louis.

PEOPLE TO KNOW

Moses Austin
Stephen Austin
Louis Blanchette
Daniel Boone
George Washington

PLACES TO LOCATE

England
France
Spain
Florissant
St. Charles
St. Louis
Cape Girardeau

WORDS TO UNDERSTAND

colony

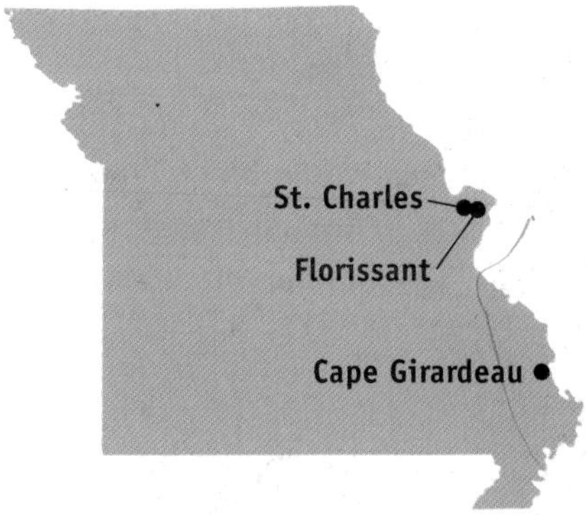

Tension With the English

A *colony* is a place ruled by another country.

Great Britain was a group of islands far across the Atlantic Ocean. England was part of one of the islands. The people in England are called British or English.

During the Spanish period, English fur traders often came into Missouri to trade with Indians. Spanish leaders tried to stop them, but the traders usually worked here anyway. This caused trouble between England and Spain. Both countries wanted to make a lot of money on the fur trade.

In 1775, the American Revolution began on the East Coast, far away from Missouri. England's American colonies fought a war to free themselves from British rule. General George Washington led America in the war against England that lasted over six years.

The American Revolution

At first, Spain did not take either side. Then France started helping the Americans. The French sent soldiers, supplies, and ships. Then Spain also helped the Americans.

When Spain entered the war, the British decided to attack the Spanish settlers in Missouri. The British sent a group of soldiers from Canada to attack St. Louis. There were only a few British soldiers, but they had the help of 1,000 Indians!

Many people today do not know that the American Revolution came to Missouri. Most of the battles were fought in the East.

George Washington was the first president of the new country.

The Battle of St. Louis

The Spanish leader in St. Louis prepared the city for attack. He organized 350 men to defend the city. They dug a trench around the small town and got cannons ready. When the British and Indians attacked, fire from the cannons kept them away from the city. The city was saved! It did not fall into English hands.

After the battle, however, some of the Indians stood outside the city. Within view of people in St. Louis, the Indians murdered 33 French prisoners. These were people who had not believed an attack was really coming, so they had not fled into the city for safety.

The United States Is Born

With help from the French, the Americans won the war in the East. The United States of America was a new country. George Washington was the first president. Missouri, however, and other land west of the Mississippi River, was not part of the United States. The people of Missouri were still ruled by Spain.

Americans had already been moving west across the continent, and many wanted to move into Missouri. At first, Spanish rulers tried to keep the Americans out. But the Spanish had few soldiers to patrol the Mississippi River. American settlers slipped across the river and settled in Missouri anyway.

North America After the American Revolution, 1783

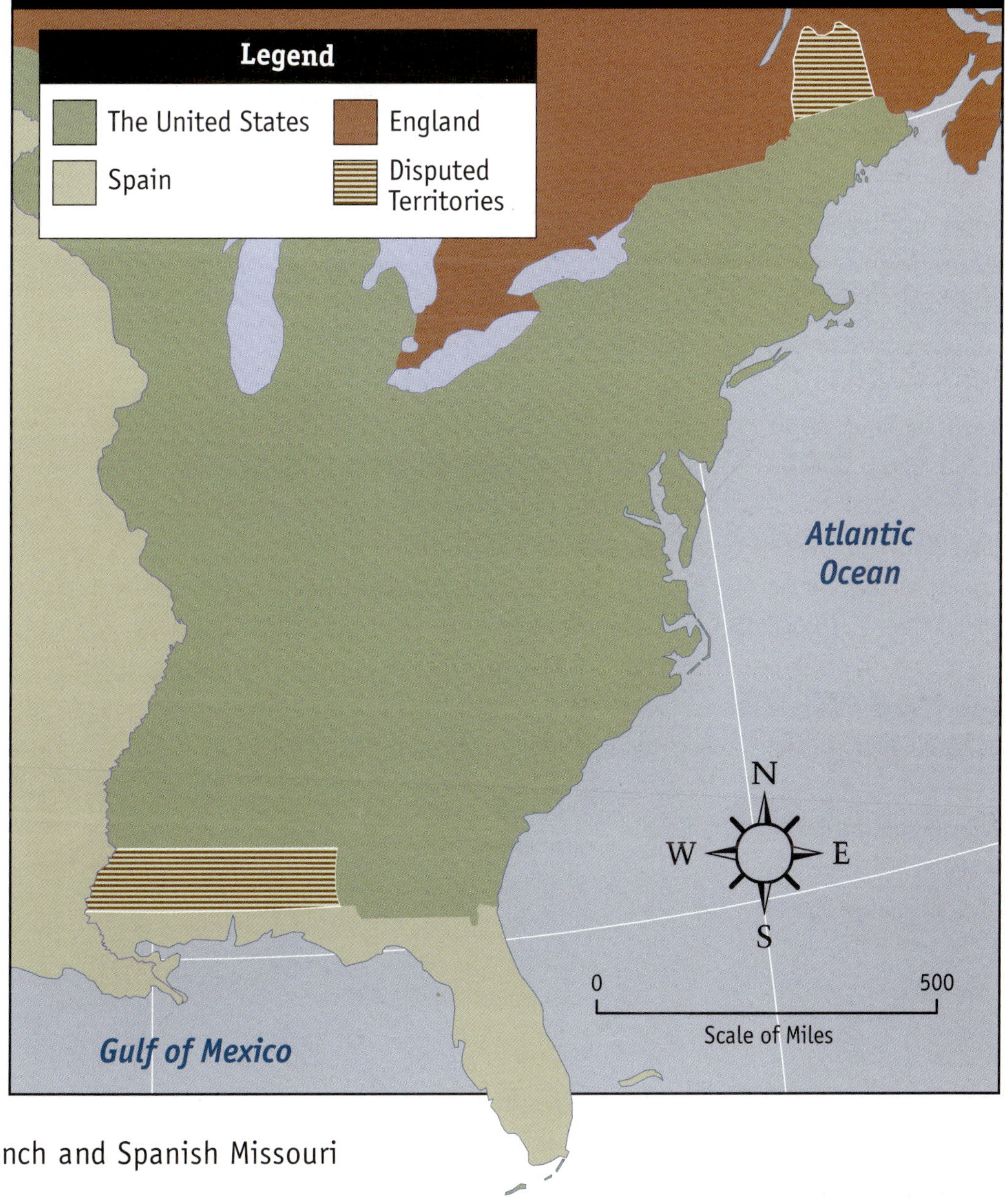

DANIEL BOONE

1734 1820

Daniel Boone is one of the most famous Missourians. He is an important part of American history and folklore. Boone was born in Pennsylvania. His family moved to North Carolina when he was a teenager. They all worked on the family farm.

Daniel, however, loved to hunt. He received his first gun when he was 13. He often went into the woods by himself for days at a time to hunt and provide meat for his family. Daniel became known as a skilled hunter and trapper.

As a young man, Boone fought in the French and Indian War. Later, he fought in the American Revolution.

Boone married his wife, Rebecca, when he was 21. As they raised their 10 children, he continued to hunt. He hunted to feed his family. He also hunted to get deerskins, which he sold.

Sometimes Boone's hunts took him away from home for up to two years at a time. He never liked living in a town. He would rather live in the woods, close to nature.

Boone is best known for leading the first American settlers over the Appalachians and into Kentucky. He and his men cut the Wilderness Road through the mountains so other settlers could travel more quickly.

During the American Revolution, Shawnee Indians who were fighting with the English kidnapped Boone. He escaped to warn others of a coming attack.

Whenever a settlement got too crowded for Boone, he moved his family west into the Kentucky wilderness and to better hunting grounds. When Kentucky became too settled, he looked farther west to Missouri.

By then, Boone's children had grown up, married, and had children of their own. The Boone families moved to Missouri. Boone was 62 years old, and he still loved to hunt. His sons, Morgan and Nathan, also hunted, trapped, and made salt. Boone's Lick was a well-known salt spring in central Missouri.

As Daniel Boone grew older, it became harder and harder for him to hunt during the cold Missouri winters. But even when he was over 80 years old, he still loved to be in the woods. After he died at age 85, he was buried in Missouri near Rebecca's grave. They were later moved to Kentucky.

The Boone's last home still stands in Defiance, Missouri. Boone will always be remembered as one of America's great frontier heroes.

Activity

Use Your Computer

The computer is a wonderful way to learn more about Daniel Boone. If you can use the Internet, look up these subjects and see what you find. Then use your computer or a piece of paper to draw a picture and write about something interesting that you learned.

- Daniel Boone
- Nathan Boone (son)
- Salt Springs, Missouri

Daniel Boone took settlers through the Appalachian Mountains into Kentucky. They cut down trees and moved rocks to make a road through a gap in the mountains.

Spain Welcomes Americans

Later, the Spanish began to welcome Americans who wanted to settle in Missouri. They changed their minds for two reasons. One, they thought the Americans would be able to help defend Missouri if the British tried to attack Missouri again.

Second, the Spanish thought the Americans were better farmers than the French settlers. They hoped the Americans would grow great crops in Missouri. The Spanish offered American settlers each 500 acres of land for a small fee. Americans began to move across the river in large numbers.

The Spanish also invited some well-known Americans to come to Missouri. Moses Austin came. He became very successful at mining lead near Potosi. He and his son Stephen later helped settle Texas.

Return to French Rule

Spain, far across the Atlantic Ocean, was a crumbing empire by 1800. The Spanish knew they could never hold Missouri and the rest of the Louisiana Territory if the English or Americans ever tried to take it. They only had 110 soldiers in St. Louis.

The French ruler decided to take back the French empire in North America. He signed a secret treaty with Spain. He gave Spain a small part of Italy in exchange for the large Louisiana Territory. France owned Missouri again.

In a later chapter you will read how the United States of America bought the Louisiana Territory from France. Missouri would change hands once again.

4 MEMORY MASTER

1. What two countries in Europe once ruled Missouri?
2. What was the American Revolution?
3. Why do we remember Daniel Boone?

Chapter 4 Review

From There to Here

At first, only different groups of Native Americans lived in the place we now call Missouri. Imagine their surprise when they saw white men in boats floating down the wide Mississippi River. They may have seen De Soto's men from Spain. Years later, they may have seen Marquette and Jolliet with Indian guides pass by in large canoes. Do you think Native American children saw La Salle and other men with him?

A huge part of North America called the Louisiana Territory was claimed by France, then Spain, then France again. These countries sent missionaries to teach the Indians. They sent explorers to make maps. They sent trappers and traders to trade metal tools, glass beads, and cloth in exchange for thick animal fur. Why did the trappers want the fur?

Some families came and farmed. From time to time, soldiers came. By 1800, France ruled the Louisiana Territory, including Missouri. The land to the east was called the United States of America.

Activity

Charting Causes and Effects

The cause is something that happened. The effects are the results, or what happened because of the cause. In the chart below, the cause is in the center bubble. Think of some effects for the empty bubbles. The first one is done for you.

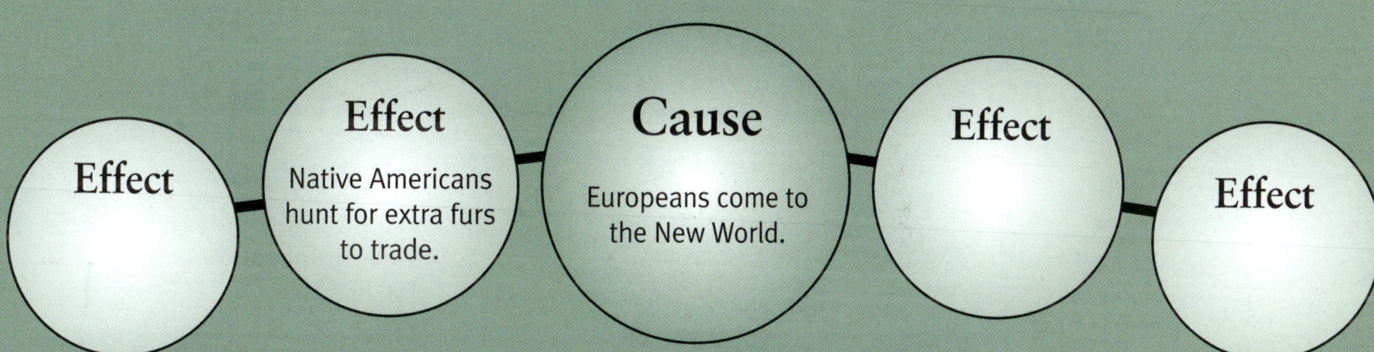

THE TIME
1800–1837

"We have lived long, but this is the noblest work of our whole lives."

— Robert Livingston, after agreeing with France to buy the Louisiana Purchase, 1803

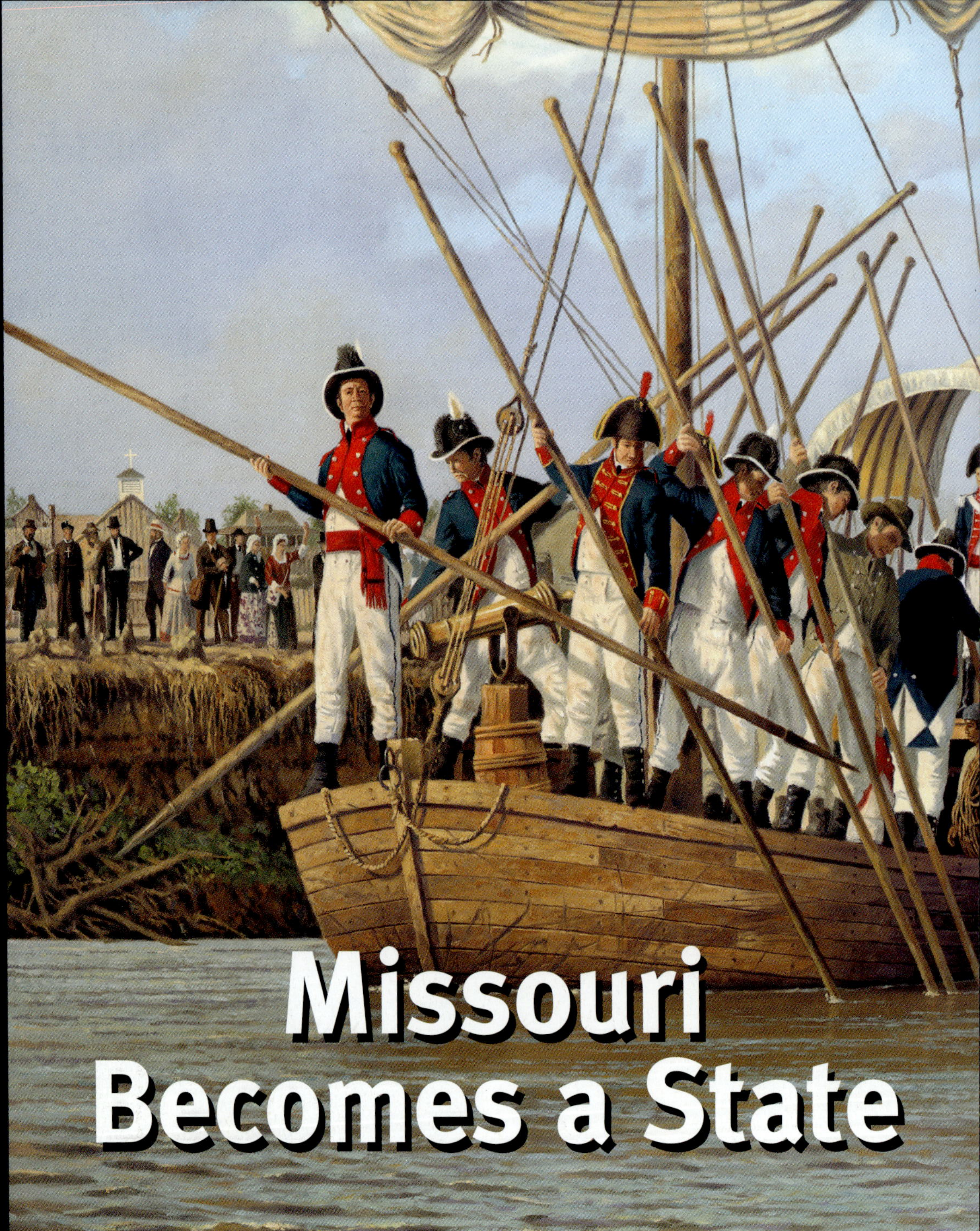

Missouri Becomes a State

Timeline of Events

1800
France gets the Louisiana Territory back from Spain.

1803
The United States buys the Louisiana Territory from France.

1804–1806
Lewis and Clark travel from Missouri to the Pacific Ocean and back.

1805–1806
Zebulon Pike leads expeditions from Missouri.

1808
Fort Osage is built.

1811
New Madrid Earthquake

1811–1812
War of 1812

1800 — 1805 — 1810 — 181

Chapter 5

In 1804 the Lewis and Clark Expedition departed from St. Charles on the Missouri River. The lists have been checked and rechecked, and goodbyes have been said. The men attended a Catholic mass and then pulled out into the water.

1819–1920
Stephen Long leads expeditions from Missouri to the West.

1820
The Missouri Compromise is approved.

1821
Missouri becomes a state. St. Charles is the capital.

1826
The state government moves to Jefferson City.

1831
Mary Easton Sibley starts a school for girls in St. Charles.

1837
The Platte Purchase becomes part of Missouri.

1820 — 1825 — 1830 — 1835 — 1840

LESSON 1

PEOPLE TO KNOW

Charbonneau
William Clark
Thomas Jefferson
Meriwether Lewis
Sacagawea

PLACES TO LOCATE

France
Spain
New Orleans
St. Louis
Mississippi River
Missouri River
Rocky Mountains
Pacific Ocean

WORDS TO UNDERSTAND

courageous
expedition
interpreter
permission

After shipping their goods in New Orleans, farmers broke up their flatboats and sold the wood for firewood. Then they walked or rode a horse back home. The trip took weeks.

The Louisiana Territory

For many years, the place we know as the state of Missouri was part of the Louisiana Territory. It was a vast stretch of land in the heart of what is now the United States. For thousands of years, the land had been the home of many American Indian tribes. Then France claimed the land. France sold the region to Spain, but very few Spanish settlers came to live. Then France got the region back.

When Americans heard that France owned the Louisiana Territory again, they were alarmed. New Orleans, at the mouth of the Mississippi River, was a very important seaport.

The American president at the time was Thomas Jefferson. He was very worried. He thought the French might try to stop Americans from shipping in and out of New Orleans. This would be a disaster. Americans needed New Orleans as a place to ship farm goods. They loaded their goods onto flatboats and floated them down the Mississippi River to New Orleans. Then they shipped the goods by sailboat to people in the eastern United States and other countries.

President Jefferson Acts

Jefferson sent two men to meet with French leaders in Paris. He asked them to try to buy New Orleans. He told them they could offer up to $10 million for the city. When the men were talking with French officials, the French made a shocking offer. They offered to sell all of the Louisiana Territory for $15 million!

The two men did not have ***permission*** to buy all of Louisiana. There was no way to contact President Jefferson and ask him if they should pay France for the land. It took weeks or months to get a message across the ocean. What were they to do?

The men decided to buy all of the land. This was one of the most important moments in the history of the United States. They were buying a huge piece of land that stretched from the Mississippi River to the Rocky Mountains. This would double the size of the United States overnight. Missouri would be part of that land. The land came to be called the Louisiana Purchase.

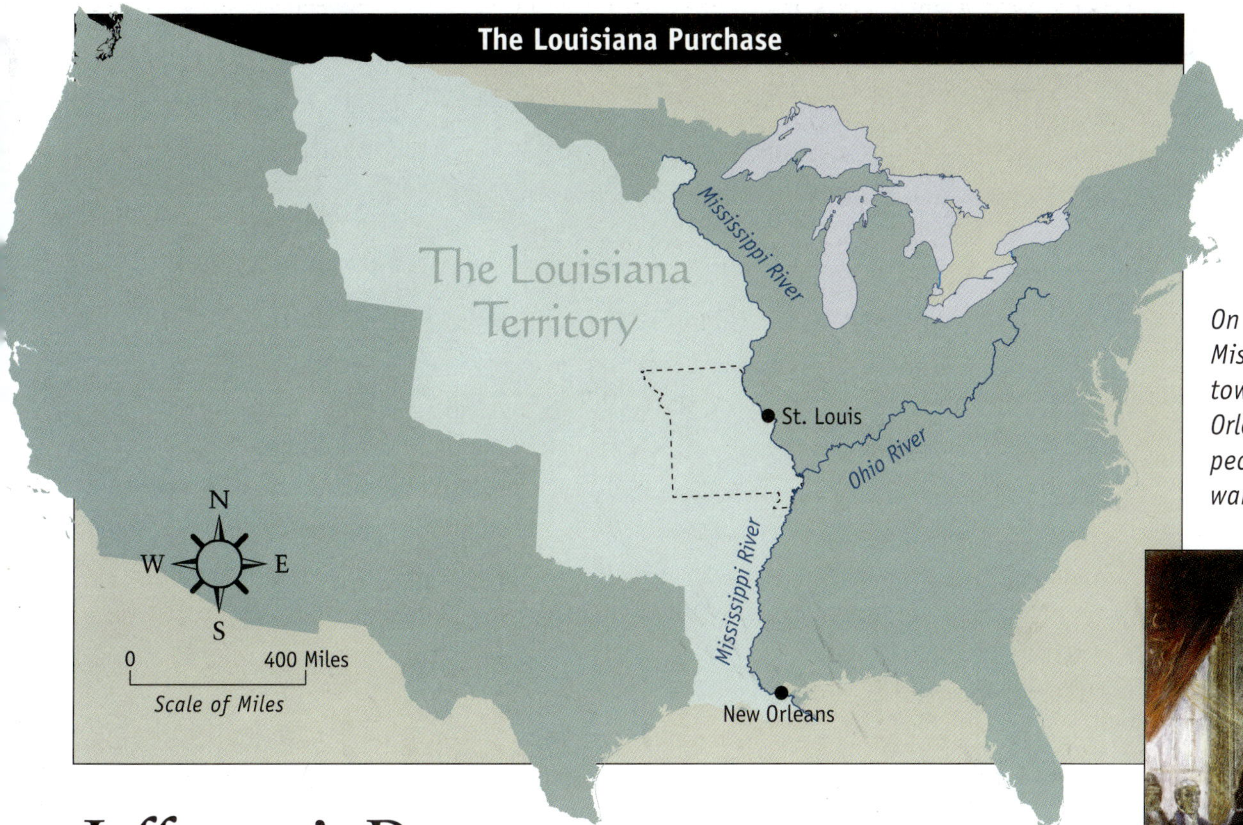

On the map, find the Mississippi River. Find the towns of St. Louis and New Orleans. Can you see why the people in the United States wanted to own New Orleans?

Americans sign an agreement to buy a huge tract of land from France.

Jefferson's Dream

President Jefferson was very pleased with the purchase. He wanted to know more about the land in the West. Once the United States bought the Louisiana Territory, Jefferson sent a team of explorers into the wilderness. No one knew what to expect. Many people believed there might still be great creatures like mastodons roaming there. There were stories of different Indian tribes that no one had ever seen.

Jefferson had no idea how long a trip from Missouri to the Pacific Ocean would take. He did not know what the explorers might find. But he had important goals for the ***expedition.*** What were they?

- Jefferson wanted the explorers to find an easy water route all the way to the Pacific Ocean. He hoped the United States could one day sell goods to China, far across the Pacific.
- Jefferson loved science. He wanted his explorers to bring back written notes about all of the new plants and animals they found. He wanted samples of plants, too.
- Jefferson wanted his explorers to meet American Indians and tell them that the people in the United States wanted to live in peace with them.
- Jefferson wanted maps of the land that now belonged to the United States.

What do you think?

When America bought the Louisiana Territory, leaders in the United States and France talked about the sale. Why were the American Indians who lived in the region not invited to the talks?

In this painting, Sacagawea is shown guiding the men through the wilderness. Historians now think that was only a myth. They think she mostly helped the men get along with Indian tribes along the route. She understood other Indian languages.

Lewis and Clark and the Corps of Discovery

President Jefferson asked his friend, Captain Meriwether Lewis, to lead the expedition. Lewis was a captain in the army and knew all about traveling in the wilderness. He knew how to live outdoors for months at a time.

Captain Lewis did not want to lead the journey by himself. He chose his friend, Captain William Clark, to help him lead the group.

The official name of the expedition was the Corps of Discovery. The word "corps" is a French word that means a team, or group of people working together. Lewis and Clark were the leaders, but they let their team vote on important decisions.

The Corps included more than 40 men. Most of the men were American soldiers, but some French trappers went too.

William Clark

York, an African American

York was part of the team. He was William Clark's slave. They had grown up together. York was strong, well liked, and a valuable member of the team. He was given a vote on important matters.

York was also a favorite with the Plains Indians. They had never seen a black man before. Sometimes they called him "Big Medicine" or "Big Magic."

After the journey, the other men were paid. York, as a slave, was not paid. He believed this was unfair and told Clark so. Clark did not pay him, but he gave him some time to go home and visit with his family. Many years later, Clark freed all of his slaves, including York.

Meriwether Lewis

Up the Missouri River

The journey of Lewis and Clark is truly one of the great adventure stories in our history and it began and ended in Missouri! The expedition left from a place near St. Louis in the spring of 1804 and did not return until the late summer of 1806. When the men did not come back after one year, most people, including President Jefferson, thought they must be dead.

The Corps had to work their way across Missouri by traveling up the Missouri River. One of the first stops was St. Charles. Clark, who was a very poor speller, described the town as having "abot 450 inhabetants principally French, those people appear pore and extreemly kind."

As they crossed Missouri, the men were amazed at all of the wild animals they saw. They hunted along the river and ate big meals around their campfire every night. But living in the wilderness was hard. Rain often soaked them to the skin. Clark wrote in his journal that bugs, especially mosquitoes and ticks, were terrible.

It was very hard work to travel up the river against the current. The Missouri River looked very different then than it does today. It was much wilder and had many hidden sandbars that could stop a boat. There were also underwater trees that could rip a hole in the bottom of a boat.

There were other problems. When the rope that men used to pull boats up the river broke, one boat spun out of control. The men feared they might lose all of their equipment. They jumped in the water and got the boat back under control. Later, the same boat floated too close to some trees, a branch caught part of the sail, and it broke off.

Also in Missouri, Lewis nearly died when he climbed high up a bluff overlooking the river. He lost his footing and began falling. He pulled out his knife and dug it into the side of the hill. Clark said that if Lewis had not caught himself, he might have been killed. That would have ended the expedition.

All of the things that happened to the Corps in Missouri helped the men become a strong team. In the wilderness, the only way to survive was to work together.

A Dog for the Journey

Before Captain Lewis left, he bought a large black dog. He named the dog Seaman. Lewis knew a dog would be a good companion for the trip, and Seaman was. One time he saved Lewis and Clark's lives. They were sleeping, and Seaman scared off a buffalo that was about to trample them.

Through the Wilderness

Lewis and Clark and their men slowly traveled up the Missouri River and spent their first winter with the Mandan Indians. There they met a French fur trapper named Charbonneau and his 16-year-old Indian wife, Sacagawea. Sacagawea was from a tribe far away in the Rocky Mountains, but years earlier she had been kidnapped by other Indians and brought east. She became an important member of the expedition.

The next year the group made the journey over the Rocky Mountains. At times they nearly froze to death. At other times they nearly starved to death. There were often no trails to follow. The land was wild and rugged. There were mountains to cross and rivers that nearly swept them away. They had to hunt and fish for food.

The men did find rivers to take them most of the way to the Pacific, but there were places where the rivers tumbled down in waterfalls or churned in dangerous rapids. The men had to get out and walk, carrying their supplies over mountains. The explorers did not find the all-water route to the Pacific Ocean that President Jefferson wanted because it does not exist.

Sacagawea

At Fort Mandan a French trapper joined the Corps. He brought along his 16-year-old wife. She was a Shoshone Indian woman. Her name was Sacagawea. She carried her baby son, Pomp, on her back the entire trip.

Sacagawea had great knowledge of the land. She was an important member of the group. She knew which plants were safe to eat. She was also an ***interpreter*** and helped Lewis and Clark talk with Indian groups.

Sacagawea helped the explorers trade some of their goods to get horses from Indians. The explorers needed horses to help them travel through the Rocky Mountains.

Lewis and Clark's Journey

Meeting American Indians

Along the journey though the Great Plains and the mountains, the explorers met many Indians. Lewis and Clark gave gifts to Indian chiefs. One gift was a medal with President Jefferson's picture on it. Lewis and Clark told the chiefs that Jefferson was their new "Great Father" in Washington, D.C. The explorers said the Great Father would protect the Indian people and trade with them if they were peaceful with white men and other Indians.

All along the way, both Lewis and Clark kept careful notes about all of the new animals and plants they saw. They drew pictures. They even kept plants and animal skins to take back to President Jefferson.

Lewis and Clark ended their trip on the Columbia River in Washington State. Can you see Sacagawea talking to Indians in the other boat? Who else is in the boat with Sacagawea?

The Pacific Ocean at Last

The explorers finally reached the Pacific Ocean as winter came. Sacagawea and the men, including York, voted on where to put their winter camp. They didn't waste any time cutting down logs and building a fort. They named it Fort Clatsop.

The Journey Home

The next spring the group began the long trip home. When they reached Missouri again, they were excited. The trip down the Missouri River was much faster and easier than the trip up the river had been.

The group had been gone for over two years. News began to reach St. Louis that they were coming. People were shocked because most thought the men were lost or dead. When the Corps arrived in the city, they were welcomed as heroes. There were parties and dances. Think of the stories they had to tell! It was almost like they had gone to the moon and back.

Thomas Jefferson was thrilled when he heard the men were safely home. Lewis traveled to the White House to see the president and tell him about the journey.

Calling from outside their burrows, prairie dogs were favorites of Lewis and Clark. They were the first explorers to write about prairie dogs. They called them "barking squirrels." Clark caught one by pouring water down into its burrow. Lewis shipped a live prairie dog to President Jefferson.

Results of the Journey

The greatest work of the Lewis and Clark expedition was just making it across the continent and back. However, Clark was a skilled mapmaker. He brought back important maps that showed rivers and mountains in the West. The maps gave people a better idea of just how large the country was.

Lewis and Clark's journals were a great gift to history. People still read them today. The news of a land of rich soil and abundant wildlife excited Americans. Many people decided to go west to trap fur and farm. They would nearly all come through St. Louis on the way.

Lewis and Clark became American heroes. They were ***courageous*** leaders who did what many thought was impossible. After their famous journey, both men took a turn as governor of the new Missouri Territory.

What do you think?

In what ways might the Lewis and Clark expedition have affected the Indian way of life?

1 MEMORY MASTER

1. Why was New Orleans important for Americans?
2. What happened in France that doubled the size of the United States?
3. Why did President Jefferson want to send explorers to the West?
4. What were some of the challenges Lewis and Clark faced?
5. How did the expedition help people learn more about the West?

LESSON 2

Zebulon Pike

St. Louis was the starting point for other explorers besides Lewis and Clark. Zebulon Pike led a team of explorers north from St. Louis. They were looking for the place where the Mississippi River began. They did not find it, but Pike explored parts of today's Wisconsin and Minnesota.

The next year, Pike left St. Louis again with a group of soldiers and headed west across the Great Plains of Kansas and Colorado. In Colorado, Pike left the Great Plains behind and came to the Rocky Mountains. He tried to climb a peak that still bears his name, but he was forced back by a blizzard.

Pike was amazed at how different the land of the Great Plains was from the eastern United States. There were very few trees, and the land was dry. For miles and miles there was nothing but tall grass that swayed with the wind. It almost looked like the ocean. He called the area "The Great American Desert."

Pike's description of the plains led many people to believe that Americans could not live and farm there. Over the next few years many Americans traveled over the Great Plains, but they did not stop until they reached California and Oregon.

Stephen Long

Major Stephen Long also led a team of explorers from St. Louis to the West. By this time, it was easier to go up the Missouri River. He and his men took a steamboat up the river to Nebraska. Then they traveled across the Great Plains and into the Rocky Mountains. Long agreed with Pike that the Great Plains would never be a good place for farmers. It was many years before people proved these two explorers wrong.

Linking the Past to the Present

Why were Pike and Long wrong when they wrote that the Great Plains were a bad place to live? Today, do people farm on the Great Plains? What crops do they grow?

PEOPLE TO KNOW

Big Soldier
Stephen Long
Zebulon Pike
George Sibley
Mary Easton Sibley

PLACES TO LOCATE

California
Colorado
Kansas
Minnesota
Nebraska
Oregon
Wisconsin
New Madrid
Great Plains

WORDS TO UNDERSTAND

boarding school

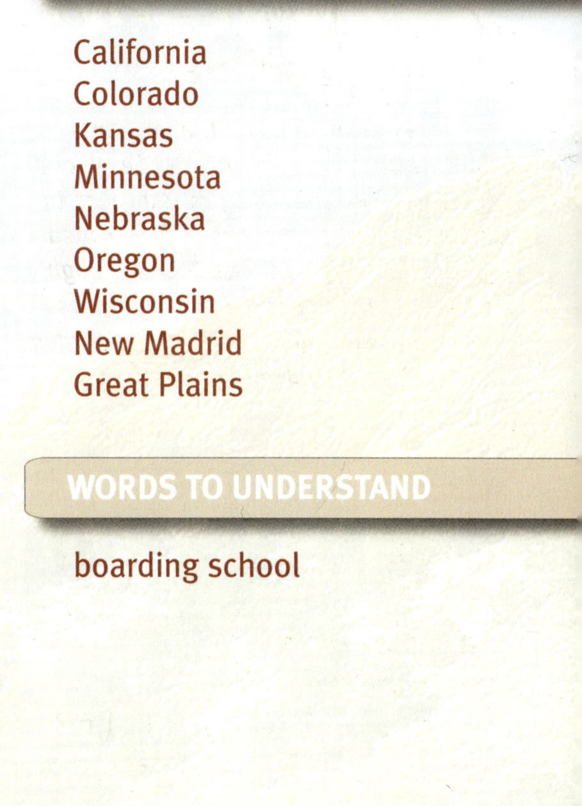

Pike's Peak in Colorado was rugged and hard to climb. Zebulon Pike had to turn back because of heavy snow.

Today, you can visit the site of Fort Osage. There is a **replica** *of the fort on the Missouri River.*

Fort Osage

At the time of the Louisiana Purchase and Lewis and Clark, there were still Indian tribes living in Missouri. The most important tribe was the Osage. The U.S. government built Fort Osage along the Missouri River. It was built so Americans could trade with the Osage. The fort could also protect settlers if there was any trouble. The Osage brought furs to Fort Osage and traded them for knives, guns, axes, blankets, and food. They could grind their corn in a mill at the fort.

George Sibley was in charge of Fort Osage. He gave supplies to the Indians. The government gave the Osage supplies in exchange for the Osage giving up much of their land in Missouri.

George Sibley's wife was Mary Easton Sibley. She worked with him at Fort Osage and opened a school for Indian children.

MISSOURI PORTRAIT

Mary Easton Sibley

1800–1878

Mary Easton Sibley was a pioneer woman who left her mark on the history of Missouri. Mary was born in New York State. Her father moved the family to St. Louis when Mary was four years old. He became the first postmaster of the city.

When she was still a young girl, Mary's family sent her to a ***boarding school*** in Kentucky. Mary loved school. She also loved to ride horses. She and her father rode their horses from Missouri all the way to Washington, D.C., when she was only 13 years old.

When Mary was 15, she met George Sibley, who was in charge of Fort Osage. They married, and she moved with him to the fort. Fort Osage was in the wilderness, with no other white people around. Mary brought an organ and as many books as she could carry.

At the fort, Mary enjoyed working with the Indians and meeting travelers who came through, including Daniel Boone. She and George never had children, but Mary loved the Indian women and their children. She helped start a school for children near the fort.

After George and Mary left Fort Osage, they moved to a farm near St. Charles. They called their farm Linden Wood. Mary started a boarding school for girls from St. Louis. She began with 20 students in a log building. At first she did all of the teaching, but the school grew, and she hired other teachers.

Mary's school became Lindenwood College, the first four-year college for women west of the Mississippi. It is now Lindenwood University and is open to men and women.

Mary Easton Sibley was a pioneer who made a difference in the lives of women on the frontier for years to come.

Activity

A Primary Source Letter: Big Soldier

George and Mary Sibley knew many Indian men and women who came to Fort Osage. One Indian man was called Big Soldier. He talked with George about how he felt about how white people lived. He compared white ways with Indian ways.

George Sibley wrote down Big Soldier's words and sent them in a letter to a friend. Here are some of the words that Big Soldier said. The words in these brackets [ ] are words that are easier to understand than the words in the real letter.

I see and admire your manner of living, your good warm houses, your fields of corn, your gardens, your cows, oxen, work horses, wagons, and a thousand machines that I know not the use of.

I see that you are able to clothe yourself, even from weeds and grass. In short, you can do almost what you choose.

You whites possess the power of subduing almost every animal to your use. You are surrounded by slaves. Everything about you is in chains, and you are slaves yourself.

As for myself, I was born free, was raised free, and wish to die free. I am perfectly content with my [life]. The forests and rivers supply [everything I need].

What does the letter mean? Talk with your class about these ideas:

1. What things did Big Soldier admire about how the white people lived?
2. What things did Big Soldier not like about how the white people lived?
3. What kinds of clothes could the people make from "weeds and grass"?
4. What did Big Soldier mean when he said that white people subdued animals?
5. What do you think he meant when he said that white people were in chains, surrounded by slaves?

Fort Osage

A Great Earthquake

In December of 1811, one of the biggest earthquakes in American history hit Missouri. It was caused by a large fault, or crack, in the earth's crust. This fault is known as the New Madrid fault because it runs under the town of New Madrid.

The New Madrid earthquake was felt as far away as New York. It even made the Mississippi River run backwards for a few hours. Trees clogged the river for weeks. The earthquake caused landslides and splits in the earth. Hundreds of farms in southern Missouri were ruined. Missourians felt aftershocks (smaller earthquakes) for weeks.

Fortunately, the New Madrid earthquake killed very few people. The population in southern Missouri was small, and people lived in one-story houses that did not fall down. But the damage was still great.

One man who was in the earthquake wrote about what happened:

> There was a great shaking of the earth this morning. Tables and chairs turned over and knocked around—all of us were knocked out of bed. The roar I thought would leave us deaf if we lived.
>
> It was not a storm. When you could hear, all you could hear were screams from people and animals. . . . It was still dark and you could not see nothing. I thought the shaking and the loud roaring sound would never stop.
>
> You could not hold onto nothing; neither man or woman was strong enough. The shaking would knock you loose like knocking hickory nuts out of a tree. I don't know how we lived through it. None of us was killed.
>
> —George Crist

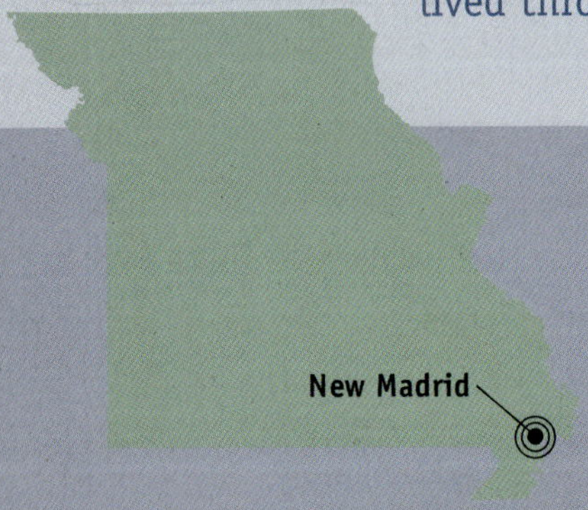

The New Madrid fault still exists, and scientists believe there will be an earthquake in Missouri again someday.

2 MEMORY MASTER

1. What was Zebulon Pike looking for?
2. How did Zebulon Pike and Stephen Long slow down settlement on the Great Plains?
3. What kind of work did George and Mary Sibley do?
4. How do we know what Big Soldier thought about how white people lived?
5. What happened at New Madrid?

LESSON 3

Missouri Grows

When Missouri first became part of the United States, about 10,000 settlers lived here. About half of the people were French.

Over the next 10 years, more Americans flocked to Missouri. They were drawn by Missouri's rich farmland. Within five years, 400-500 settlers were crossing the Mississippi River into Missouri every day.

By 1820, there were thousands and thousands of people in Missouri. Only a small number of them were French. Most of the new settlers came from Tennessee, Kentucky, and Virginia. Many families brought slaves with them.

Besides St. Louis, one of the fastest growing areas of Missouri was the "Boonslick" region. It was named after the salt springs in the center of Missouri that Daniel Boone and his sons had used. They had boiled water to get salt. The town of Franklin quickly had 1,000 people. The town of Boonville also sprang up.

PEOPLE TO KNOW

Henry Clay
Alexander McNair

PLACES TO LOCATE

Boonville
Franklin
Jefferson City
St. Charles
Washington, D.C.
Platte River

WORDS TO UNDERSTAND

argument
compromise

The Missouri Compromise

Finally, Missouri had over 60,000 people. That was enough people to become a state. The people were ready to write a state constitution.

At this time, the United States was divided by the issue of slavery. The states in the South allowed slavery, and the states in the North no longer allowed people to own slaves. At the time, there were 11 slave states and 11 free states in the United States of America.

Many people in Missouri wanted to enter the United States as a slave state. There had been slavery here since French days. People in the North, however, did not want Missouri to become another slave state. People in the South did. A new slave state would give slave states more votes and more power in government.

The Missouri Compromise was created by Henry Clay, a senator from Kentucky.

Two New States

The men in Congress had strong ***arguments*** about whether or not Missouri should become a state. Then Congress found a way to come to an agreement. Members made a ***compromise.*** Each side gave up some things they wanted. Each side also got some things they wanted.

The compromise was the idea of Henry Clay, a great U.S. senator from Kentucky. He said that two states should be allowed to join the United States. One would be slave and one would be free. Missouri and Maine would be allowed to become states. This would keep the number of slave and free states the same.

After the Missouri Compromise, there was still a balance of free states and slave states in the country. Maine became a free state. Missouri became a slave state.

One other part of the Missouri Compromise was that Congress decided that a line would be drawn along the southern border of Missouri through the whole Louisiana Purchase. No slavery would be allowed north of this line, except in Missouri.

The Missouri Compromise

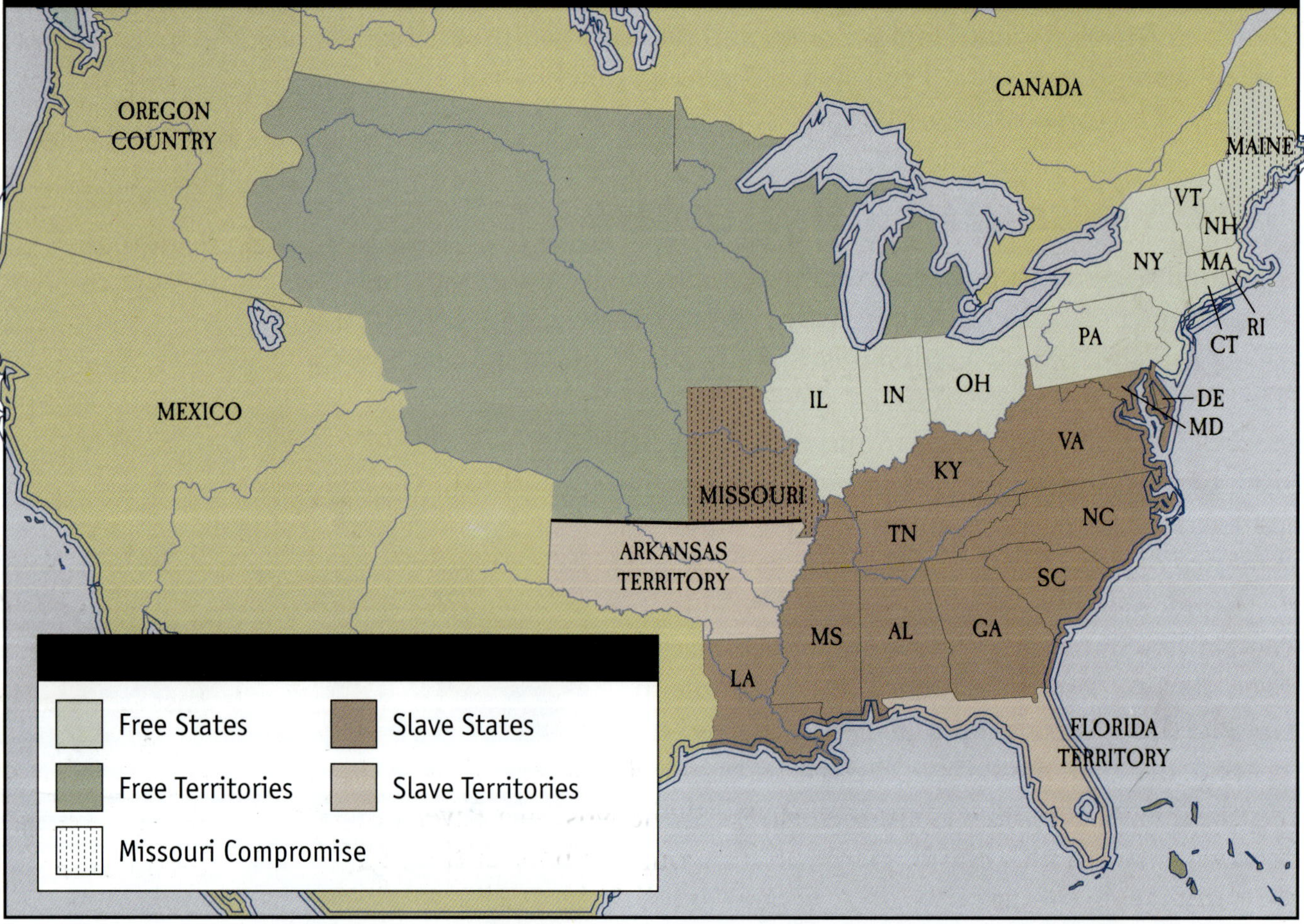

The United States also had land that was divided up into territories. Territories were different from states. Fewer people lived in territories. They could not elect their own leaders. They could not help make laws in Washington, D.C. Slavery was against the law in some territories but not in others.

The first state government met in this building in St. Charles. You can visit it today.

A State at Last, 1821

Leaders in Missouri wrote the first state constitution. Congress approved the constitution, and Missouri became the 24th state.

Then Missouri men elected leaders of the first state government. Alexander McNair became the first governor. The government leaders met in St. Charles. St. Charles was the first state capital. You can still visit the small room in St. Charles where the legislature met.

A Capital City

The state constitution said the state's capital city should be in the middle of the state. So a place overlooking the Missouri River in central Missouri was chosen. A new city would be built at the site.

Some people wanted to call the new capital "Missouriopolis." But instead, the legislature chose to call it "The City of Jefferson," after President Jefferson. The name of our capital city is still officially the City of Jefferson, but most people call it Jefferson City.

Linking the Past to the Present

Missouri became the 24th state. How many states are there today? Could our country add more states in the future?

Activity

Who Lived Here? Population Graph

Graphs help us "see" facts more clearly. Graphs help us see how facts have changed over time.

To understand the information on a graph, do these things:

- Read the words and numbers along the LEFT side of the graph.
- Read the words and numbers along the BOTTOM of the graph.

Missouri's Population Growth, 1800 to 1840 (not including American Indians)

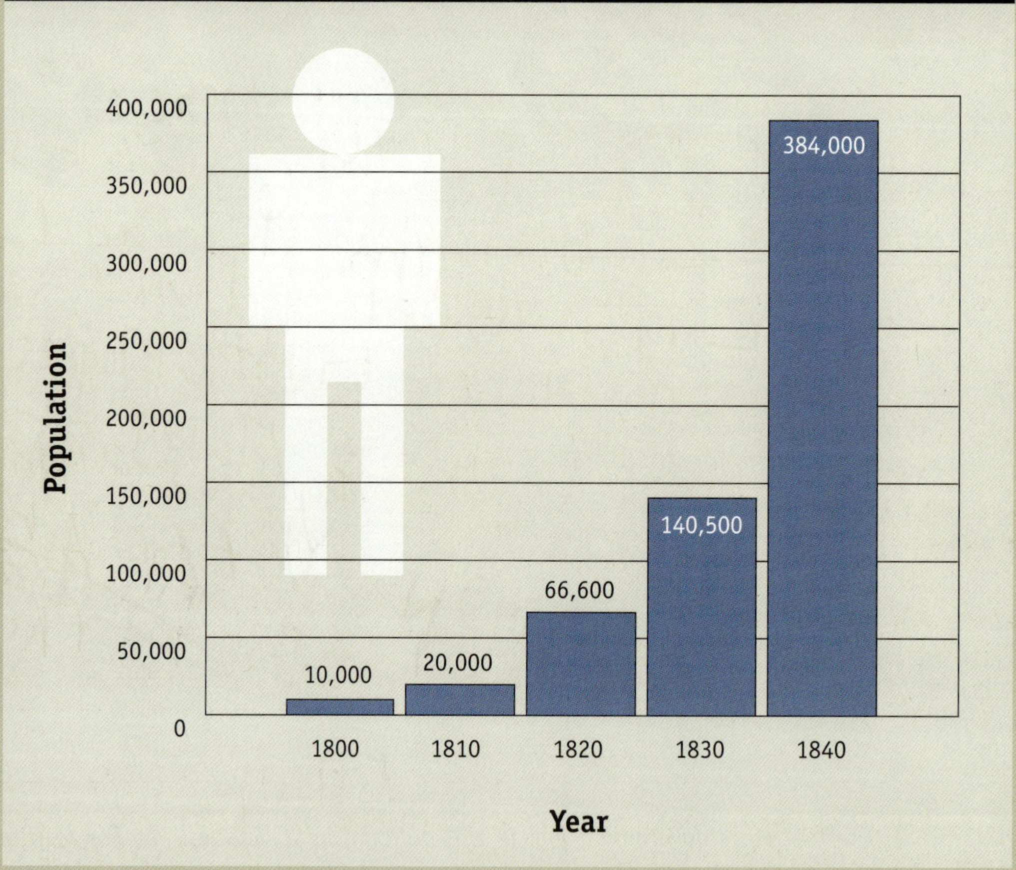

On a separate piece of paper, answer the questions below. Remember that many American Indians lived here, but they were not included in these figures.

1. In 1800, France owned the Louisiana Territory. Missouri was part of that land. About how many people lived in Missouri then?
2. In order to become a state, at least 60,000 people had to live in Missouri. In 1821, Missouri was made a state. How many people lived here then?
3. In 1840, about how many more people lived in Missouri than in 1820?
4. A decade is 10 years. In which decade did our state's population grow the most?

3 MEMORY MASTER

1. List two reasons new settlers came to Missouri.
2. How did the Missouri Compromise help Missouri become a state?
3. What city was our first state capital?

Chapter 5 Review

From There to Here

At the beginning of this chapter, Missouri was part of the Louisiana Territory. It was not a state. By the end of the chapter, Missouri was the 24th state in the United States of America. Finally, our state's people could vote for their own leaders and make their own state laws. At first, St. Charles was the capital. Then Jefferson City was built as a new capital city.

What happened that helped Missouri's population grow enough to become a state? Lewis and Clark's Corps of Discovery and other explorers made people in the East more aware of Missouri. Many people passed through on their way to the West. Farmers heard about the fertile land in Missouri. Laws were passed that allowed slavery in our state, so more farmers came and brought slaves with them.

The issue of slavery almost stopped Missouri from becoming a state. Then the Missouri Compromise was agreed on. People on both sides of the issue gave in a little so that the country would have new states and still have a careful balance between free states and slave states.

Activity

Missouri's Borders

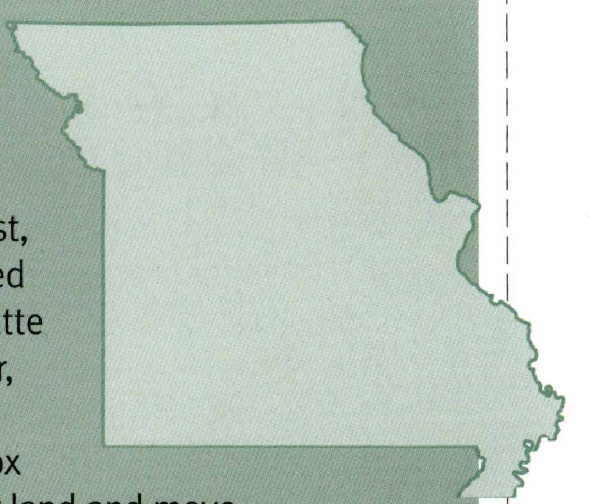

Have you ever noticed that Missouri's "boot heel" looks out of place? It became part of Missouri because a man named J. Walker, who owned land between two rivers, wanted his land to be part of the new state.

Our western border also changed after Missouri became a state. At first, our western and southern borders were straight. Then more farmers moved into the region where the border juts out as it follows the Missouri and Platte Rivers. They wanted the good land and the water from the rivers. However, this was Indian land.

William Clark and other men met with the Sioux, Iowas, and Sac and Fox Indians to talk about the land. Clark told the Indians they should sell their land and move farther west. The Indians did not want to move, but they did. The farmers kept coming. The land became part of Missouri.

1. Look at the map closely for a minute.
2. Shut your eyes and draw the shape of the new state from memory. How close were you? Did you include the "boot heel" and the uneven part of the western border?

THE TIME
1807–1860

Oh, don't you remember sweet Betsey from Pike,
Who crossed the big mountains with her husband Ike,
With two yoke of cattle, a large yellow dog,
A tall Shanghai rooster and one spotted hog?

—*from an American folksong*

Timeline of Events

1805

1807
The Missouri Fur Company starts in St. Louis.

1817
The *Zebulon Pike* is the first steamboat to dock in St. Louis.

1820

1821
Missouri becomes the 24th state of the Union.

1821
William Becknell opens the Santa Fe Trail.

1822
William Ashley founds the Rocky Mountain Fur Company.

1825

Gateway to the West

Chapter 6

An artist painted this scene of St. Louis in 1846. Notice the buildings along the river, many kinds of boats, and the pioneer wagons across the river in Illinois. What does the painting show about life around St. Louis during that time? If the artist were painting this view today, how would the painting look different? How long ago was the painting made?

1836 The Whitmans travel to Oregon Country.

1838 Mormon settlers are driven from Missouri.

1842 John C. Fremont explores the West.

1843 Peter Burnett leads settlers on the Oregon Trail.

1848 Gold is discovered in California.

1849 A cholera epidemic hits St. Louis.

1849 Forty-niners leave Missouri for California gold fields.

1855 Freight service begins across the Great Plains.

1856 The steamboat *Arabia* sinks in the Missouri River.

1857 Stagecoach service between Missouri and California begins.

1859 The first railroad crosses Missouri.

1860 The Pony Express begins mail service between Missouri and California.

1835 — 1840 — 1845 — 1850 — 1855 — 1860

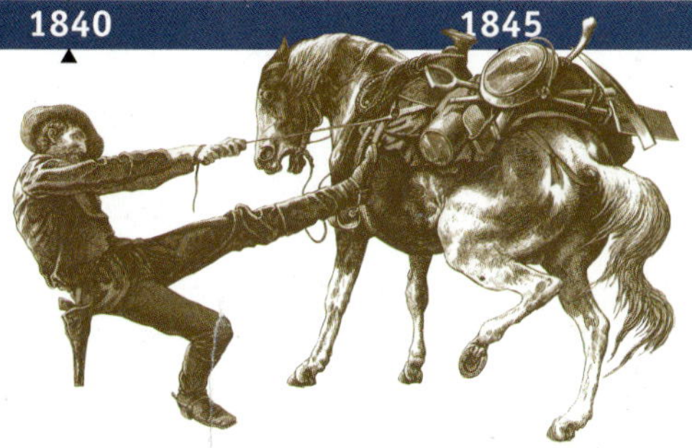

Today, the tall Gateway Arch welcomes visitors to St. Louis. Although the arch wasn't built during pioneer times, St. Louis welcomed weary visitors who stopped to rest and get supplies for their trek to the West.

LESSON 1

Gateway to the West

Today, people from all over the world come to St. Louis to see the Gateway Arch. A gateway means an open gate, or door, into a place. In pioneer times, Missouri was a gateway to all the beautiful land in the West.

PEOPLE TO KNOW

James Beckwourth
Jim Bridger
Kit Carson

PLACES TO LOCATE

Kansas City
St. Louis
Rocky Mountains
Yellowstone National Park

WORDS TO UNDERSTAND

exaggerate
petrified
rendezvous
wilderness

The Fur Trade Moves West

The fur trade had been important to the French and the Indians. It was still important when Missouri became a state. It was especially important to St. Louis.

Beaver hats were still very popular in Europe. But beavers were getting harder and harder to find. Almost all the beavers in Missouri had already been killed, so fur trappers had to go farther and farther west to find the animals. The trappers had to go all the way to the Rocky Mountains.

St. Louis Fur Companies

Fur companies in St. Louis sent men to the Rockies to trap beaver. One of the first companies to do this was the Missouri Fur Company. The company had helped supply Lewis and Clark with supplies for their long journey. When the explorers came back, their stories excited men in the company. They wanted to trap beavers and other animals in the West.

Another company was the Rocky Mountain Fur Company. It advertised in Missouri newspapers for brave young men. The men could earn money by trapping animals in the Rockies and then selling the fur. The ads said the men would be gone for up to three years.

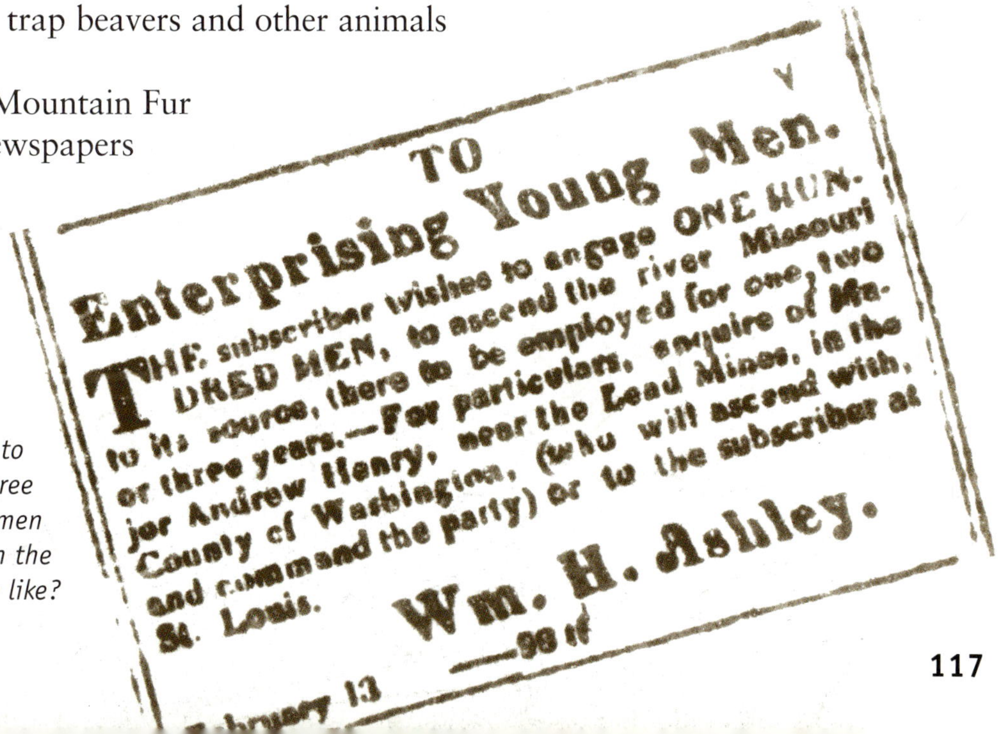

TO

Enterprising Young Men.

THE subscriber wishes to engage ONE HUNDRED MEN, to ascend the river Missouri to its source, there to be employed for one, two or three years.—For particulars, enquire of Major Andrew Henry, near the Lead Mines, in the County of Washington, (who will ascend with, and command the party) or to the subscriber at St. Louis.

Wm. H. Ashley.

February 13 —98 tf

This old newspaper ad says men are needed to "ascend the river Missouri for one, two, or three years." What does that mean? How many men were needed? What do you think their life in the wilderness would be like?

Both trappers and Indians enjoyed a rendezvous. It was a time for trading, playing, and relaxing after a long season of hard work.

Mountain Men

Young men from Missouri joined the fur trade and went west. They hoped to make money fast. They wanted to live in the ***wilderness*** and see new lands that no white men had ever seen before. They would be facing very cold and very hot weather. There would be wild animals. Some men found the danger exciting. The trappers were called "mountain men."

Trapping was dangerous, hard work. Mountain men spent the fall and spring of each year standing in cold mountain streams. They set traps and waited for beavers to get caught in them. Then they took the dead beavers from the traps and skinned them. Many Indians did not like the trappers because they took too many animals. Sometimes the Indians attacked and killed the mountain men.

Other times the mountain men became friends with Indians. Winters in the mountains were long and cold, but the trappers stayed warm in Indian lodges. Many mountain men married Indian women and had children. The whole family helped with the work.

The Rendezvous

In the summer, animal furs were not very thick, so they were not worth trapping. Summer was a good time for mountain men to gather at a ***rendezvous*** to trade their furs. Rendezvous is a French word that means "a place and time of meeting."

Trappers met in the valleys of the Rocky Mountains. There was a lot of buying and selling. Mountain men and Indians sold their furs to fur companies and used the money to buy supplies. They needed blankets, coffee, gunpowder, knives, and rifles for the coming year.

The rendezvous was also a time of great fun. Many men spent months alone in the mountains. It was great to be around other trappers and Indians for storytelling, feasts, races, and gambling. By the end of the rendezvous, some mountain men had spent all the money they had earned.

Jim Bridger

Mountain Men Heroes

Several Missouri boys who became mountain men became famous American heroes. Boys and girls back East read about them in books called dime novels. These were small books of stories that sold for only a dime. The adventures of men like Jim Bridger and Kit Carson made people in the East want to see the West. Many stories about mountain men were ***exaggerated.*** That means the stories sounded much more exciting than the truth.

Linking the Past to the Present

Do people still tell tall tales to make us laugh? Do you know a tall tale?

Tall Tales

When they sat around campfires at the rendezvous, mountain men told tall tales about places they had been. Many of the stories were not true. They were meant to make other people laugh.

One of the great mountain men was a Missourian named Jim Bridger. He told stories of glass mountains and how he had been to Pike's Peak in Colorado "when it was still a hole in the ground."

One of Bridger's most famous stories was of seeing:

> peetrified birds a sittin' on peetrified trees a singin' peetrified songs in the peetrified air. The flowers and leaves and grass were peetrified, and they shone in a peculiar moonlight. That was peetrified too.

People laughed at this story, but in fact, Bridger was probably the first white man to see the ***petrified*** trees in what is now Yellowstone National Park! A petrified tree is one that has turned to stone over thousands of years.

When Jim Bridger was an older man, he lived on a farm near Kansas City. He still told tall tales of his days in the mountains.

Kit Carson spent most of his childhood near Boone's Lick, Missouri. As a young man, he trapped, explored, and guided other explorers throughout the West.

Kit Carson

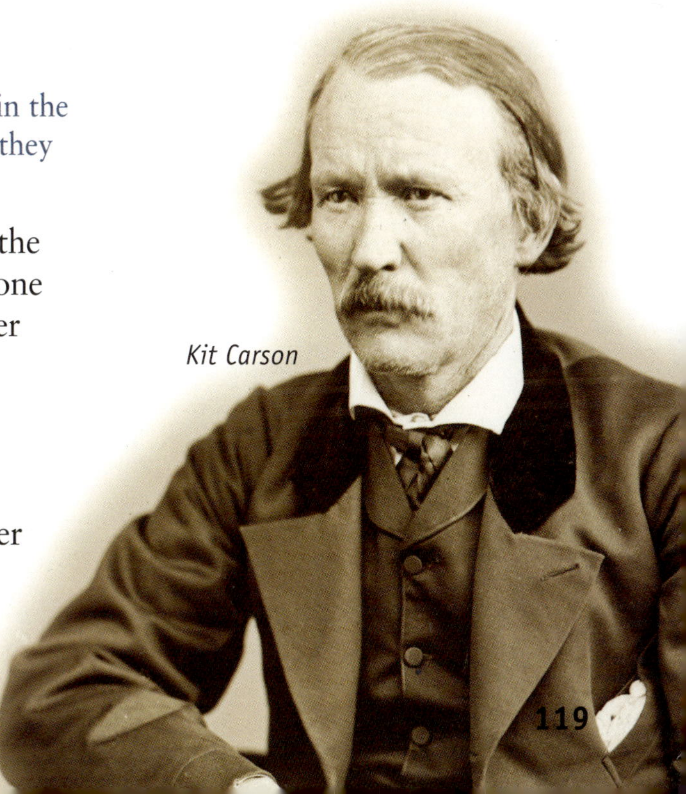

MISSOURI PORTRAIT

James Beckwourth
1798–1866

James Beckwourth was an African American slave who grew up near St. Charles. His father was white and sent Jim to St. Louis to school when he was 10 years old. Jim learned to read and write, which was something most slaves were not allowed to do.

Later, Jim read an ad in a newspaper. The ad asked men to go west to trap fur. Jim wanted to go. Before he left, Jim's father gave him his freedom.

For years Jim Beckwourth traveled through the West. He trapped animals and explored new places. He found a pass through the steep mountains on the way to California that was named for him. Thousands of people later used the pass to move to California.

Beckwourth got along well with American Indians. He wore Indian clothing. He was accepted by the Crow tribe and lived with them for years. He married a Crow woman. The Crow came to think of Jim as one of their leaders.

Later in life, Jim Beckwourth was an important scout for the army. He knew the West like few other men.

An author wrote about the trapper's adventures in a book titled *The Life and Adventures of James P. Beckwourth: Mountaineer, Scout, and Pioneer, and Chief of the Crow Nation of Indians*. Many of the stories in the book are exaggerated, but the book made Jim famous. The boy who started out as a slave became one of the most famous mountain men.

The Fur Trade Ends

Mountain men are important to our history. They helped map the West. They taught people in the East about the American Indians, animals, and the beautiful land in the West.

When people in Europe started wearing silk hats instead of beaver hats, the fur trade ended. Then some of the great mountain men became scouts for the U.S. Army in the West. Others guided families going to Oregon or California through the hard mountain passes.

1 MEMORY MASTER

1. Why was Missouri called the Gateway to the West?
2. Why did young men want to work as fur trappers?
3. What kinds of work did the fur trappers do?
4. Describe what went on during a rendezvous.
5. What was unusual about the life of Jim Beckwourth?

A Jumping-Off Point

When Missouri became the 24th state, it was farther west than any other state in the country. Many people wanted to come to Missouri to live and farm, but many others wanted to go even farther west to places like Oregon and California.

Oregon and California were a very long way from the rest of the United States. They were across the Great Plains and over the rugged Rocky Mountains.

Missouri was the last settled region the ***pioneers*** went through before making their long journey. When they left Missouri, the pioneers felt like they were jumping off the map and into a vast wilderness. Many places in Missouri became known as jumping-off points. First St. Louis, then Franklin, Independence, St. Joseph, and Westport (an early name for Kansas City) all became known as jumping-off points.

The song at the beginning of this chapter is "Sweet Betsey of Pike." Pike refers to Pike County in Missouri. This song tells us that many Missourians also got caught up in the excitement of moving west. Why did the pioneers make the hard trip?

- Some went for adventure. They wanted to see beautiful new places unlike any place they had ever seen.
- Most went for land. They knew they could find cheap, fertile farmland in the West.

PEOPLE TO KNOW

William Becknell
Peter Burnett
Jean de Smet
John C. Fremont
Nancy Kelsey
Marcus Whitman
Narcissa Whitman

PLACES TO LOCATE

California
Idaho
Oregon
Washington
Franklin
Independence
Kansas City
Lathrop
Santa Fe, New Mexico
Pike County

WORDS TO UNDERSTAND

emigrant
ferry
missionary
pioneer

St. Louis was a jumping-off point for many pioneers. Here on Broadway Street pioneers could buy supplies for their trip to California or Oregon.

Independence

Of all of the jumping-off points, Independence was the most popular. Every spring, the town was busy with families getting ready to go west. Companies in town made a fortune selling supplies. Men were busy getting wagons ready for the long journey.

One man described what Independence looked like in his book, *Oregon Trail*. He wrote about ***emigrants.*** Emigrants are people who leave one place to move to another place.

> The town was crowded. [Many] shops had sprung up to furnish the emigrants and Santa Fe traders with necessaries [supplies] for their journey; and there was . . . hammering and banging from a dozen blacksmiths' sheds, where the heavy wagons were being repaired, and the horse and oxen shod.
>
> The streets were thronged with men, horses, and mules. While I was in town, a train of wagons from Illinois passed through to join the camp on the prairie. . . . Children's faces were peeping out from under the covers of the wagons.

Ho for California

"We crossed the mountains and camped. It was my 18th birthday." The young woman who wrote those words was Nancy Kelsey, the first white woman to cross the high mountains into California. She crossed the snow-covered mountains barefoot, carrying her infant baby daughter in her arms and leading her packhorse behind her.

Nancy and her husband were among the first pioneers to set out for California from Missouri in 1841. Nancy, her baby, and 31 men completed the trip. "Where my husband goes, I go," said Nancy when she was told that the trip would be too hard for a woman.

What do you think?

What do you think the children on the trails were thinking? Were they excited? Nervous? Scared? Homesick?

If you visit Independence today, you can visit the National Frontier Trails Center and learn about what it was like to leave Independence on a pioneer trail.

Pioneers circled their wagons at night. They could keep animals safely inside the circle.

Wagons Ho!

Pioneers usually traveled from Missouri to the West in a wagon train. It was safer to travel with a group than alone. At night the men took turns staying awake to guard the wagon train. They made sure the animals did not wander off or get stolen.

At first, pioneer trails went across flat land, so the wagons moved along without much trouble. But even over flat land, the trip could be very hard. The pioneers faced storms of rain, dust, and hail.

There were also rivers to cross. There were no bridges. Sometimes travelers found a shallow place to wade across the river. Other times they had to stop and build a wooden raft called a *ferry* to carry their wagons and animals across a river. Sometimes the ferries tipped over, and animals drowned in the swift water.

When the wagons got to the mountains, the journey was even harder. Pioneer families had to take their wagons through the high mountains. If they left home too late in the summer, they might face terrible snowstorms.

Linking the Past to the Present

Going to Oregon or California from the East took six months. How far could you travel in six months? Where would you go? How would you travel?

Wagons and Chores

Large groups of settlers traveled on the trails. Families loaded their things into wooden wagons. One wagon followed another, making a long wagon train. The whole group moved very slowly, often just 12 miles a day. Today you can travel 12 miles in 12 minutes by car.

Covered wagons were only big enough to carry the food, tools, and clothes a family needed. There was little room left for anyone to ride inside, so most people had to walk. Some families tried to take furniture, but most of it had to be dumped along the trail because it was just too heavy.

During the daytime there was work to do. Children gathered firewood as the wagons moved slowly along. Some members of the wagon train rode off on horseback to hunt. If they were lucky, they would find a deer or a buffalo.

At night the wagons formed a large circle. In the center of the circle, each family built a fire and cooked a simple dinner. After eating, people often sang songs and shared stories. They slept in the wagons or on the ground. The next morning they started walking again.

Horses, Mules, or Oxen

People on the trails used three kinds of animals to pull their wagons: horses, mules, or oxen. Horses and mules moved the fastest, but they were not as strong or as tough as oxen.

Horses were the most expensive. They needed better food and better care to keep them going. Mules were cheaper. They could eat tougher, drier grasses. They could pull more than horses, but they could also be very stubborn.

Covered Wagons

The first pioneer wagons were called Conestoga wagons. They were too heavy and got stuck easily. They were about the size of a small truck. People complained about the heavy wagons, so wagon makers made changes.

They made the wagons smaller and lighter. They covered the tops with white canvas. The canvas could be pulled tight to keep out some of the dust, rain, wind, and sun. From far away the round canvas tops looked like the sails of ships. In those days a sailing ship was called a schooner. Soon people began calling covered wagons prairie schooners, especially when the tall prairie grasses rippled in the wind like the waves of the ocean.

Oxen were the cheapest to buy. They moved much slower than horses or mules, but they could pull a heavier load. Oxen were not picky eaters either. They could eat almost any grass along the trail.

What do you think?

Imagine you are leaving your home forever. You are moving to a place that has no stores and no hospitals. That is just what the pioneers did. As a class, talk about the ways pioneers showed courage.

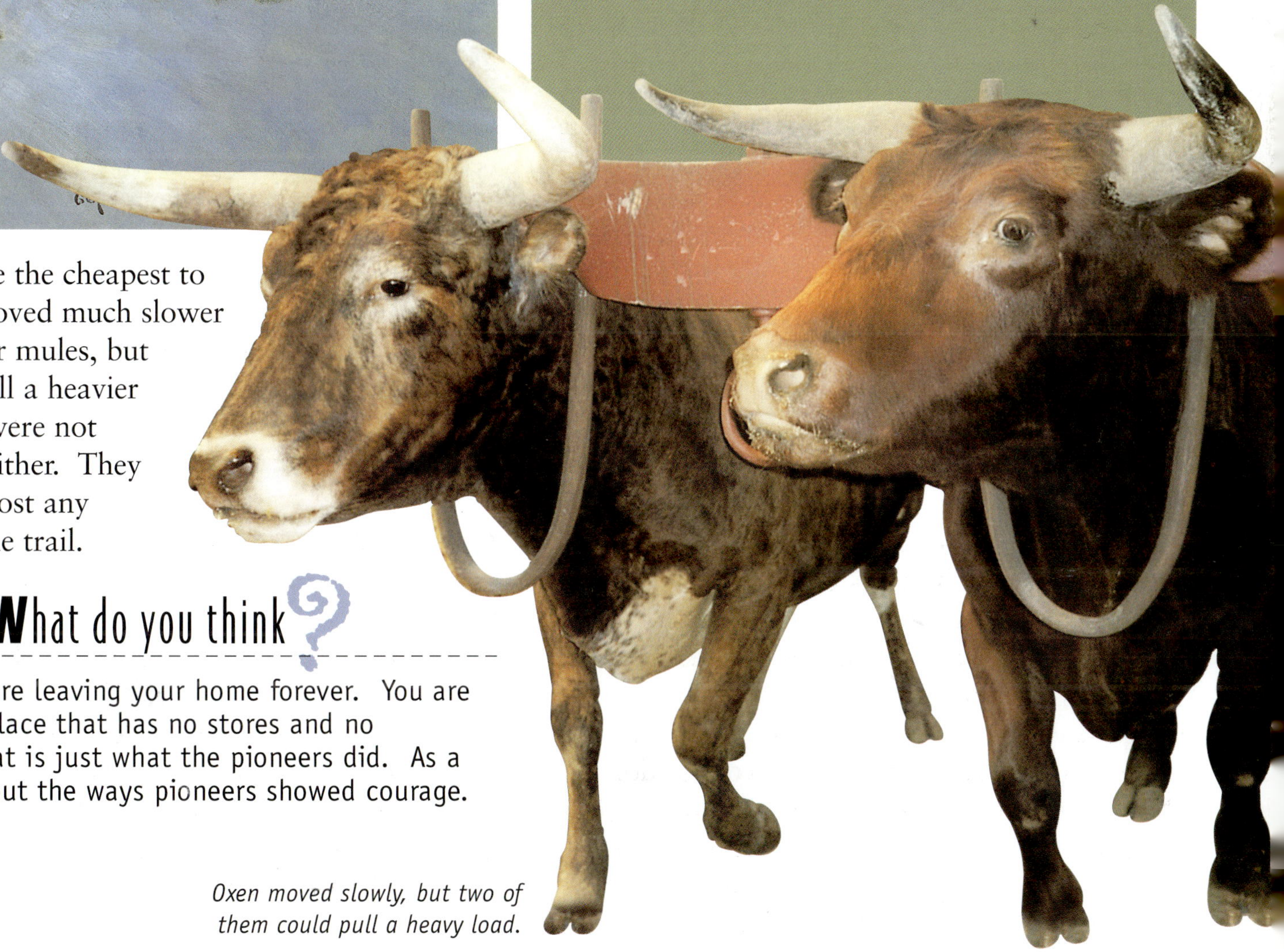

Oxen moved slowly, but two of them could pull a heavy load.

The Santa Fe Trail

The Santa Fe Trail

Santa Fe is one of the oldest cities in the United States. It was very hard for the people of Santa Fe to get supplies like tools, knives, and cloth. It was hard because they were so far from other cities.

American traders thought they could make money by selling supplies to the people of Santa Fe. They were willing to go 600 miles from Missouri to Santa Fe to sell goods and to buy things such as silver and horses.

The trip to Santa Fe in freight wagons took about six weeks. It was a hard journey over the Great Plains and desert land. Rivers were very dangerous to cross.

The Missouri Mule

One important result of the Santa Fe trade was Missouri's state animal, the Missouri mule! Mexican burrows from Santa Fe and strong Missouri horses had baby mules.

For over 100 years, Missouri was famous for its mules. They were known as smart animals that were hard workers on farms and strong pack animals for armies. No other animals could carry such large loads of supplies. Missouri mules from towns such as Lathrop and Clarence were sent all over the world.

William Becknell

William Becknell, a Missouri man, is known as the Father of the Santa Fe Trail. He left Franklin and made the long trip to Santa Fe. Becknell took wagons full of supplies to sell.

Becknell found he could sell goods in Santa Fe for five times as much as he could sell them for in Missouri. Then he brought back silver and horses and sold them in Missouri. When others saw how rich Becknell became, they wanted to go to Santa Fe themselves.

Wagon Caravans

Within a few years, wagon caravans were leaving Franklin and Independence for Santa Fe every spring. Up to 25 large wagons were in a caravan. Teams of oxen or mules pulled the wagons.

Not many people took part in the Santa Fe trade, but it was still important. Missourians learned to take wagons across the Great Plains. That would be helpful in the future.

Settlers celebrate their arrival into Santa Fe.

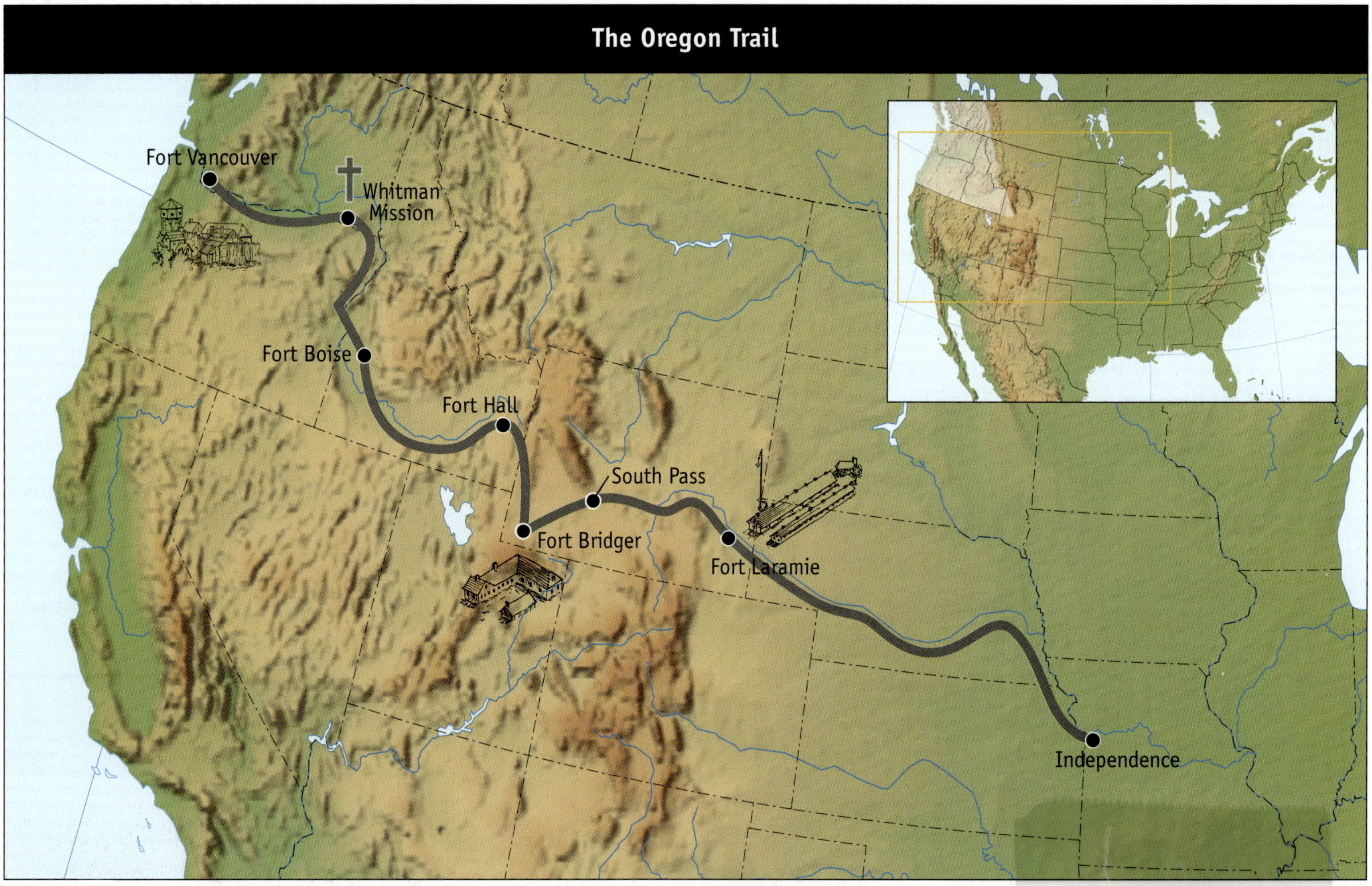

The Oregon Trail

Oregon Country was a large region of land on the other side of the Rocky Mountains. It included most of today's Oregon, Washington, and Idaho.

After the Lewis and Clark expedition, Americans began to dream about traveling to Oregon Country. They heard stories about the forests, mountains, and fertile green valleys. Oregon Country seemed far better than the Great Plains. People still thought of the Great Plains as a great desert.

The Missionary Spirit

What first got Americans interested in Oregon? Four Indian men from Oregon traveled all the way to St. Louis and asked to see William Clark. Clark still lived in Missouri and was in charge of Indian Affairs.

The men told Clark that some white men had come to Oregon and told them the Indians were not pleasing God. The white men had told the Indians that the people "in the land of the rising sun" (the East) could teach them about God. Newspapers told the story of these Indians who wanted to learn more about the white people's God. The newspapers called these Indian men the "Wise Men of the West."

What do you think?

How do you think the missionaries felt about leaving their homes behind to go to Oregon?

The stories made some people want to go west and share their Christian religion with American Indians. These people were called ***missionaries.***

The Whitmans

Some famous missionaries who left St. Louis for Oregon Country were Marcus and Narcissa Whitman. They traveled with another missionary couple, Henry and Elizabeth Spalding. Marcus Whitman was a doctor. The missionaries wanted to set up a mission in Oregon to help Indians read the Bible and learn about Christianity.

Fur traders guided the missionaries. They told the missionaries that the wagons and women would never make it to Oregon Country. The fur traders were partly right. The wagons broke down, but the women made it all the way. The Whitmans and the Spaldings built missions in Oregon Country.

Soon more people made the journey to Oregon. The fur traders and missionaries helped set up a route for them to travel on.

Narcissa Whitman

Marcus Whitman

MISSOURI PORTRAIT

Father Jean de Smet
1801–1873

Jean de Smet was born in Europe. He came to America as a young man and became a Catholic priest. He helped start an Indian school. It later became St. Louis University.

De Smet is most known for his missionary travels to the American West and Canada. He went from St. Louis up the Missouri River. He set up Indian missions in Nebraska, Montana, and Oregon Country.

The American Indians called the priest Chief Black Robe. Many trusted him when they trusted no other white man. He would not sell whiskey or guns to Indians. He thought these things were very harmful. The U.S. government often called on him to help make treaties with American Indians.

When he came back to St. Louis from his many trips, Father de Smet told stories about his life:

> I have been several years a wanderer in the desert. I was three years without receiving a letter. . . . I was two years in the mountains without tasting bread, salt, coffee, tea, or sugar. I was four years without a bed, without a roof.
>
> I have been six months without a shirt on my back, and passed whole days and nights without a morsel of anything to eat, not even a drop of water to quench my thirst. I thank God for it, and most gladly would exchange my present situation for the life again.
>
> —Father de Smet

Oregon Fever

Soon "Oregon Fever" swept the country. Everyone talked about moving to Oregon. Many Missourians were caught up in the excitement. People were saying that Oregon had some of the best farmland in the world.

People wanted to go to Oregon, but they did not have a map. How would they know where to go? There were no road signs and no towns along the trails. People wanted a good map and a guidebook for their journey.

John C. Fremont

The government sent John C. Fremont to plot a route to Oregon. Fremont traveled on trails used by Indians and fur traders. He took a team of artists and mapmakers to prepare a guidebook. Kit Carson, a mountain man, went along as Fremont's guide.

When Fremont returned from his many trips to the West, he and his wife, Jessie, wrote a report. The report caused a great deal of excitement. People wanted to move to Oregon and start new farms. The report gave people a better idea of how to prepare for the journey.

Peter Burnett's Stories

One Missourian who made the trip to Oregon was Peter Burnett. He got other Missourians to go with him by going from town to town and telling fantastic stories about how wonderful Oregon was. In one speech he said:

> They do say, gentlemen, they do say that out in Oregon the pigs are running about under the great acorn trees, round and fat, and already cooked, with knives and forks sticking in them so that you can cut off a slice whenever you are hungry!

Burnett led a wagon caravan of 875 people to Oregon. Thousands of people followed. They all began their trip in Missouri, where they bought their last supplies before "jumping off" on their journey.

2 MEMORY MASTER

1. In what ways was Missouri a jumping-off place?
2. Why was the Santa Fe Trail important?
3. How did missionaries open up the way to settlement in Oregon Country?
4. Who helped map the West to make it easier for new settlers to find their way?

LESSON 3

PEOPLE TO KNOW

Lilburn Boggs
Joseph Smith
Brigham Young

PLACES TO LOCATE

California
Illinois
New York
Ohio
Utah
Far West
Caldwell County
Clay County
Jackson County

WORDS TO UNDERSTAND

apology
epidemic
persecute

The California Trail

Fur traders had been to California and talked about it as a place where the land was rich and the weather was perfect all year. But when gold was discovered in California in 1848, a new fever swept Missouri and the nation. People called it "gold fever."

Men from all across the nation and around the world flocked to California. Most left their homes and families behind in the hope that they could "strike it rich." Since many of these men left for California in 1849, they were known as "forty-niners."

Some forty-niners left New York and took a ship all the way around South America to get to California. But most men made the trip across the Great Plains. They had to go through Missouri. They bought supplies for the long trip in Missouri stores.

People going to southern California took a split off the Santa Fe Trail. Those going to northern California took a split off the Oregon Trail. This became known as the California Trail.

Few people actually got rich by finding gold. Some people, however, did get rich in other ways. They sold tents, clothes, and other supplies to thousands of gold seekers.

What do you think?

- Why do people leave home and move today?
- Are the reasons the same or different from the reasons pioneer families or gold-seekers went west?

Trails to the West

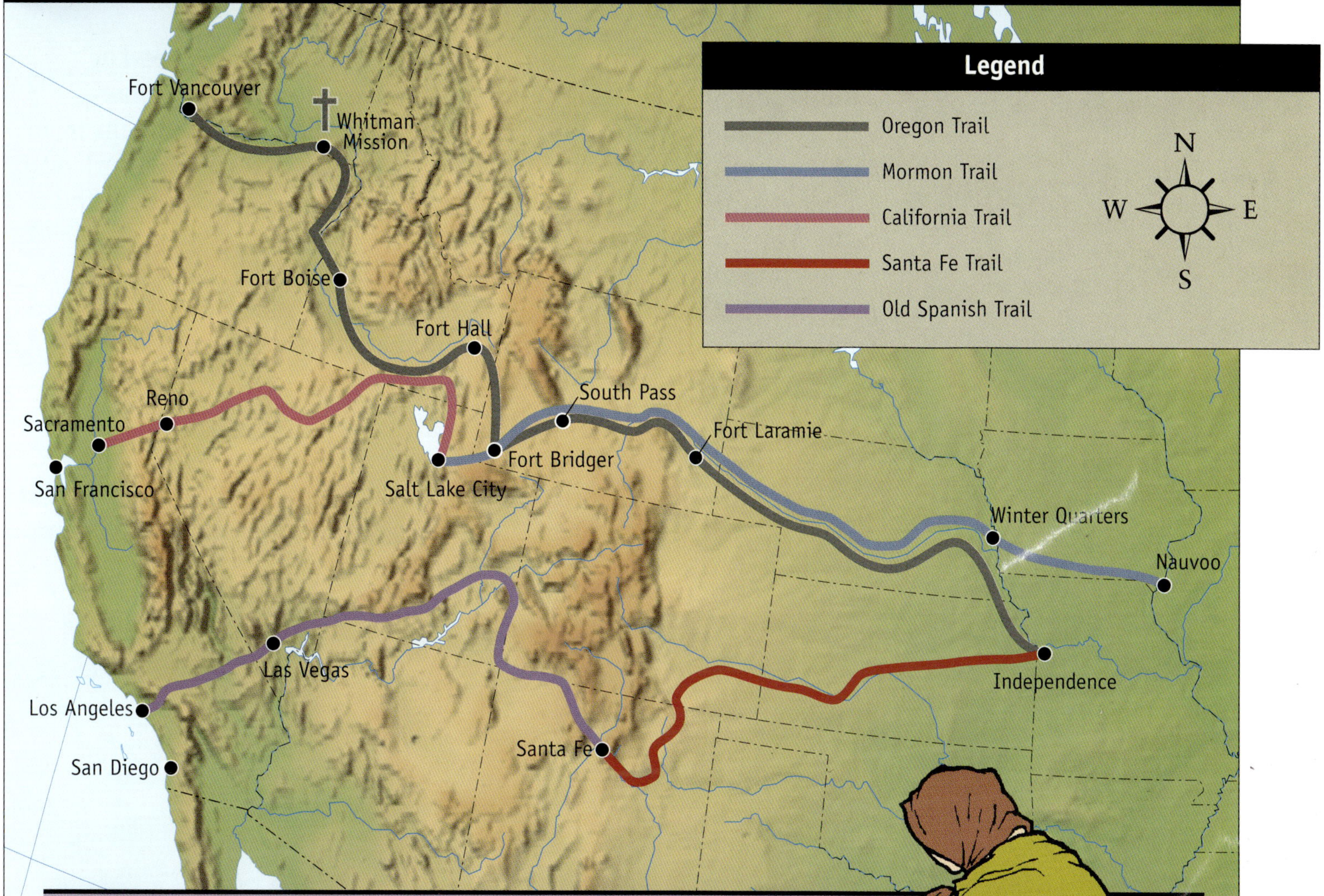

Hardships on the Trail

One tragedy that struck people going to California was a cholera ***epidemic.*** Cholera is a sickness caused by drinking unclean water. An epidemic is when many people get the same disease at about the same time.

The cholera epidemic hit St. Louis as the forty-niners came through. Many people got sick in St. Louis, and thousands died there. Others died along the trail. They never made it to California.

There were other hardships. Sometimes food and water were scarce. People got bitten by snakes and swarms of mosquitoes. Rain, snow, or blazing sun made travel hard.

The Mormon Trail

Another group also made the journey west. Members of The Church of Jesus Christ of Latter-day Saints, also called Mormons, wanted freedom of religion. Some of their beliefs were different from most other Christians, so they were not treated well in New York and Ohio. A large group of Mormons came to Missouri hoping to find a better life.

Joseph Smith was the leader of the Mormons. He went to Independence and told his followers that they should also move there. Smith believed Jackson County would be a perfect place for the Mormons to farm and raise their families in peace.

Hardships in Missouri

Over a thousand Mormons came to Jackson County. They bought farms and businesses. They cut down trees and built cabins to live in. They hoped to stay for the rest of their lives.

Angry mobs forced the Mormons out of their homes and out of Missouri.

Sadly, some people in Missouri began to ***persecute*** their Mormon neighbors. They did not accept the Mormons for several reasons. First, they feared the Mormons might control the county because they were such a large group. Second, the Mormons were against slavery, and most Missourians supported slavery. But the biggest problem was that the Mormons had different religious ideas.

The people of Independence demanded that the Mormons leave. When they did not, a mob of angry men beat some Mormon leaders and destroyed their newspaper presses. When this happened, the Mormons left.

The Mormons left their cabins and farms behind and moved to Clay County, but their new neighbors also persecuted them. Then the Mormon families moved to Caldwell County. It was not easy to start over and build new homes and plant new crops, but the people built a new town called Far West. Soon over 5,000 Mormons lived in this region of Missouri. They came from other states and other countries in Europe.

As more and more Mormons came to Missouri, they moved into other counties. When other Missourians would not let them vote, fights broke out. This almost started a war. The Mormons raised an army to defend themselves. Missourians surrounded them and attacked with guns. Dozens of people, including children, were killed.

The governor of Missouri at the time was Lilburn Boggs. He wrote that all the Mormons needed to be either killed or driven from Missouri:

> The Mormons must be treated as enemies and must be exterminated [killed] or driven from the state if necessary.

Linking the Past to the Present

The story of the Mormons in Missouri is one of the worst cases of religious persecution in American history. In 1976, another Missouri governor, Kit Bond, issued an ***apology*** to the Mormons. He said the people of Missouri were sorry for what had happened long ago.

What do you think?

Do people still persecute others today because of religion?

Not all Missourians were against the Mormons. Alexander Doniphan was a lawyer, government leader, and a general in the state militia. He was ordered by Governor Boggs to kill Joseph Smith and others. He was very angry at the order and bravely refused. He felt the Mormon leaders were not being treated fairly. Several years later, Doniphan visited the Mormons in Utah and was treated as a hero.

Some Mormon immigrants from the United States and Europe formed handcart companies. They loaded up supplies and pushed or pulled the carts along the trail. Thousands of poor immigrants who could not afford wagons or animals to pull the wagons made the trip this way.

Fleeing Missouri

Once again, the Mormons had to flee. They crossed the Mississippi River into Illinois. They built a city next to the river. Once again they planted crops. Their new city became one of the largest cities in Illinois. For a while, they lived in peace.

Sadly, the Mormons still had enemies. This time a mob killed Joseph Smith and his brother. The Mormons knew they would never be safe unless they moved to the far, far West.

On to Utah

Brigham Young was the new leader of the Mormons. He led over 3,000 pioneers on the long trip to Utah. They did not want to be on the same trail as other pioneers, so they traveled on the other side of the Platte River. Their trail was called the Mormon Trail.

At first, they went in covered wagons. Many wagon trains of Mormons traveled that way, year after year. After several years, more Mormons wanted to go to the West. Many of them had traveled from England and other countries in Europe. They had no money left to buy wagons, horses, or oxen, so they made wooden carts.

They loaded up the handcarts with flour, sugar, cornmeal, dried meat, blankets, and a few clothes. They couldn't carry much. Only a baby or small child could ride in the handcart. Everyone else walked.

The Mormons settled in a place they named Salt Lake City, Utah. They worked together to build a great city in the wilderness.

Some Stay Behind

One group of Mormons did not follow Brigham Young to Utah. They returned to Independence and formed a church called the Reorganized Latter-day Saints. Today, they call the church the Community of Christ. The center of their church is still in Independence.

Freedom of Religion

Part of the rules for our country is a document called the Bill of Rights. It lists freedoms that cannot be taken away from people in the United States. One is freedom of religion. People in our country can live any religion they choose.

3 MEMORY MASTER

1. Why did people think they could get rich in California?
2. How did people travel to California?
3. How does our Constitution's Bill of Rights protect religious freedom?

LESSON 4

PEOPLE TO KNOW

Robert Fulton

PLACES TO LOCATE

Boonville
Hannibal
Lexington
Sacramento, California
San Francisco, California
St. Joseph
Washington

WORDS TO UNDERSTAND

freight

Steamboats Make Travel Faster

Fur traders had used keelboats to move furs up and down the Mississippi and Missouri Rivers. The boats were not easy to use. They tipped over easily. Piles of furs spilled into the river.

People needed an easier way to go upriver. Robert Fulton had developed a steamboat back east. The first steamboat to come to St. Louis was the *Zebulon Pike*. It came to the city about 10 years after Fulton built his first steamboat.

By the 1830s, steamboats were a common sight up and down Missouri's two great rivers. The steamboats helped people travel west by taking them 2,000 miles up the Missouri River. Some boats were huge. They could carry 400 passengers.

The large paddlewheels and engines spewing smoke were quite a sight! Some boats were like floating palaces, with carpets on the floors of guest rooms and sparkling lights in the dining rooms.

Danger on the Water

The boats were a great way to travel, but they were dangerous. The Missouri River was especially dangerous. Steamboat pilots had to know every bend of the river. They had to know where the sandbars and underwater trees were.

The boats could explode when their steam engines overheated. The *Saluda* blew up near Lexington, and over 100 people died. Many were Mormons heading for Utah. Children whose parents died in the explosion were adopted by Missouri families in the area.

How a Steam Engine Works

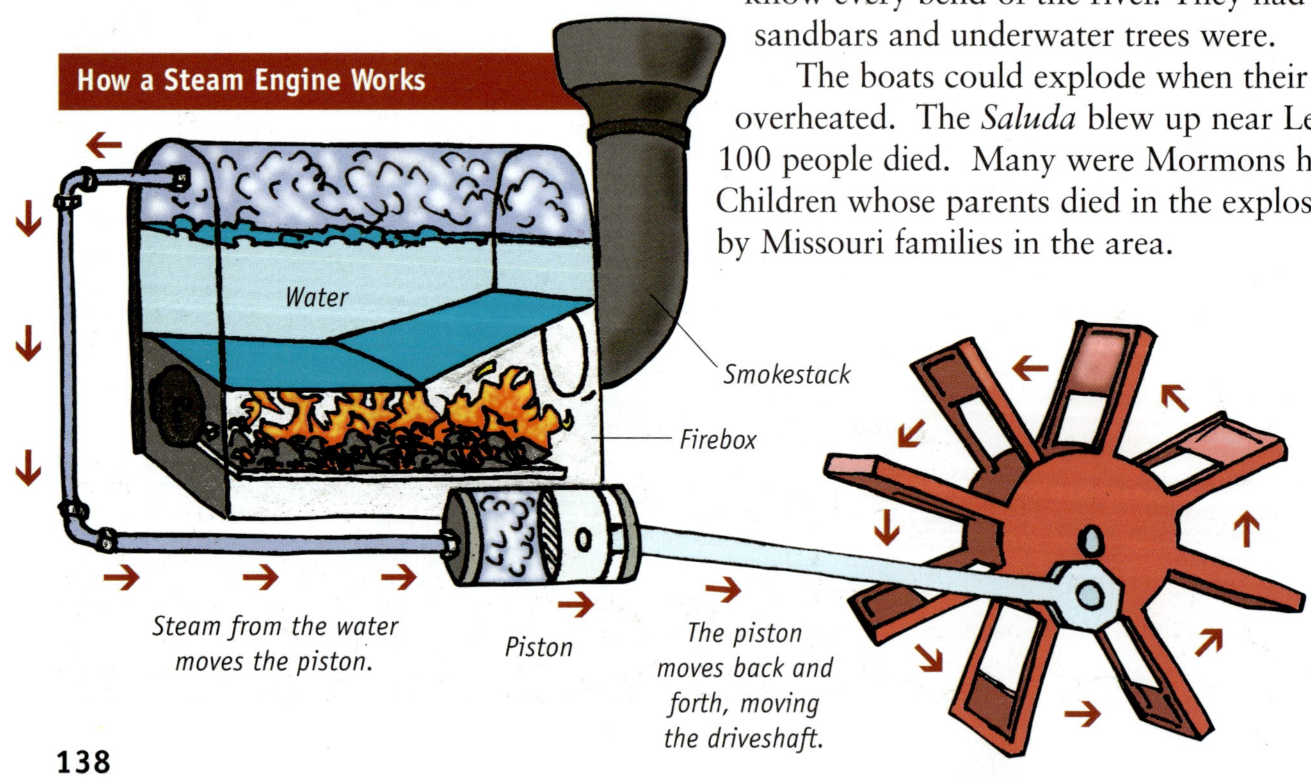

Steamboats had tall smokestacks where the steam escaped. They had decks where passengers could sit and watch the scenery go by.

Steamboat Ports

Steamboats were very important to Missouri. Over 3,000 boats docked in St. Louis every year. Many Missourians got jobs building boats and working on boats as they traveled. Towns like Washington, Boonville, and Lexington along the Missouri River became important steamboat ports. Boats stopped to unload and pick up passengers and supplies. They traveled all up and down the river.

The *Arabia*

The steamboat *Arabia* sunk in the Missouri River just north of Kansas City. A tree snag had torn a hole in the bottom of the boat. All of the passengers got off safely, but a mule on board died.

The ship sunk in the muddy Missouri River. Over the years, the river changed course, and the boat ended up 100 feet beneath a farmer's field. It was not until 1988, 132 years after it sank, that a team of archaeologists decided to raise the boat.

They finally dug down to the *Arabia*. All of the supplies were still in almost perfect condition! There were guns, clothing, tools, buttons, and many other things. Bottles of fruit and pickles were still good enough to eat! All of these supplies had been put on the boat to be taken to stores along the river.

Today, the Arabia Museum in Kansas City displays all of the treasures found on the boat that sunk long ago.

This pitcher was found in the boat that had been under the ground for 132 years.

Riders were happy to finally stop at a stagecoach station. They could stretch their legs, get a drink, and eat a meal of beans or soup. Sometimes they could even stay overnight!

Stagecoaches Move People

Companies took people west in stagecoaches. The Butterfield Overland Mail Company carried both people and mail from Missouri all the way to San Francisco. Travelers could only take a few things with them in a trunk. People could get on and off in different towns along the route.

A ride on a stagecoach was rough. Roads were dusty, and the dust covered people's clothes and made it hard to breathe. When the roads were muddy the wooden wheels got stuck, and everyone had to get out and help push. The trails and roads were nearly always rocky. People bounced up and down on hard seats.

Freight Lines Carry Goods

Steamboats took supplies to people as far as the rivers went. Another way to get supplies to people was to send them with a ***freight*** company. Freight is a lot of anything that needs to be moved from one place to another. A freight company in Lexington sent supplies across the prairie by wagon. The company was Russell, Majors, and Waddell. They had 3,500 wagons and over 40,000 oxen.

Day after day, the oxen pulled their heavy load. They stopped in towns to sell the things on the wagons. Then they loaded up again with more things to sell in other towns and cities. Each time someone bought something, the men who ran the freight companies made money.

The Pony Express Moves the Mail

One of the most famous examples of travel was the Pony Express. The government asked Russell, Majors, and Waddell to start a service that would take mail from St. Joseph, Missouri, to Sacramento, California, and back.

The company took out a famous ad to get men to take this dangerous job. The riders could not weigh over 125 pounds or their weight would slow down the horses.

The mail was carried along the 2,000-mile trip almost without stopping. Each man rode 75 miles a day. There were rest stops, called way stations, about every 10 miles where the riders got off their horses, got a quick bite to eat, and changed horses. Then off they went again.

The Pony Express could get a letter from Missouri to California in 10 days or less. This amazed people. However, it was used only for very important mail because the Pony Express charged $5.00 for a half-ounce letter! That was a lot of money in those days. It would be an expensive way to send mail even today.

The Pony Express lasted only 18 months. When the telegraph came along, people could get messages across the country in a matter of minutes.

PONY EXPRESS!

CHANGE OF TIME! REDUCED RATES!

10 Days to San Francisco!

LETTERS

WILL BE RECEIVED AT THE

OFFICE, 84 BROADWAY,

NEW YORK,

Up to 4 P.M. every TUESDAY,

AND

Up to 2½ P.M. every SATURDAY,

Which will be forwarded to connect with the PONY EXPRESS leaving ST. JOSEPH, Missouri,

Every WEDNESDAY and SATURDAY at 11 P.M.

TELEGRAMS

Sent to Fort Kearney on the mornings of MONDAY and FRIDAY, will connect with PONY leaving St. Joseph, WEDNESDAYS and SATURDAYS.

EXPRESS CHARGES.

LETTERS weighing half ounce or under $1 00

For every additional half ounce or fraction of an ounce 1 00

In all cases to be enclosed in 10 cent Government Stamped Envelopes,

And all Express CHARGES Pre-paid.

PONY EXPRESS ENVELOPES For Sale at our Office.

WELLS, FARGO & CO., Ag'ts.

New York, July 1, 1861.

SLOTE & JANES, STATIONERS AND PRINTERS, 93 FULTON STREET, NEW YORK.

Men placed heavy poles into the ground. Then they strung telegraph wires along the poles. Once wires were strung across the country, people could send messages in minutes. The Pony Express soon ended. Letters were too slow.

Linking the Past to the Present

- Why do you think the Pony Express charged by weight?
- How much does it cost to mail a letter today?

A Terrible Day

The Union Pacific Railroad was being built across the state from St. Louis to Kansas City and beyond. Finally, after a lot of hard work, tracks were laid all the way from St. Louis to Jefferson City, the state capital.

To celebrate, the railroad company invited a few hundred people from St. Louis to ride the train to the capital city. People were excited to ride a train for the first time. They were excited to see the sights out of their windows on the train.

Then the train started to cross a new bridge. The bridge crossed the Gasconade River near Hermann. The bridge started groaning. It was not strong enough to hold the train. People screamed as the bridge crashed to the ground. Ten train cars fell into the river. Thirty-one people were killed. More than seventy people were hurt.

Even this terrible accident did not stop people across the state from trying to get railroad tracks to their towns. Everyone knew trains were a great boon to transportation.

The Railroads

After railroad tracks were laid from city to city, the fastest way to travel was on a train. The first railroad to cross Missouri went between Hannibal and St. Joseph. At the time, most people still traveled by boat, horse, or wagon.

But as the railroads grew, they changed the way people traveled. People stopped traveling to the West by wagon and took the train instead. It was much faster and more comfortable. It was a real adventure to ride a train!

4 MEMORY MASTER

1. How did steamboats improve transportation?
2. How did freight lines help people get supplies?
3. Describe a stagecoach ride.
4. Describe how the Pony Express helped move the mail.
5. Why did people like the new railroads?

Chapter 6 Review

From There to Here

If you were a rugged mountain man like those who left Missouri at the beginning of this chapter, you traveled west in a boat. You would take food, traps, and guns. You would be going a long way to earn money by trapping animals and selling their fur.

If you were a pioneer child on the Oregon Trail, the California Trail, or the Mormon Trail, you would go west in a covered wagon. You would take supplies of food, tools, seeds, and blankets. Your family's large brown dog would run beside you on the trail.

No matter when and how you traveled, your life changed. How did you feel about going into the wilderness? What problems did you have as a trapper or a pioneer? What were the great parts about living outdoors? What new sights did you see? What new people did you meet?

Then, new ways of travel made going west easier. Steamboats, stagecoaches, and railroads took people and goods farther and faster than ever before. Life changed for everyone.

Activity

Record Information on a Chart

On a separate piece of paper or on the chalkboard, copy this chart. Use the information you have learned in this chapter to fill in the chart.

Type of Transportation	Advantages	Disadvantages
Covered wagon		
Stagecoach		
Horseback. pack train		
Steamboat		
Railroad		

Geography Tie-In

The people in this chapter traveled a lot! They went a great distance by boat, horseback, wagon, and on foot. On their trips, the people crossed flat grassy prairies, rolling wooded hills, deserts, high mountains, and rich green valleys. Follow the map of pioneer trails on page 133 and draw a picture of three kinds of land along one of the trails.

THE TIME
1820–1860

"We live here as in Germany, surrounded by Germans. Missouri is becoming Germany for America."

—German immigrant Emil Mallinckrodt in a letter from Missouri, 1847

Frontier Life

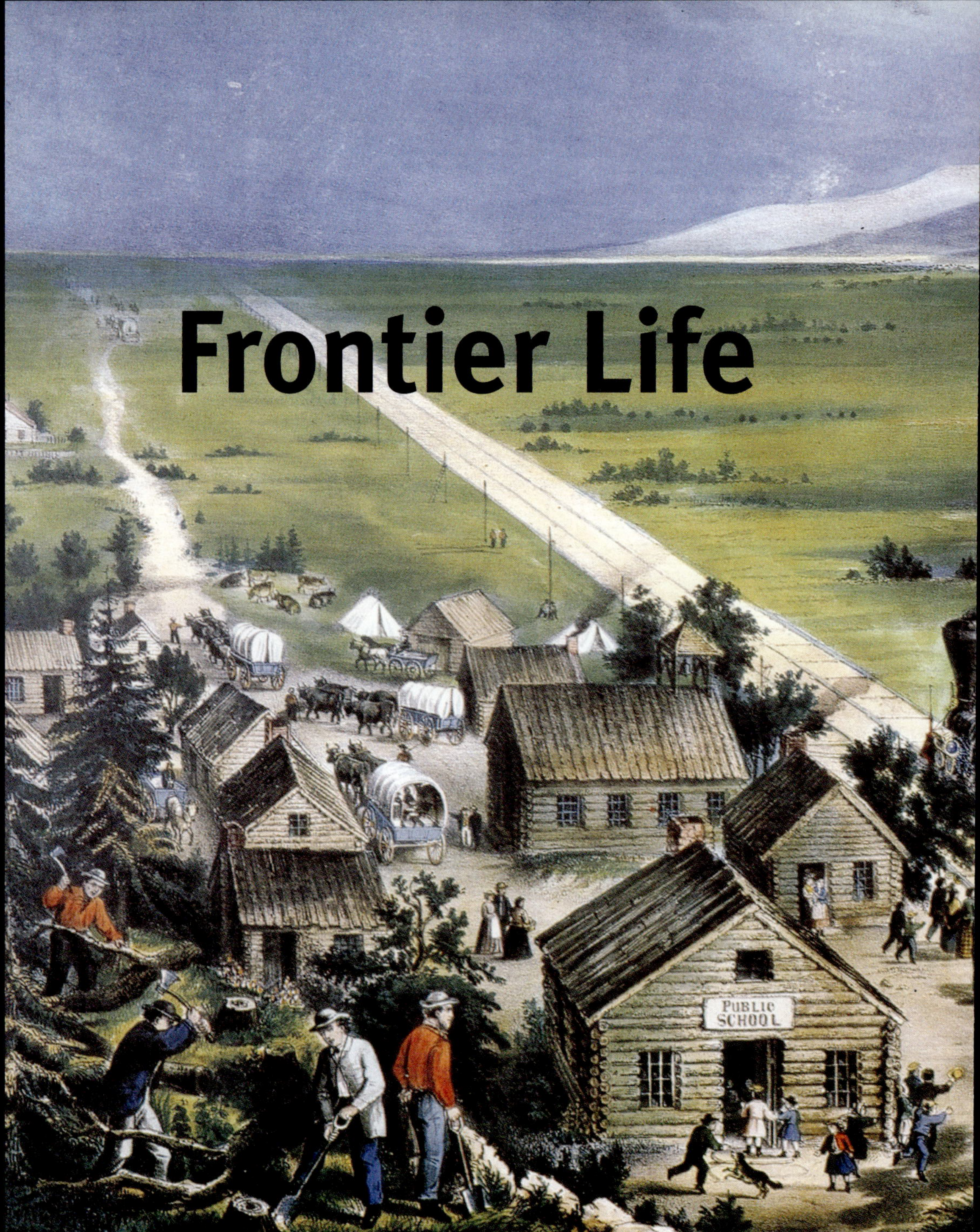

Timeline of Events

1820 · 1825 · 1830 · 183

1821
The Missouri government passes Slave Codes.

1830s
Germans come to Missouri.

1832
Cholera causes evacuation of St. Louis and thousands of deaths.

Chapter 7

Choo! Choo! Trains crossed North America, changing life for everyone. New towns were built near the tracks. Farmers and factories shipped food and goods to faraway cities on trains. How do you think the trains changed life for Native Americans?

1840s
An Irish potato famine drives immigrants to the U.S. and Missouri.

1847
John Berry Meachum starts the Freedom School on a steamboat.

1858
John Brown raids Vernon County.

1840 — 1845 — 1850 — 1855 — 1860

1837
- Elijah Lovejoy is killed in Illinois by a mob.
- German immigrants start the town of Hermann.

1849
- Fire destroys buildings on the St. Louis riverfront.
- Cholera outbreak

1853
Cholera outbreak

LESSON 1

PLACES TO LOCATE

Kentucky
Tennessee
Virginia

WORDS TO UNDERSTAND

auction
folktale
identify
squatter

Life in Frontier Missouri

People who moved to Missouri were moving to the American frontier. There were few large cities. Most people were farmers. The people were happy to live in a place where they could own their own farm.

Most new settlers built their homes near the large rivers, just as the French had done many years earlier. Newcomers first settled along the Mississippi and Missouri Rivers. Then they started towns next to other rivers like the Gasconade, Osage, White, Current, Chariton, and Grand Rivers.

Settlers bought land at ***auctions.*** The government gave land to the highest bidder. Some land sold for $1.25 an acre, but other land could be as high as $20 an acre. A farm family needed about 80 acres.

Some families did not buy their land. They simply moved to a place no one else owned and started farming. This was called "squatting." The settlers were called ***squatters.*** Sometimes they bought the land later. Other times someone else made a legal claim to the land, and the squatter family had to move.

Clearing the Land

When a frontier family started a farm, the first chore was to prepare the land for planting. This meant cutting down trees if the land was wooded. Cutting trees and removing stumps was very hard work.

First a farmer removed a ring of bark around the tree trunk. This was called "girdling" a tree. When the tree died, the leaves fell off and sun could get to the soil. Then the farmer planted corn or wheat around the tree.

The farmer cut down the tree in a year or two after it was rotten.

The farmer dug up the stump and the roots or left them in the ground to rot.

Building a Home

Frontier families built simple homes. They chose a place on their land, often near a spring. The spring would provide fresh water and a cool place for milk, butter, or meat.

To build a home, the men stacked heavy logs on top of each other. Then they put clay or a mix of mud and straw between the logs. This sealed the cracks and kept out the wind and rain. If there were neighbors nearby, everyone would help build the cabin. This was called a "raising." People talked and sang as they worked. The women cooked food for everyone. The cabin was built in a day.

The men built a fireplace along one wall. It kept the cabin warm in the winter. A pot over the fire cooked food. Most cabins were only one room, but they often had a loft where the children slept. The children climbed a ladder to get to the loft and then went to sleep as the fire crackled in the fireplace below. On winter nights, the fire was low by the time the children got up in the morning. They could see their breath as they got out of bed!

The furniture in the cabin was simple. Most families had only a table, benches, and one or two beds. There might be a few chairs and a cradle for the baby.

After a few years, families often built a larger home out of stone or brick. Then the cabin was used as a barn for animals or a storage shed for tools and food.

Linking the Past to the Present

How are homes built today? How are they different from homes built by the settlers?

A farm family gathers pumpkins and shucks corn in the fall. Some of the food would be dried and some would stay fresh in a cool cellar. Everyone had to work on the farm.

Growing Food for the Family

All the food the family ate was grown or raised on the farm. Growing food began when the farmer plowed the soil. Plowing the land for the first time was very hard. The roots of prairie grasses went deep into the soil. Farmers used wooden or iron plows pulled by a mule or an ox. After plowing, farmers planted the seeds.

Next to the house, the mother kept a small garden. She grew pumpkins, squash, beans, potatoes, and other vegetables.

Corn

All Missouri farmers grew corn. Corn grew well in Missouri's climate. Corn could be roasted and eaten on the cob. Corn could also be ground into cornmeal and used to make corn bread or mush. Frontier families ate corn nearly every day. They even fed corn to their animals. Many farmers made whiskey from the corn.

Families made use of the entire corn plant. They dried the green corn shucks and used them for mats and brooms. They stuffed a mattress with them. They burned the cobs for fuel. They even made dolls for the children from corn cobs.

Frontier families also grew wheat and ground it into flour. Then they baked bread and cakes with the flour.

A hunter stays hidden behind a tree. At just the right time, he will shoot the wild turkeys. There will be delicious meat for dinner.

Animals

Frontier families raised animals. Cows provided milk and beef. The cream on top of the milk was churned into butter. Hogs provided bacon and ham. Chickens provided eggs and meat. Sheep provided wool for clothing.

Many families let their cattle and hogs roam freely through the woods. They marked the ears of the animals with a family mark. This helped ***identify*** animals later. Men and boys also hunted deer, wild turkeys, squirrels, and rabbits to provide meat for the family.

Cash Crops

Besides growing crops for food, farmers grew some crops to sell for cash. Along the Missouri River, farmers grew tobacco and hemp. Hemp was used to make rope and twine. Farmers who grew these crops often owned slaves to help with the hard work.

Frontier Women

Life on the frontier was very hard work. Work for mothers and their daughters was never done. They took care of the children. They cooked the meals. They made the clothing. They sewed quilts. They helped work in the gardens and fields. They milked the cows and made butter and cheese. They dried corn, vegetables, and fruit in the hot sun and stored it for long winters. They smoked and salted meat so it would last for months.

It took hours to prepare a meal. Cooking was done over an open fire in the fireplace. When the mother finished cleaning up after one meal, it was often time to begin another meal.

A person pushed and pulled the tall handle up and down in a butter churn. After a long time, the cream in the rich milk had turned to butter.

▲ Courtesy of PVMA, Memorial Hall Museum, Deerfield, MA

▶ Photo ©Kindra Clineff

Making Clothes

The mother of the family spent hours and hours making wool cloth. First she cleaned the wool and spun it into yarn. Then she wove the yarn into cloth on a small loom. She cut the cloth and sewed it into shirts, pants, or dresses. She knitted wool yarn into hats, gloves, and socks. Because it took so long to make clothes, people owned only a few pieces of clothing.

People wore their clothes for a long time before washing them. But when clothes were washed, it was a lot of work. The women washed clothes in a creek by scrubbing them against rocks. Some families used washtubs, washboards, and hot water. After washing, the clothing had to be hung outside to dry on a tree branch or on a long rope.

Making Soap and Candles

To make soap, women saved ashes from the fireplace. They kept the ashes in barrels and added water. The liquid that oozed out the bottom was called lye. The women put the lye in a big kettle, added animal fat, and cooked the mixture over the fire. After it cooled, they molded the gooey liquid into soap cakes. The soap was strong and smelly, but it got clothes clean!

Women made candles from beeswax or animal fat. There were no electric lights like we have today, so candles and oil lamps were a way to produce light. Most people could not afford to waste candles, so when it was dark they went to bed.

Wool clothes were not as soft and comfortable as your clothes today. Wool clothes were itchy and hot. To make the wool, the mother cleaned the sheep's wool and spun it into yarn. Then she knitted the yarn or wove it into wool cloth.

Linking the Past to the Present

How are the chores divided in your house? What jobs do you do?

Pioneer life in Missouri in 1820 is shown in this drawing. How many different activities can you find in this picture? Do you do any of these activities?

Frontier Children

Children were expected to work hard on the farm. Everyone had chores to do. Parents were strict. Children had to be polite. They did whatever their parents asked and were not allowed to complain.

Girls helped their mother prepare meals, sew, do the laundry, and work in the garden. Boys helped their fathers tend crops, feed the animals, chop wood, and hunt and fish. Everyone had to work together. Because of this, children grew up fast and had very little time for simple play.

Families were large. Many children were needed to work on the farm.

Time for Fun

Just because work was hard did not mean frontier families never had fun. After a hard day on the farm, the family might relax by singing songs. They might also play fiddles, banjos, or flutes. They might even dance to the music.

Children loved to sit in front of the fireplace on a winter evening and hear their parents and grandparents tell stories. They heard stories from the Bible, ghost stories, or ***folktales.*** The folktales might be funny, or they might be about brave people and their adventures.

The fiddle is our state instrument.

Families looked forward to Sunday. They took a day off from farm work to rest. They walked, rode horses, or rode in a wagon to church. It was fun to be around other families to share news from the week.

Families also combined helping each other with fun. "You help me, and I'll help you," was the way people worked on the frontier. If a cabin or barn needed to be built, families came together to help.

When the corn crop was ready, families took turns having husking bees. Husking bees were part work, part party. Husking the corn meant pulling the husks off the ears. Everyone laughed, told stories, and sang as they worked. Someone might bring a fiddle so the neighbors could dance after the work was done. Young unmarried men and women often played a game. If a man found an ear of corn with red, instead of yellow, kernels, he got to kiss the girl of his choice!

Activity

Child's Play

When children were finished with their chores, they might have time to play. They played with toys like dolls, marbles, or dominoes. They also made up their own games. They played group games like Button, Button. This is how it worked:

> The children sat in a circle. Everyone held the palms of their hands together. One child was "It." She held a button between the palms of her hands. Then she went from one player to another and passed her hands between their hands. She left the button in one of the children's hands. She tried to do this secretly, so the other children would not know where the button was. Then she said, " Button, button, who has the button?" All the children took a guess, and the one who got it right was "It" next time.

Now it is your turn. As a class, play Button, Button. After you finish playing, answer these questions:

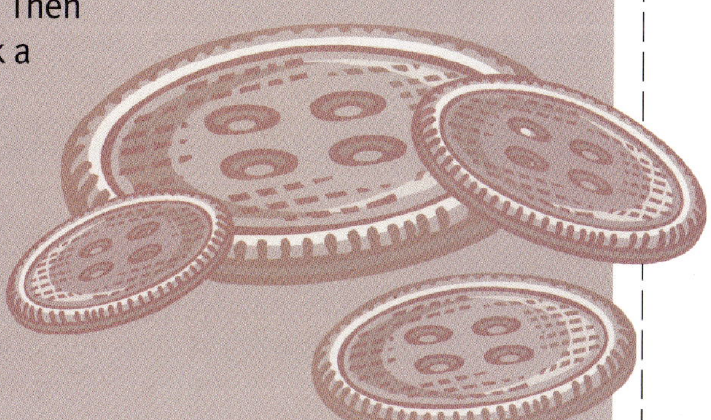

1. What do you like to do for fun? Make a list of five activities.
2. Of those five activities, which ones could settler children have played?

School

Some children went to school, while others did not. Some families needed their children to work on the farm. Those families taught their children reading, writing, and arithmetic (the "three R's") at home. Other parents did not know how to read and write. They did not think their children needed to learn how if they were only going to farm when they grew up. Many other families wanted their children to learn. They worked together to provide schools.

Early schools were one-room buildings for all grades. Most schools did not have desks. Students sat on hard benches. The families helped pay the teacher. They took turns letting the teacher live with them. Would you like your teacher to live with your family for a few months?

School usually lasted only a few months a year when children were not needed to plant or harvest crops. Children walked or rode a horse to school and took their lunch in a pail. It was fun to get away from the hard work on the farm and be around other children.

The teacher was often very young. He or she might be only 16 years old! In some places, if a female teacher got married, she was no longer allowed to teach.

There were few books, and students did not have their own paper. They had a piece of slate (like a little chalkboard) and a piece of chalk to write with. The subjects included spelling, reading, writing, arithmetic, history, and geography.

Linking the Past to the Present

Why do you think the modern way of having school vacation in June, July, and August began?

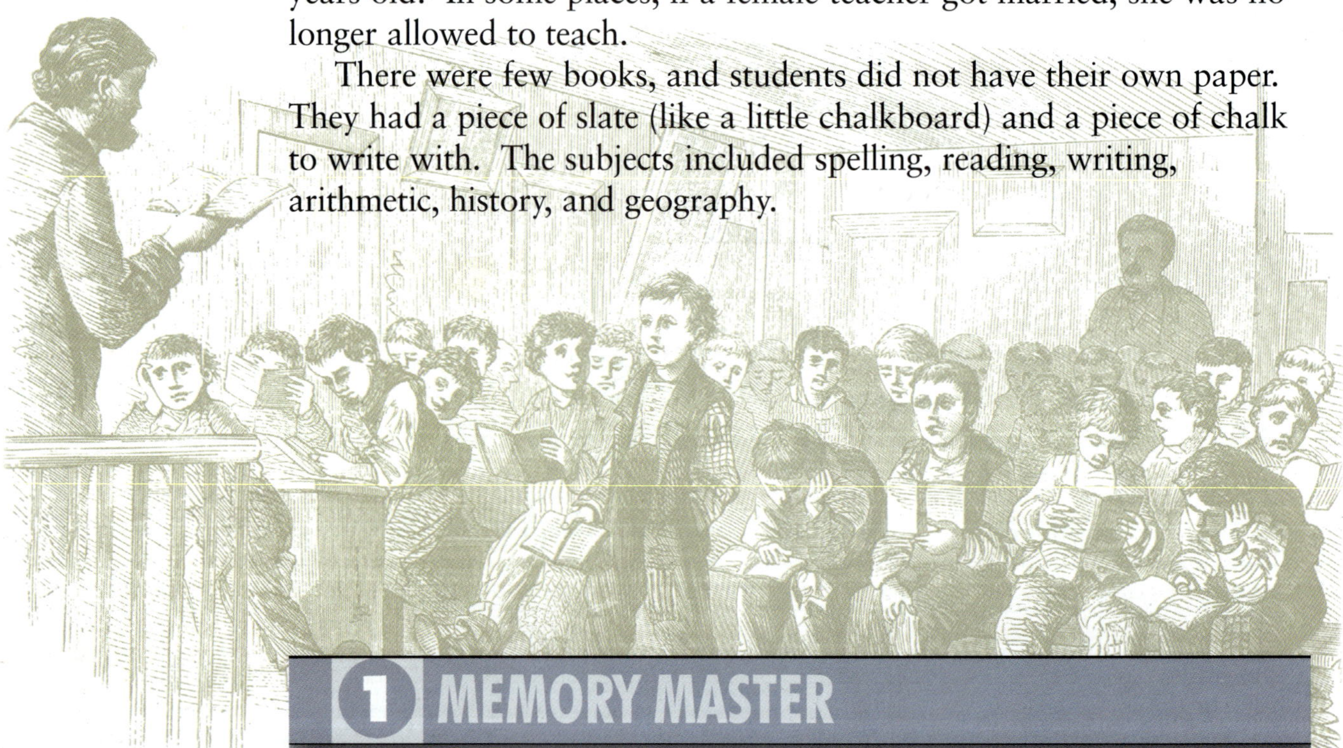

Students took turns standing and saying their lessons out loud.

1 MEMORY MASTER

1. In what ways did families get land?
2. How did farmers clear trees off their farms?
3. Describe how a cabin was built.
4. How did the people get food and clothes?

Early Manufacturing

Although most families lived and worked on farms, other people lived in towns. They worked in ***manufacturing.*** Small workshops made barrels, shoes, furniture, and clothing.

St. Louis grew rapidly. Most of the state's manufacturing took place there. Steamboats were also built in the city. People who moved to St. Louis to work made the city crowded and dangerous. Hogs and dogs roamed the streets.

Diseases spread because drinking water was not clean. Cholera hit St. Louis every 10 years or so, killing thousands of people. When the disease started to spread, families fled the city. It was years before people understood that dirty drinking water carried the germs that caused cholera.

Other smaller manufacturing towns also grew up along the rivers. Towns such as St. Joseph, Hannibal, and Kansas City had meat packing plants and rope factories. Rope and cloth bags were made from hemp, a Missouri crop.

Fire!

In large cities such as St. Louis, houses often caught fire. There was not a good system to put the fires out. In 1810, the city leaders divided all men over age 18 into two fire companies. Every family was told to keep at least two buckets on hand at all times in case they were needed to help put out a fire.

The Great Fire of St. Louis started on a steamboat. The fire spread to other steamboats. Twenty-three of them burned. Then the fire jumped to freight on the dock. From there the flames roared from building to building along the river. Most of downtown was burned. Many people were out of work for a long time. Hundreds of people were homeless.

PEOPLE TO KNOW

Henriette Bruns
John Henry Gall

PLACES TO LOCATE

Germany
Ireland
Hannibal
Hermann
Kansas City
St. Louis
St. Joseph
Washington
New Orleans, Louisiana

WORDS TO UNDERSTAND

famine
manufacturing

Immigrants say goodbye to their families and friends in the 1800s.

Emigrants or Immigrants?

A dictionary defines the words like this:

emigrant: a person who leaves a country to live somewhere else

immigrant: a person who moves into a country to live

So, a person who packs up all his furniture, clothes, and photographs and moves from one place to another is both!

Books written a long time ago usually called all the new people who moved to our country and our state "emigrants." Did the authors of those books use the word correctly?

Travel by Sea

New people came to Missouri from faraway lands. The two largest groups at that time were the Germans and the Irish.

Some people came to Missouri so they could own their own land. Others came because their governments in Europe did not allow them freedom of religion or freedom of speech. It took a lot of courage for these people to travel across the huge Atlantic Ocean and to a new country. They knew they might never see their families and friends in the old country again.

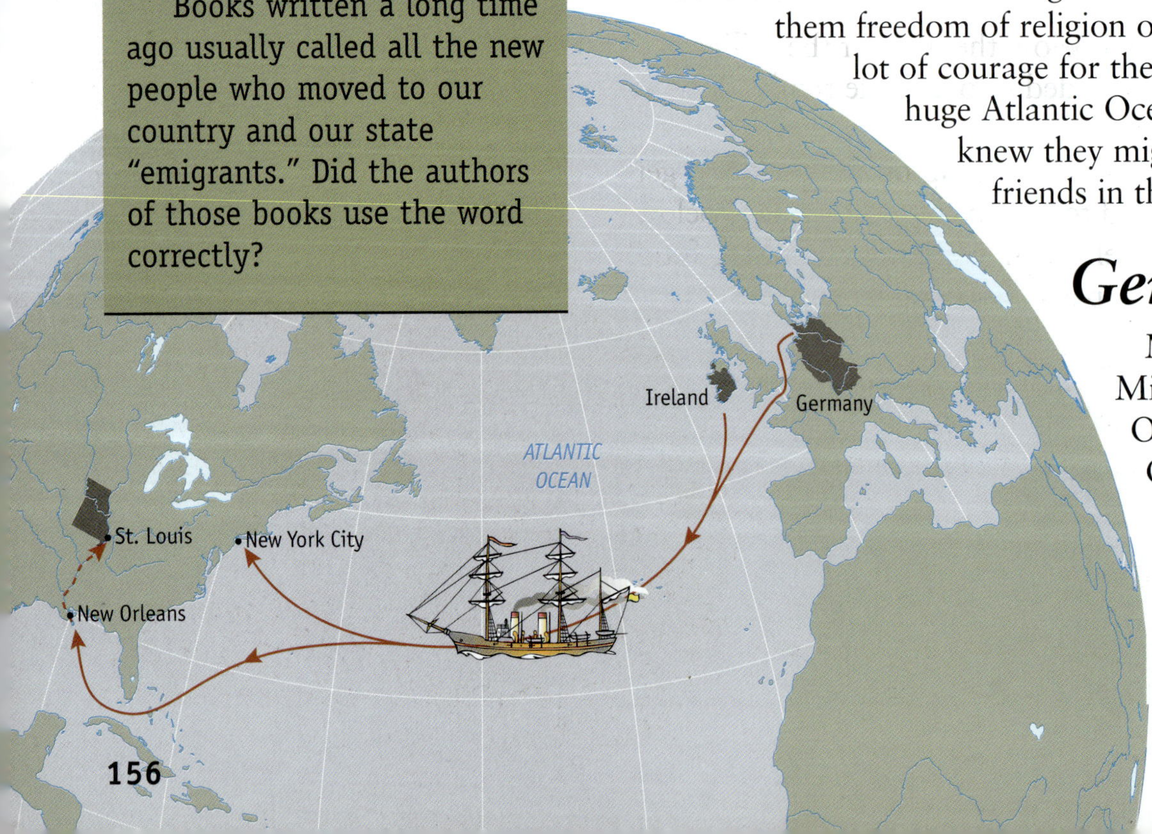

German Immigrants

Most Germans who came to Missouri sailed across the Atlantic Ocean to the busy seaport of New Orleans. Then they rode in boats up the Mississippi and Missouri Rivers.

What was the trip across the ocean like? People had to bring their own food and cook it on

Many immigrants entered the United States at New Orleans.

the ship. Families had to share space below the deck of the sailing ship. Often four or more people crowded into a single bunk. There was one toilet for every 50 people.

If the weather was nice, people could walk up on the deck and get fresh air. During storms, people had to stay below. The smells below deck were horrible. There were smells from smoke and cooking food. There were also smells from seasick passengers and from the toilets.

Another problem was sickness. With so many people living close together, diseases like cholera and typhoid often broke out. Many people died before they made it to the United States.

What do you think?

Would you make a trip to a new country if you knew you would never see your grandparents, aunts, uncles, or cousins again?

A German Family

John Henry Gall came to Missouri from Germany. In 1857 he sailed across the Atlantic Ocean to New Orleans. The trip took 55 days. He made his way up the Mississippi River. Then he rode on the Missouri River to the town of Liberty. He got a job working on a farm. After a time he bought a farm of his own.

John Henry married a 17-year-old Missouri girl. The next year she died while giving birth to a baby boy. The baby also died.

After a time, Gall married another young woman, and they had 13 children. Sadly, six of the children died very young. A smallpox epidemic hit Missouri, killing John Gall's wife and three children.

John Henry had to take his children to the cemetery, dig their graves, and bury them himself because his neighbors were afraid they would catch the horrible disease.

This is an ad for a German zither. A player held the zither and strummed the strings to make music.

German Farms and Villages

Immigrants often lived near each other in the new country. They could speak their own language. They could celebrate holidays together like they did back home.

The Germans liked the land around the Missouri River because it reminded them of the river valleys back in Germany. They were excellent farmers who taught other farmers better ways to grow food.

German families often lived in villages and then went out to their farms each day, just like they had done in Europe. Towns like Washington and Hermann had so many German people that the schools were taught in the German language for many years.

German settlers in St. Louis became some of the city's finest furniture makers. They also brewed and sold beer. Settlers in Hermann grew grapes and produced some of the finest wine in the United States. Germans in Washington started factories that produced corncob pipes. Most of the world's corncob pipes are still made there.

Germans in Washington also made instruments called zithers. Zithers were played in Germany. When the people sailed for America, they often danced on the deck of the ship to zither music. German settlers made some of the finest zithers in the world. The zithers were even bought by people back in Germany!

Homesick in America

Henriette, called Jette, came with her husband, Bernhard Bruns, from Germany. About five years later, three of their four children got sick and died. The couple had more children, but two more children also got sick and died.

Like Jette, many immigrant women were lonely and homesick. Their work was hard. They had to have a big breakfast ready for the family before sunrise. Then they spent the rest of the day taking care of children, keeping up the house, cooking, working in the fields, and tending the garden.

In a letter, Jette wrote to her brother about her struggle to learn to speak English:

> Today I was alone all day long with my little ones. And I thought that I would write you a lot. I talked with you in my thoughts all morning. But here comes an American on horseback, and I have to try to speak English with him. He is waiting for Bruns, who will not return until this evening. I have progressed with my English speaking so far that I can understand . . . a few common little sentences. . . . I must really learn more, for it annoys me when I stand there like a blockhead and cannot answer. . . .

Men on a log raft watch a riverboat tow a passenger barge. Irish immigrants found work building the riverboats.

Irish Immigrants

Missouri's other large immigrant group during this time came from Ireland. There was a flood of Irish immigrants to America during the 1840s because of a terrible potato *famine* in Ireland. Growing potatoes was the way the Irish earned a living. They ate potatoes and sold potatoes. When the potato crops became diseased, a million people in Ireland died. Another million left. Most of them came to the United States. Many Irish stayed in the eastern part of the country, but thousands came to Missouri.

Most of the Irish immigrants were too poor to buy land. Instead, they settled in St. Louis or other towns. The men worked in manufacturing, on wharves unloading boats, or building steamboats. Others got jobs working on the state's first railroads.

What do you think?

America is a nation of immigrants. People have come here from all over the world. Where did your ancestors come from? Where are immigrants coming from today?

2 MEMORY MASTER

1. What products were manufactured in St. Louis?
2. Who were our state's two largest immigrant groups?
3. What kinds of work did the Germans do in Missouri?
4. Why did the Irish leave their country and come to the United States?
5. What work did the Irish do in Missouri?

LESSON 3

PLACES TO LOCATE

Kentucky
Tennessee
Virginia

WORDS TO UNDERSTAND

rebel
resist

Some slaves broke the law and learned to read and write.

Slavery

During the early years of Missouri statehood, slavery was a cruel fact of life. French settlers had brought enslaved people to Missouri in the 1700s. Americans who moved to Missouri in the 1800s from Kentucky, Tennessee, and Virginia often brought slaves with them.

Families all over Missouri had slaves, but certain regions of the state depended on slavery more than others. Most slaves worked on tobacco and hemp farms along the Missouri River.

Work in Town

The work slaves did varied from farm to farm and town to town. A slave in St. Louis might be a highly skilled carpenter or blacksmith. He would have lots of freedom to move around the city and find work. At the end of each day he would return to his master's house and give the master the money he had earned.

Most slaves did not live in the city. They worked on farms from sunup to sundown six days a week. All workers usually had Sundays off. They rested, washed their own clothes, and cleaned their own cabins. It was a time for slave families to be together.

Slave Codes

The Missouri government passed laws called Slave Codes. The codes stated that slave owners could buy and sell their slaves like any other property. Enslaved people had no rights. Slaves could not talk in court, could not carry weapons, and could not meet in groups without a white person present. It was also against the law for anyone to teach slaves to read and write.

Free African Americans

Masters rarely freed slaves, but a few were freed when the master died. In some cases, slaves worked on their own time and made enough money to buy their freedom.

A few thousand free African Americans lived and worked in St. Louis. Some owned businesses and earned enough money to live well. But even these free blacks were not allowed to vote or hold a government job. Missouri laws prevented this.

"Part of the Family"

Most Missouri families who owned slaves owned no more than five. Sometimes they owned a slave family.

Masters and slaves often worked side by side in the fields. A slave woman worked with the master's wife, cooking meals and making clothing. She helped raise the master's children and worked in the garden. Slave children often played with the master's children.

Some slaves lived in the master's farmhouse in a small room off the kitchen. They slept on a mat they rolled out on the floor each night. Others were given a small cabin behind the master's house. Each slave usually got two shirts and two pairs of pants a year. Children went barefoot in the summer, but everyone got one pair of shoes for the winter.

Masters and slaves could develop close bonds. The masters often told people that the slaves were "part of our family." The slaves might even have affection for the master and his family.

Men, women, and children were sold to the highest bidder at an auction. This woman is pleading with a buyer to let her stay with her husband.

Sold!

Slavery, however, was still cruel. Slave traders marched slaves in chains through the streets of St. Louis, Liberty, and Boonville. The slaves lived in fear. They knew that at any time the master might decide to sell them or a member of their family. Slave parents might be separated from their children forever.

> Yes suh, there was ten children and we was all separated. I was sold when I was four years old, they said for three hundred and fifty dollars. I seen my brothers and sisters [later] but they had different names.
>
> —Gus Smith, a Missouri slave

Surviving Slavery

As cruel as slavery was, slaves in Missouri showed an amazing ability to survive. They did this by finding ways to adapt and ***resist*** this horrible system. It was very rare for the slaves to ***rebel.*** They knew they were outnumbered and had very little chance of living if they attacked their masters.

Slaves resisted by finding ways to get out of work. They might pretend to be sick or might work slowly. Sometimes they broke tools or burned barns as a way to resist their masters.

Masters gave slaves very simple food. Slaves could add to their diet by growing their own small garden next to their cabin. Sometimes they had time to fish and hunt on Sunday. In this way, they could make their lives a little better. Slaves also secretly resisted by stealing food from the master's kitchen.

Singing for Freedom

Enslaved people developed their own culture. They adapted the master's Christian religion and made it their own. They believed God would one day send someone to free them, just like Moses delivered the people from slavery in the Bible.

Music was important. Slaves sang about their faith in God and their hope for freedom. People who were suffering under slavery gave us many great American gospel songs. The songs are also called Negro spirituals.

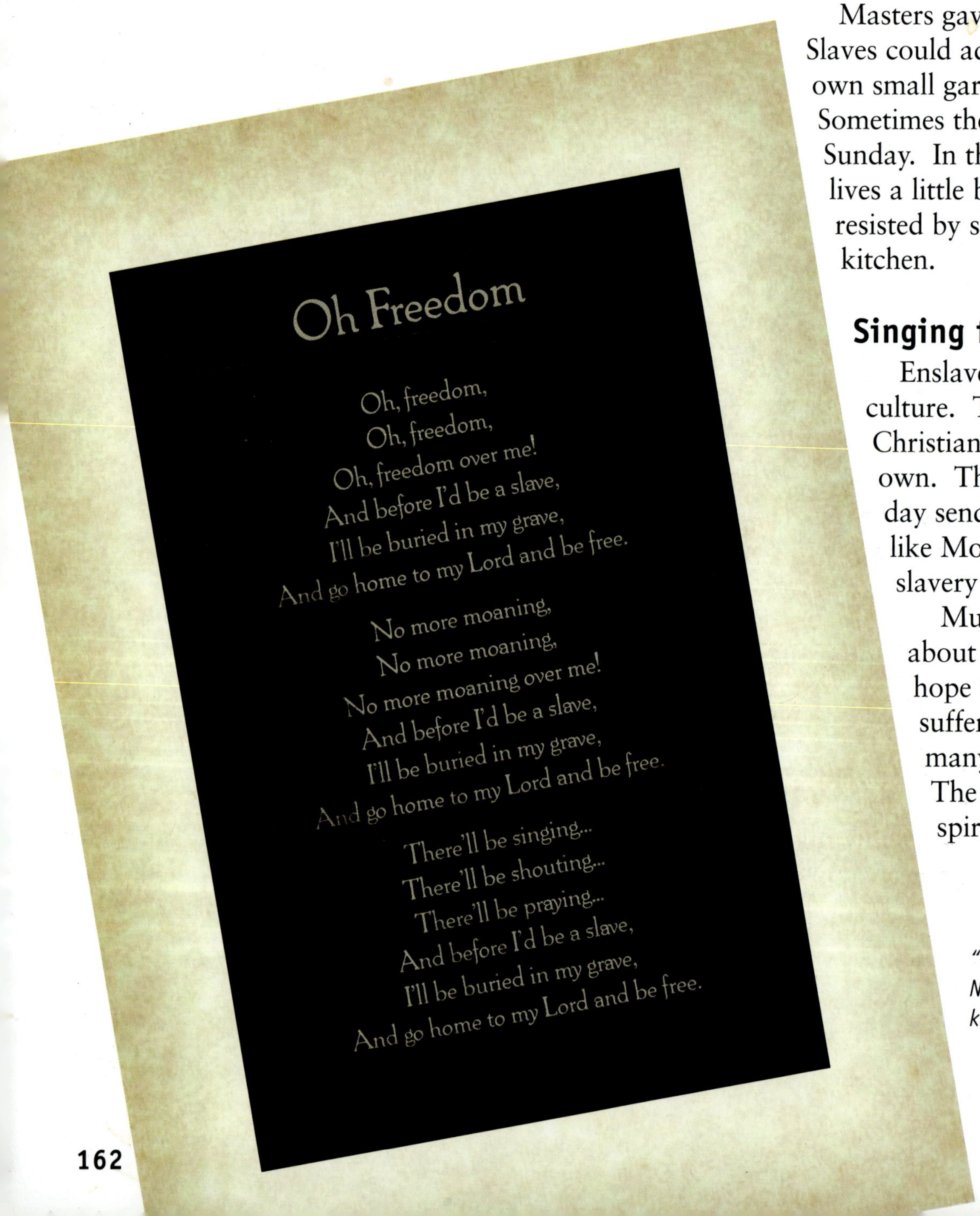

"Oh Freedom" is one Negro spiritual. Do you know any others?

Escape!

The most direct form of resistance was escape. Missouri slaves knew there were free states and territories on three sides of Missouri—Illinois, Iowa, and Kansas. Many slaves escaped, but it took great courage. To do so often meant leaving loved ones behind. They knew if they were caught, they would be whipped or killed.

Mark Twain, an author who lived in Hannibal, captured this in *The Adventures of Huckleberry Finn*. As Huck, a runaway white boy, and Jim, an escaped slave, float down the Mississippi River on a raft, Huck notes the following about Jim:

> He was thinking about his wife and his children, away up yonder, and he was low and homesick; because he hadn't ever been away from home before in his life; and I do believe he cared just as much for his people as white folks do for their'n. It don't seem natural, but I reckon it's so.
>
> He was often moaning that way nights, when he judged I was asleep, and saying "Po little 'Lizabeth! Po little Johnny! It's mighty hard; I s'pec I ain't ever gwyne to see you no mo', no mo'!

What do you think?

At the time, white people were taught that enslaved people were so different from white people that they didn't have the same feelings.

- Why do you think Huck was surprised that Jim missed his family?
- Why do you think Jim ran away from slavery if it meant leaving his family behind?

3 MEMORY MASTER

1. Give two examples of Slave Codes.
2. In what ways did some enslaved people become free?
3. Describe how slaves lived and worked.
4. In what ways did slaves resist slavery?
5. What famous Missouri author wrote *The Adventures of Huckleberry Finn*?

LESSON 4

PEOPLE TO KNOW

John Brown
William Wells Brown
Elijah Lovejoy
John Berry Meachum

PLACES TO LOCATE

Canada
Chillicothe
Platte City
Weston

WORDS TO UNDERSTAND

abolish
criminal
legal

Working Against Slavery

Missouri was a slave state. Slavery was ***legal*** here. However, within a few years after Missouri became a state, a movement to ***abolish,*** or end, slavery spread across America. It grew mostly in the northern states.

The people who worked to stop slavery were called abolitionists. They were deeply religious people who thought slavery was evil. They believed God wanted all people to be free. They also believed slavery was wrong in a country like ours. Our country was founded on the idea of freedom.

Elijah Lovejoy

There were only a few abolitionists in Missouri. It took great courage for them to do what they thought was right. Elijah Lovejoy was a Presbyterian pastor who started a newspaper in St. Louis. In his newspaper, he wrote about his views against slavery. His words made other people angry. A mob attacked him and threw his newspaper presses in the Mississippi River.

Lovejoy moved his paper to Illinois and published it from there. Missourians crossed the river and attacked him again. This time the mob shot and killed him.

Preachers from churches in Chillicothe and Platte City taught that slavery was wrong. They were forced by angry mobs to leave town.

In Weston, an abolitionist was taken by a mob and tarred and feathered. The mob covered the man's body with hot, black tar. Then they covered the tar with white feathers. This was done to strike fear into anyone who would speak out against slavery.

A mob destroyed Elijah Lovejoy's printing press.

Linking the Past to the Present

Freedom of the press and freedom of speech are important in our country today. What do these freedoms mean?

Underground Railroad: A Secret Path to Freedom

Other Missourians secretly helped slaves escape to freedom on the Underground Railroad. The Underground Railroad was not really underground, and it was not a railroad. It was a secret system run by whites and free blacks to help slaves escape.

The route to freedom was very dangerous. Slaves traveled at night, using the moon and stars to guide them. During the day they hid in the woods. Friendly people called "conductors" sometimes hid runaways in their barns or cellars. Then they gave the slaves instructions on how to get to the next safe house. The safe houses were called "stations."

Some Missouri slaves escaped to Illinois, Iowa, or Kansas. Some kept going all the way to Canada.

Some runaways were clever. They found ways to stop barking dogs who were trying to follow them. One man later wrote about how they stopped the dogs, called bloodhounds, with a plant called Indian turnip.

> They would take this [plant] and dry it, . . . and tie it around their feet to keep off the trail of the bloodhounds. No bloodhound could trail a bit farther after smelling it. It was strong like red pepper, burns like everything, and colored folks who were running away used it all the time.
>
> —Gus Smith, a Missouri slave

People who worked with the Underground Railroad were breaking the law. The law said that people who found slaves had to return them to their owners. The people who helped slaves escape wanted to obey the law, but they also believed slavery was terribly wrong.

MISSOURI PORTRAIT

John Berry Meachum

Missouri was a slave state, but there were Missourians who worked bravely to help slaves. One of those heroes was a former slave.

John Berry Meachum was born a slave in Virginia. As he grew up there, he was trained to be a carpenter. Over the years, he worked on his own time to save enough money to buy his freedom. He also bought the freedom of his father.

Once he was free, Meachum moved to Kentucky. Then he moved to St. Louis. He began a small factory that made wooden barrels. He used the money he made to buy slaves. Over a period of many years, Meachum bought 20 slaves. He let them work in his factory until they could pay him back and earn their own freedom. He taught them important skills that would help them make a living after they were free.

John Berry Meachum is best remembered for his Freedom School. He started a Sunday school for black men, women, and children in his church. He taught eager students to read and write. Then the Missouri government made it against the law to teach African Americans to read and write, whether they were slave or free.

Meachum bought a steamboat in St. Louis and anchored it in the Mississippi River just off the shore. Since it was not on Missouri soil, the Freedom School was not against the law. Black students could take small boats out to the steamboat and go to school. This made many white people angry, but John Berry Meachum wanted to do what was best for his people.

Meachum was also a preacher. He started the First African Baptist Church in St. Louis. When he died there were 500 members in his church.

William Wells Brown

William Brown was a Missouri slave who became a world-famous abolitionist. He was born in Kentucky, but when William was two years old, his master took the young boy and his mother to Missouri. As he grew up, William worked on his master's farm.

When William was a teenager, his master moved to St. Louis. He started renting William out to other white people. William worked at many jobs, including work on steamboats up and down the Mississippi and Missouri Rivers.

On one trip up the Ohio River, William escaped from his boat when it docked. He fled to northern Ohio. He spent a few years working on a steamboat on Lake Erie. He also helped other slaves escape to Canada. Then he moved to Buffalo, New York, and started speaking to abolitionist groups. They were moved by his stories of how cruel slavery in Missouri really was.

William learned to read and write. He wrote the story of his life and had it published in a book. Then people all over the North and in Europe could read about slavery. William wrote:

> All I demand for the black man is that the white people shall take their heels off of his neck, and let him have a chance to rise by his own efforts.

John Brown

John Brown was an abolitionist living in Kansas. He rode into Vernon County, Missouri, with a group of followers. Their plan was to free slaves.

On one farm, a farmer tried to stop John Brown and the men who were with him. The abolitionists killed the farmer and led his 11 slaves to freedom. They also took money and supplies from the farm and gave them to the slaves to start their new lives. Abolitionists believed John Brown was a hero. Other people believed he was a ***criminal.*** He was breaking the law.

The next year, John Brown shocked the nation when he and his followers attacked Harper's Ferry, Virginia. They tried to capture a storehouse for weapons and give guns to the slaves so they could fight for their freedom. Hiding inside, John Brown was shot and taken prisoner. He was hanged for trying to free slaves.

4 MEMORY MASTER

1. What does the word "abolish" mean?
2. How did the Underground Railroad help slaves?
3. List two things John Berry Meachum and William Wells Brown did for African Americans.

Reward!

Masters offered money for the return of their slaves. People often read newspaper advertisements for runaway slaves. An 1832 advertisement in Boone County read:

$100.00 Reward

Lost on the night of 6 and 7 of April last . . . . A Negro woman and her four children. Her name is Betsy. The children range in age from 9 months to 6 years of age.

What do you think?

How much courage did it take for Betsy to escape with her children? What hardships might she have faced?

Chapter 7 Review

From There to Here

In 1821 Missouri was a finally a state. People in the East thought that places such as Missouri were good places to start over. They could get good land. They could farm. They could raise a family near the wide rivers.

At the same time, other people far across the Atlantic Ocean were in trouble. They needed a new home. Families left Germany and Ireland to start a new life. They said goodbye to their relatives and friends and began the long trip across the ocean. Once they got to the United States, many of them traveled all the way to Missouri. They farmed or worked in cities.

Other people came to Missouri against their will. They were enslaved people who were brought to work on farms and in cities. Resisting their masters was very hard, but many tried. Some ran away. They got help from good people who wanted slavery to end. Some of the people who helped slaves died for their efforts. However, life was about to change. Soon a terrible Civil War would be fought. After the war, all slaves would be free.

Activity

Make a Book: People on the Frontier

Fold four pieces of plain white paper in half. Then put the four pieces of paper together to make a book. Place two staples along the fold.

The first page will show the title of the book and the author (you). For the other pages of the book, choose groups of people from this chapter. You might have pages about frontier families, German immigrants, Irish immigrants, or enslaved people. You might have pages for specific people you read about. You might want to make your book all about children. Use the Internet to find information.

For each page, write words and draw a picture. Include pages that:

- Show some of the work the people did. You could write about how the work in those days was the same or different from how people work today.
- Show a problem the people had. You could write about how they tried to solve the problem.

Activity

Dictionary Corn Clues

Missouri farmers grew a lot of corn. They couldn't have lived without it.

Use a dictionary to learn more about corn. Find the first time the word "corn" appears, and then keep reading all the words that have to do with the yellow vegetable. Skip over the words that really don't have anything to do with corn, such as "corner."

Make a list of at least six "corn" words, separating the syllables with small dots, just like the dictionary does. Next to each word, write down its meaning. Then draw small pictures of some of the words.

Now search for "Missouri corn" on your computer. What can you learn about corn, a very important crop?

Activity

Answer with Art

You have read about people who came to live in Missouri from other places. In this chapter, people moved here from Germany and other countries. They also moved here from other states in the United States. Some people came to find land, jobs, and freedom. Enslaved people were brought here against their will. They came to work for masters.

No matter where they came from, or why they came, the people brought their art and music with them. Answer the questions below, but in different ways. Choose two of these questions, and give your answers in the form of a drawing or a very short poem that could be sung as a song.

- How did the settlers build a home?
- How did the settlers get food?
- How did the settlers prepare the land for planting?
- What work did pioneer men, women, and children do?
- What kinds of work did the Irish immigrants do?
- What kinds of work did the German immigrants do?
- In what ways did African American slaves rebel?
- What instrument did the pioneers play?
- How did the Underground Railroad help slaves?
- What kinds of work did the African American slaves do?
- Choose one person from this chapter and show how he or she helped others.

THE TIME
1854–1865

"My wife and I came through Johnson, Cass, and Jackson Counties and for miles and miles we saw nothing but lone chimneys to mark the spot where happy homes once stood. It seemed like a vast cemetery—not a living thing to break the silence. . . . Man no longer existed there."

—Reverend George Miller describing the scene in western Missouri just after the Civil War

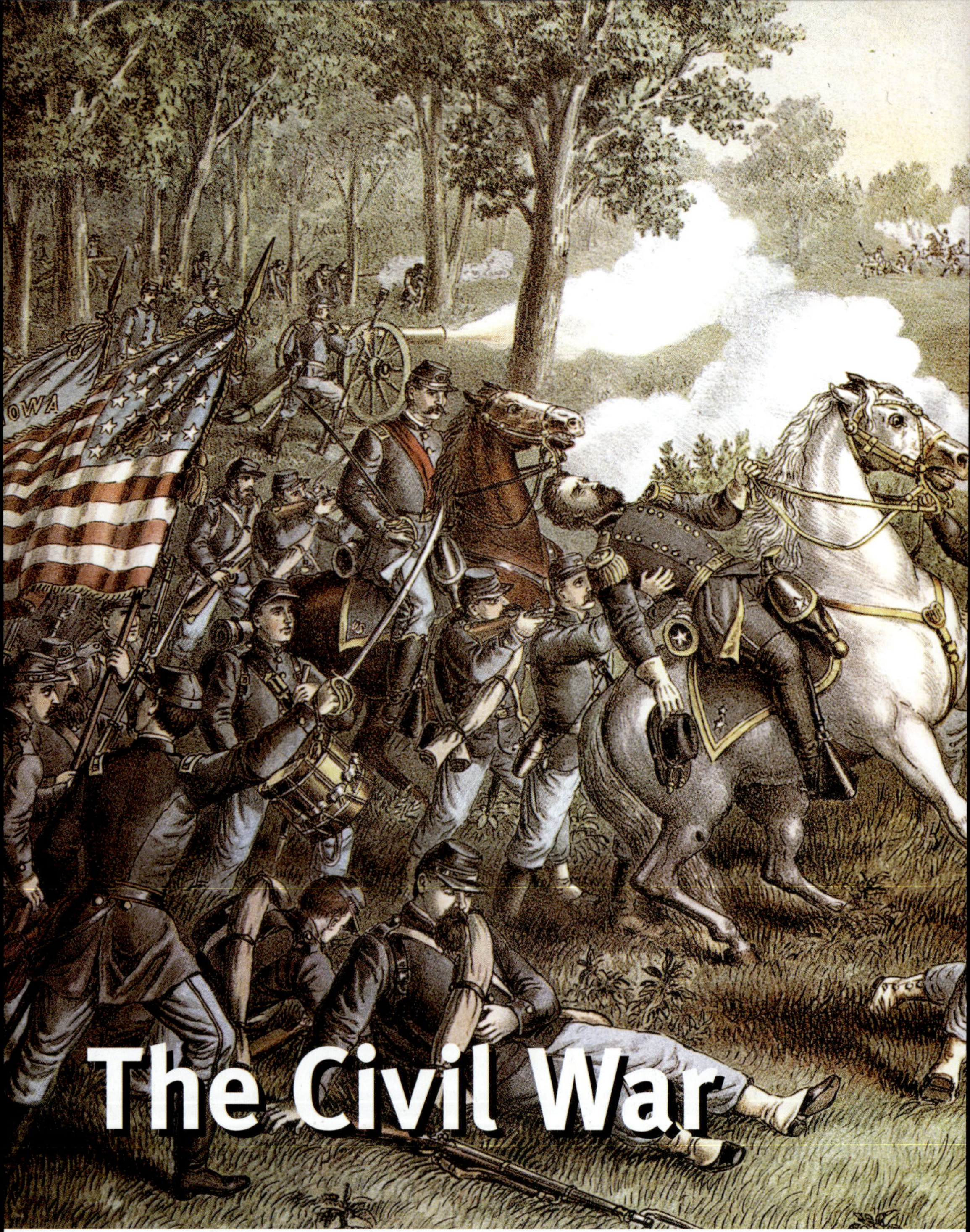

The Civil War

Timeline of Events

1854-1856 "Bleeding Kansas"

1854 — 1855 — 1856 — 1857 — 1858

1857
The U.S. Supreme Court rules against Dred Scott.

Chapter 8

Union General Nathaniel Lyon was shot and fell off his horse at the Battle of Wilson's Creek. He gave his life to fight for the Union in Missouri.

1859

1860 Abraham Lincoln is elected president. Claiborne Fox Jackson is elected governor of Missouri. South Carolina secedes from the Union.

1861-1865 Civil War

April 12, 1861 The South attacks Fort Sumter. More states secede.

1861 Missouri Civil War battles of Boonville, Wilson's Creek, and Lexington

1862 Missouri Civil War battles of Kirksville and Lone Jack

1863
- Lincoln issues the Emancipation Proclamation.
- The Kansas City Jail collapses.
- Quantrill attacks Lawrence, Kansas.
- General Ewing issues Order Number ll.

1864 Missouri Civil War battles of Pilot Knob and Westport

1865 Abraham Lincoln is shot.

1865 Missouri frees all slaves in the state.

1866

LESSON 1

PEOPLE TO KNOW

Dred Scott
Harriet Scott

PLACES TO LOCATE

Kansas
Nebraska
Lawrence, Kansas

WORDS TO UNDERSTAND

decision

"Bleeding Kansas"

Government leaders in Washington, D.C., could not decide whether people in Kansas and Nebraska could or could not own slaves. Congress decided to let the people who moved to these places vote on whether or not to allow slavery. Thousands of farm families moved to Kansas so they could vote against slavery.

Slave owners in Missouri felt differently. They wanted to be able to move to Kansas and take their slaves with them. For each election, thousands of Missourians crossed the border into Kansas and voted for slavery. They should not have been allowed to vote because they did not live in Kansas. They broke the law and voted anyway. This led to a small war in Kansas.

Missouri men crossed over the Kansas border to vote in elections. They hoped to make Kansas a slave state.

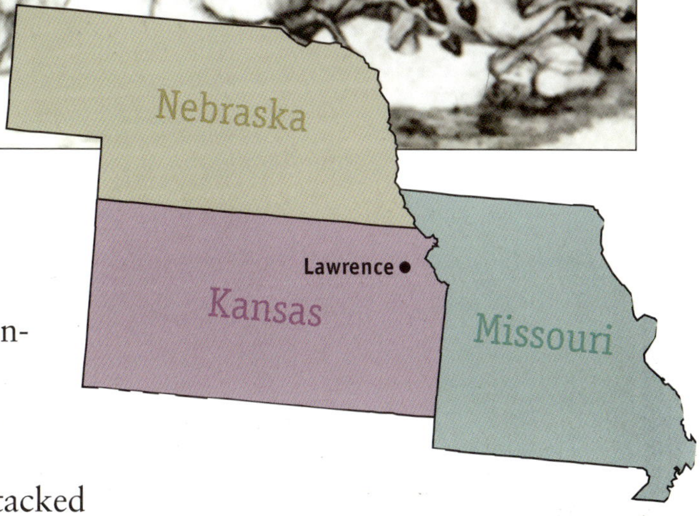

More Trouble

Abolitionists worked to end slavery everywhere. They kept moving into Kansas to keep it free. Many brought guns.

Missourians who were pro-slavery tried to stop the abolitionists from getting to Kansas. The two groups were constantly fighting with each other. Many innocent settlers on both sides were killed.

One day some men from Missouri rode into Kansas and attacked the city of Lawrence. Lawrence was home to many abolitionists. The men from Missouri burned buildings and killed several settlers.

Finally, the national government sent soldiers to the Kansas-Missouri border to keep the peace. But many of the people there had come to deeply hate one another. There would be more killing to come.

When you see the prefix "pro" before a word, it means "for." When you see the prefix "anti" before a word, it means "against." What did people who were pro-slavery or anti-slavery want?

What do you think?

What are some ways people can solve serious problems without fighting and killing?

This letter states in handwriting that the "public mind" was not "in a condition to listen to reason." In other words, people were not thinking clearly about how unfair it was to think of men and women as property.

Baltimore Nov. 9th 1857

My Dear Sir

I have been away from Washington since the 28th of October – engaged in holding the circuit courts for Delaware and Maryland. The latter is still in session; owing to my absence from Washington I did not receive either of your letters or speeches until a day or two ago.

I thank you for them – and have read them with much pleasure – Your argument in each of them is maintained triumphantly by the clearest proofs of facts and constitutional law: and if the public mind were in a condition to listen to reason, one might look for a change of opinion

Dred Scott

Dred Scott

As Americans argued about slavery, they learned the names of a Missouri slave named Dred Scott and his wife, Harriet. Scott had been a slave in Virginia. Then he was sold to an army doctor. The doctor moved to Missouri and brought Scott with him. Over the years, the doctor took Scott with him on many trips into free states.

When Scott's master died, Scott wanted to be free. He went to court to get his freedom. Abolitionists in St. Louis helped him. They argued that Scott should have been freed when his master first took him to a free state.

The Missouri Supreme Court in St. Louis heard the case. The court ruled against Scott. The judges said Scott had returned to Missouri, and since Missouri was a slave state, Scott was still a slave.

Scott's last chance was the United States Supreme Court. It is the highest court in the nation. The judges of that court heard his case. The nation watched and waited for the court's decision. It would have a big effect on other slaves.

The U.S. Supreme Court decided Dred Scott was not free. The judges said that a slave was only a piece of property. They said owners of property could take their property anywhere they wanted.

Most people today believe this is one of the worst ***decisions*** ever made by the U.S. Supreme Court. It meant there was almost no way to stop people from taking slaves to the new lands in the West.

After the painful loss in court, friends in St. Louis bought Dred and Harriet Scott gave them their freedom.

1 MEMORY MASTER

1. Why did Missourians go to Kansas?
2. What did abolitionists want?
3. What did the U.S. Supreme Court decide in the Dred Scott case?

The Beginning of the Civil War

The most painful time in our nation's history was the Civil War. A *civil war* is one in which groups of people in the same country fight against each other. Sometimes neighbors fought against neighbors, and brothers fought against their own brothers. Hundreds of thousands of Americans died in the war.

PEOPLE TO KNOW

Jefferson Davis
Claiborne Fox Jackson
Abraham Lincoln
Sterling Price

PLACES TO LOCATE

Arkansas
Lexington
Wilson's Creek
Charleston, South Carolina

WORDS TO UNDERSTAND

civil war
secede

The Election of 1860

In the election for president, most Missourians did not vote for Abraham Lincoln because he was against the spread of slavery. Lincoln did not say he would end slavery in the slave states. He believed, however, that there would be more problems in the country if some of the states allowed slavery and some did not.

Even though Lincoln lost the election in Missouri, he won enough votes in the rest of the country to win. He became the new president of the United States of America.

The new president faced many problems. The people in the South did not want to stay in the United States with Lincoln as president.

Abraham Lincoln was president during the Civil War.

What do you think?

Earlier, Lincoln had quoted the Bible when he said, "A house divided against itself cannot stand." What do you think he meant by that statement? Is it important to support a leader even if you did not vote for him or her?

This cartoon was published before the Civil War. What is it trying to show?

What do you think?

The Union, or the North, was at war with the Confederacy, or the South. What would our country be like today if President Lincoln had let the Southern States leave the Union?

The First Battle

After Lincoln was elected president, the slave states in the South thought about ***seceding,*** or breaking away, from the United States of America. They thought the national government was too powerful. They wanted states to be able to decide important issues such as slavery for themselves.

Lincoln felt very strongly that states could not leave the Union. The United States was often called the Union. Lincoln believed the Union would break apart and die if any of the states left.

Some states, however, did not listen to President Lincoln. They seceded soon after the election. South Carolina was the first state to leave. South Carolina was also where the first battle of the Civil War took place. What caused the battle?

Fort Sumter was a U.S. fort in South Carolina. President Lincoln wanted to keep soldiers at the fort. He wanted the fort to fly the U.S. flag. South Carolina wanted the U.S. soldiers to leave and to take their flag down. Lincoln refused to turn over the fort.

South Carolina soldiers fired cannons at the fort. People in Charleston came out to watch as soldiers fired. One boy wrote: "I had a splendid view. A perfect sheet of flame flashed out. There was a roar, a rumbling, and the war was on."

Union soldiers surrendered and headed north, carrying their flag. No one had been killed in the battle.

Confederate troops fired on Fort Sumter in Charleston Harbor, South Carolina. It was the first battle of the Civil War.

A Nation Divided

After the battle, other slave states in the South left the Union. The states formed what they hoped would be a new country. They called their country the Confederate States of America, or the Confederacy. Jefferson Davis was the president of the Confederacy.

It was a very sad time in history. Each side formed an army to fight for their beliefs. Each side chose a general to lead their army. The Union fought to keep the country together. The Confederacy fought for the right to be a separate country.

A Nation Divided—the Civil War

North		South	
Name: Union		**Name:** Confederacy	
Nickname: Yankees		**Nickname:** Rebels	
Color: Blue		**Color:** Gray	
Number of States: 23		**Number of States:** 11	

President: Abraham Lincoln

General: Ulysses S. Grant

General: Robert E. Lee

President: Jefferson Davis

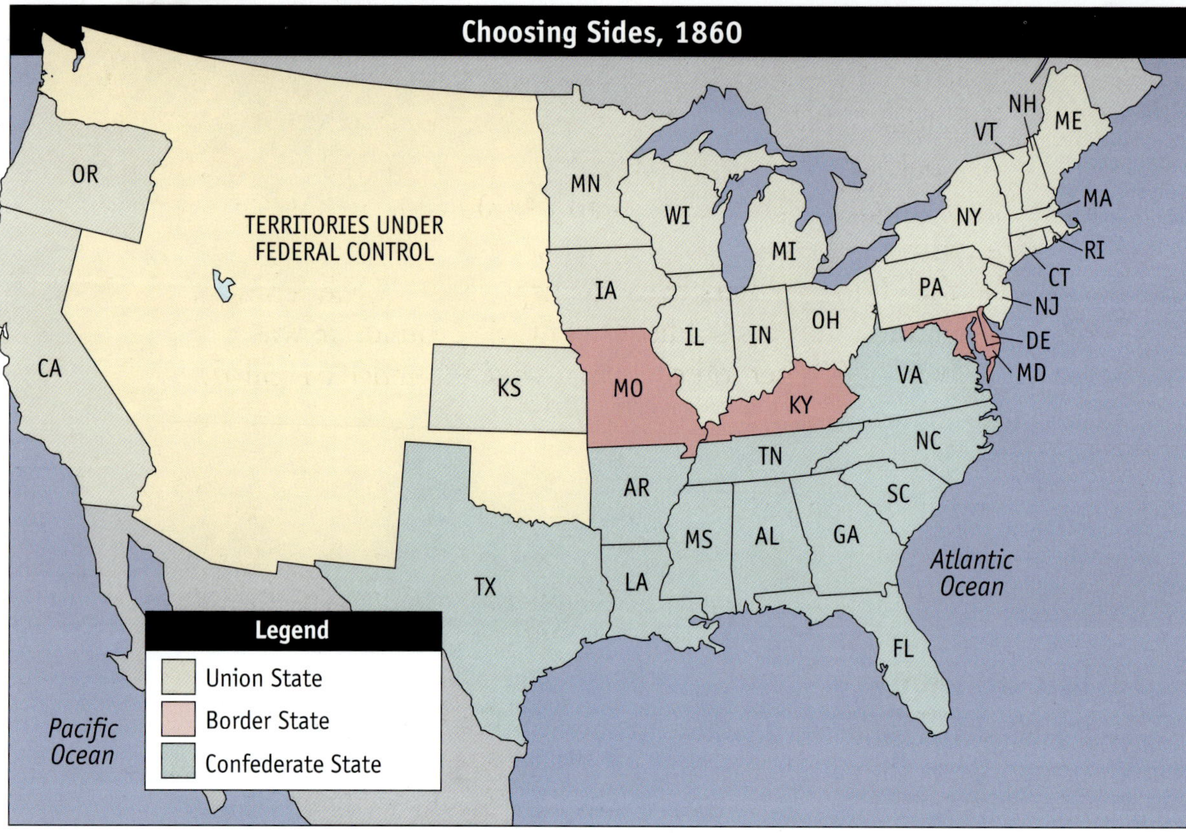

The border states were part of the Union, but people there still owned slaves. Can you find Missouri on the map? What are the four border states?

The Border States

Eleven slave states in the South seceded. Four slave states, however, stayed with the Union. Because they were between the Northern states and the Southern states, these states were known as the border states.

People who lived in these states were divided about how they felt about the war. This was very true in Missouri. Some Missourians fought with the North to save the Union. Other Missourians fought with the South.

Governor Claiborne Fox Jackson wanted Missouri to join the Confederacy.

Governor Jackson

Missouri's governor was Claiborne Fox Jackson. He supported the South. He wanted Missouri to secede from the Union.

When President Lincoln asked each state to send men to stop the South from seceding, Governor Jackson refused. In fact, he ordered the Missouri militia to train for war. They were led by General Sterling Price. He hoped to use the soldiers to aid the South.

Then Missouri men who supported the North formed their own militia in St. Louis. This meant that the state was preparing to fight for both the North and the South.

Union troops moved toward Jefferson City to capture the governor. Knowing he could not win, Governor Jackson and his army fled.

Battle at Wilson's Creek

Union soldiers followed Jackson and Price. One of Missouri's biggest Civil War battles took place near Springfield at Wilson's Creek. There were 7,000 Union soldiers. Price had 14,000 men because his army had been joined by soldiers from other states.

In the battle, the Union soldiers tried to surprise the Confederates in an early morning attack. Price's soldiers held their ground. It was a terrible battle. Over 1,000 men on each side were wounded or killed.

Battle of the Hemp Bales

After winning at Wilson's Creek, Governor Jackson and General Price met Union troops at Lexington. They had 15,000 soldiers. The Union army had only 3,000 soldiers. Price's army surrounded the town and cut off all supplies of food and water. They also began to fire cannons on the Union forces.

For the final attack, the army moved toward the Union troops. To protect themselves, the Confederates rolled large bales of hemp leaves in front of them. Some people called this the "Battle of the Hemp Bales."

Union soldiers had to surrender. They were forced to give up thousands of guns and hundreds of horses.

Later, General Price and Governor Jackson left the state and went into Arkansas. The next year, Governor Jackson died there.

2 MEMORY MASTER

1. Who was president of the United States during the Civil War?
2. What does "secession" mean?
3. What made Missouri a border state?

Battle of the Hemp Bales

LESSON 3

PEOPLE TO KNOW

"Bloody Bill" Anderson
George Caleb Bingham
Adaline Couzins
Thomas Ewing
Mary Whitney Phelps
Martha Jane Tolton
William Quantrill

PLACES TO LOCATE

Lawrence, Kansas

WORDS TO UNDERSTAND

disloyal
guerrilla warfare
revenge
volunteer

What do you think?

What freedoms did the people of Missouri lose? How important are these freedoms to people today?

Guerrilla Warfare

There were few major battles fought in Missouri during the war. Instead, Missouri had a different kind of war that was perhaps even more horrible. Missouri lived through four years of ***guerrilla warfare.*** A guerrilla fighter is part of a small band of men who fight on their own. They are not part of a regular army. They attack the enemy in surprise raids, and then they disappear into the woods.

Disloyal to the Union

After the Battle of the Hemp Bales, more Union troops came. Union soldiers did not trust Missourians and treated them all as if they were ***disloyal*** to the Union. Missourians had to live under strict laws. These people lost basic freedoms that had been protected by the Bill of Rights in the U.S. Constitution. Newspapers could not print anything against the Union. To travel in the state, Missourians had to get a pass. Military leaders could arrest people and keep them in jail for a long time if they thought the people might be disloyal to the Union.

Attacks from Jayhawkers

Missourians faced another problem. When the war began, groups of men from Kansas crossed the border and attacked Missouri. These groups were called "Jayhawkers."

Some of these groups were seeking ***revenge*** for killings by Missouri men. They believed all Missourians were their enemy. They attacked farms across western Missouri. They came onto a farm, murdered the farmer and his oldest sons, and stole his tools and animals. After burning the farm, they carried the stolen goods back into Kansas and sold them.

> In the morning burned another house, then went to [a home] and took breakfast. . . . Allowed them to carry out clothing before burning. . . . Marched north again, burning a few more houses, and rested for the night. . . .
>
> —Sherman Bodwell, a Kansas Jayhawker

Bushwhackers Fight Back

Facing both the Union troops and attacks from Jayhawkers was more than some people could take. Some young men became so angry they fought back.

Many of these young men had seen their farms attacked or their fathers murdered. They began to form their own guerrilla bands. These bands were led by men such as William Quantrill and "Bloody Bill" Anderson.

Many people called these guerrilla fighters "Bushwhackers." This was because they hid in the bush, or the woods, after they attacked. The Bushwhackers wore colorful "guerrilla shirts" with many pockets to hold their many pistols. They rode fast horses.

Most Bushwhackers wanted Missouri to join the Confederates. They attacked rail lines or telegraph lines used by the Union troops. At other times, Bushwhackers attacked groups of Union soldiers.

Bushwhackers also attacked farmers they believed were loyal to the Union. They often murdered people who were just trying to live their lives in peace. As the war went on, Bushwhackers attacked Missouri families just to steal their food and supplies. They brought terror to the hearts of people who never knew when they might attack.

"Bloody Bill" Anderson led the Bushwhackers.

These Jayhawkers crossed into Missouri to rescue a friend.

Quantrill Attacks Lawrence

Union troops tried to stop the Bushwhackers by punishing their families. General Thomas Ewing was in charge of Union troops in western Missouri. He put many of the wives, sisters, and mothers of Quantrill's Bushwhackers in the Kansas City Jail. The jail was in the basement of an old brick building that was falling down. The building did fall in, and five women were killed. Others were badly hurt.

Quantrill's men went crazy with hatred and anger. They wanted revenge. They rode all night and arrived at the town of Lawrence, Kansas, at daybreak. Lawrence was a quiet town, but Quantrill believed many Jayhawkers lived there. Quantrill ordered his men to kill every man and boy "old enough to carry a gun."

What happened that day was horrible. Quantrill's men killed over 150 men and boys. They also burned 185 buildings and left the town in ruins. This raid of revenge shocked the nation.

Quantrill's men burned the Free State Hotel during the attack in Kansas.

What Did the Women Do?

During the Civil War, women took care of their families and their homes. If their husbands were away at war, the women also had to run the farm. They got jobs as nurses.

Many women ***volunteered.*** They worked without pay to help soldiers. They sewed uniforms. In hospitals, the women washed patients, changed bandages, and gave food to wounded soldiers. They washed sheets and clothes. They talked to men who were dying or in pain. They wrote letters to send to wives and mothers back home.

Adaline Couzins worked on a floating hospital on the Mississippi River. One time a bullet was fired from shore. It hit her knee, but she didn't stop working on the floating hospital.

Mary Whitney Phelps from Springfield also cared for wounded soldiers. After the war, she opened a home for children whose fathers had died in the war. She also took in children of both Union and Confederate soldiers whose mothers could not care for them.

A woman writes down a letter from a wounded soldier. Notice that the men were outdoors or in tents.

MISSOURI PORTRAIT

Martha Jane Tolton
1833-1911

Martha was a slave in Kentucky. At age 16, she was given to a young white bride as a wedding gift. The family soon moved to Brush Creek, Missouri. Martha worked for the family in the tobacco and hemp fields and in the house.

Martha married Peter Paul Tolton, and they had children. When the Civil War started, the Tolton children were Charles, age eight, Augustine, six, and Anne, two months old. Augustine later said that he learned to sing and pray with his mother.

During the war, Martha Tolton and her children escaped and walked 20 miles to Hannibal. They crossed the Mississippi River in a rocking rowboat and arrived safely in Illinois, a free state. The young family walked another 20 miles to find work in a tobacco factory. Everyone but the baby worked 10 hours a day, 6 days a week. There were no schools for black children. On Sundays, the family went to a Catholic church.

Augustine Tolton grew up, went to Rome, and became the first African American Catholic priest born in the United States.

Order Number 11

Once Quantrill's men escaped back to Missouri, General Ewing decided to take strong action. He believed the Bushwhackers were getting help from many farmers along the Missouri-Kansas border.

He gave a military order called "Order Number 11." He ordered farmers all along the Missouri-Kansas border to leave their homes within 15 days. They had to give their crops to the Union army. Ewing thought this would put an end to the terrible work of the Bushwhackers.

This was a terrible order for the farmers. They had to leave farms they had spent years working on. They could only take what they could get in their wagons. Over 20,000 farmers and their families had to move. Many had nowhere to go.

Smoking Ruins

Once the farm families left, Kansas men entered the area to get their own revenge for what had happened in Lawrence. They burned every house in sight and stole anything left behind. For miles and miles, all that was left were smoking ruins of houses with chimneys sticking in the air.

Ewing's Order Number 11 caused anger across the nation. After a few months he took back the order, but by then it was too late. Those families who had been forced from their homes could not go back and had nothing to eat. Many faced a winter of starvation.

3 MEMORY MASTER

1. Describe guerrilla warfare.
2. Who were the Jayhawkers?
3. Who were the Bushwhackers?
4. How did Order Number 11 affect families?

A Soldier Paints *Order Number 11*

After the war, one of Missouri's most famous artists painted a picture he titled *Order Number 11*. His name was George Caleb Bingham. He painted daily life in Missouri from his home in Arrow Rock.

Even though Bingham himself was a Union soldier, he thought Ewing's order was cruel. The painting shows a Missouri family being forced from their home while all of their property is being stolen by Union troops. In the background of the painting you can see the smoking remains of houses. For years this painting reminded Missourians of that horrible time.

LESSON 4

PEOPLE TO KNOW

Archer Alexander
Abraham Lincoln

PLACES TO LOCATE

Washington, D.C.

Final Battles

As the war came to a close, Union troops hunted down and captured most of the Bushwhackers. "Bloody Bill" Anderson and William Quantrill tried to escape, but they were captured and killed.

General Price led his Confederate army into Missouri one last time. He led his troops toward St. Louis, but Union soldiers slowed him down at the Battle of Pilot Knob. Finally, Price led his army toward Kansas City. There he met Union forces in the Battle of Westport. The battle raged for three days. The Union forces won the battle, and Price led his army back to Arkansas.

By this time, most Missourians were tired of war and wanted it to end. There had been 400 small battles in the state during the war. No other state had more small battles. Thousands of Missourians on both sides had died.

A Message Through Wire

Many people call the Civil War the first modern war because there was a lot of new technology used in the war. Telegraphs were the fastest way to send a message. A letter could take weeks to arrive, but a message from a telegraph arrived in minutes. Armies could communicate faster. Newspaper reporters could send their stories to their printers more quickly.

Telegraph machines sent messages over an electric wire. Telegraph wires were strung for many miles between towns. Messages were tapped into the telegraph machine by using a system of dots and dashes. It was called the Morse code. An operator touched a key quickly for a dot and held it down longer for a dash.

Morse Code

A • —	S •••
B — •••	T —
C — • — •	U •• —
D — ••	V ••• —
E •	W • — —
F •• — •	X — •• —
G — — •	Y — • — —
H ••••	Z — — ••
I ••	1 • — — — —
J • — — —	2 •• — — —
K — • —	3 ••• — —
L • — ••	4 •••• —
M — —	5 •••••
N — •	6 — ••••
O — — —	7 — — •••
P • — — •	8 — — — ••
Q — — • —	9 — — — — •
R • — •	0 — — — — —

Figure out this famous Morse code signal:
••• — — — •••

Missouri Slaves Are Freed

Late in the Civil War, a group of government leaders met in Missouri to write a new constitution for the state. One of the first things the men did was vote to end slavery in Missouri. The new state constitution said that all Missouri slaves would be freed. Can you imagine what it would be like to finally be free after a lifetime of being a slave? You will read more about the new constitution in the next chapters.

By the time Missouri's slaves were freed by the state, many had already sought freedom on their own. The war had given thousands of slaves a chance to escape. With their masters away fighting, the slaves had run away to free states. Some enslaved men had been given freedom when they joined the Union army.

More Americans died in the Civil War than in any other war, before or since. More men died from disease than from wounds. Doctors at the time didn't know how important it was to keep hospitals and operating tools clean.

The War Ends

After four long years and many battles, the Civil War finally ended. Confederate General Robert E. Lee surrendered to Union General Ulysses S. Grant. Some families celebrated as their husbands, fathers, and sons came home from war. In other families, tears were shed because loved ones had died in the war.

The war had shown everyone that Americans could not split their country in two. They had to stick together and work out their problems.

General Robert E. Lee's surrender meant the end of the Civil War.

Archer Alexander and President Lincoln

A minister asked freed slaves to give money to help build a monument. The monument would show Abraham Lincoln removing the chains of slavery from a black man. A sculptor used Archer Alexander, a Missouri slave, as a model for the statue. Today, if you visit Lincoln Park in our nation's capital city, you can see the monument.

John Wilkes Booth shot President Lincoln at Ford's Theater in Washington, D.C.

All Slaves Are Freed

After the war, the U.S. Congress freed all enslaved men, women, and children in the country. No longer could one person own another person. It was a time of great rejoicing among African Americans. However, prejudice was still strong in the hearts of many people. In the next chapter you will read how former slaves still lived very hard lives.

President Lincoln Is Assassinated

Just days after the war ended, a terrible thing happened in Washington, D.C. President Lincoln and his wife, Mary Todd Lincoln, were watching a play when an actor named John Wilkes Booth shot Lincoln. Booth blamed Lincoln for the South losing the war. Lincoln was taken to a home across the street. He died early the next morning.

4 MEMORY MASTER

1. How were slaves in Missouri finally freed?
2. How long was the Civil War?

Chapter 8 Review

From There to Here

When groups of people strongly disagree about very important issues, what can they do? Sometimes they talk together. They compromise so both sides give in a little and both sides win a little. Sometimes, however, the two groups decide to fight for what they think is right.

In this chapter, people failed to compromise. They failed to find solutions to problems. Instead, they went to war. War is always a terrible thing for both sides. During the Civil War, families in Missouri, a border state, suffered greatly. It was a very hard time for everyone. At the end of the Civil War, all of the states in the United States of America came together once again. Soon all slaves were freed.

Activity

Hardly Worth Eating

Many soldiers ate hardtack during the Civil War. It was a hard cracker that would not spoil or go bad. It was called hardtack because it was very hard. A soldier once wrote home that he bit into his hardtack and found something soft. It was a nail! Of course, that was just a joke, but the story hints that hardtack was very hard to bite and chew.

With the help of an adult, you can make your own hardtack. Here is the recipe:

Mix 2 cups of flour, 1 cup of water, and a pinch of salt into a dough. Spread dough out on a cookie sheet. Divide the dough into 3-inch squares with a butter knife. Then use a fork, or a big nail, to poke holes in the dough. Be sure not to leave the nail in the dough! Bake at 375 degrees for one hour. You've got hardtack!

THE TIME
1865–1900

"When I was a boy, there was but one ambition among my [friends] in our village on the . . . Mississippi River. That was to be a steamboat pilot."

—from Mark Twain's Old Times on the Mississippi, *1875*

Reconstruction and Growth

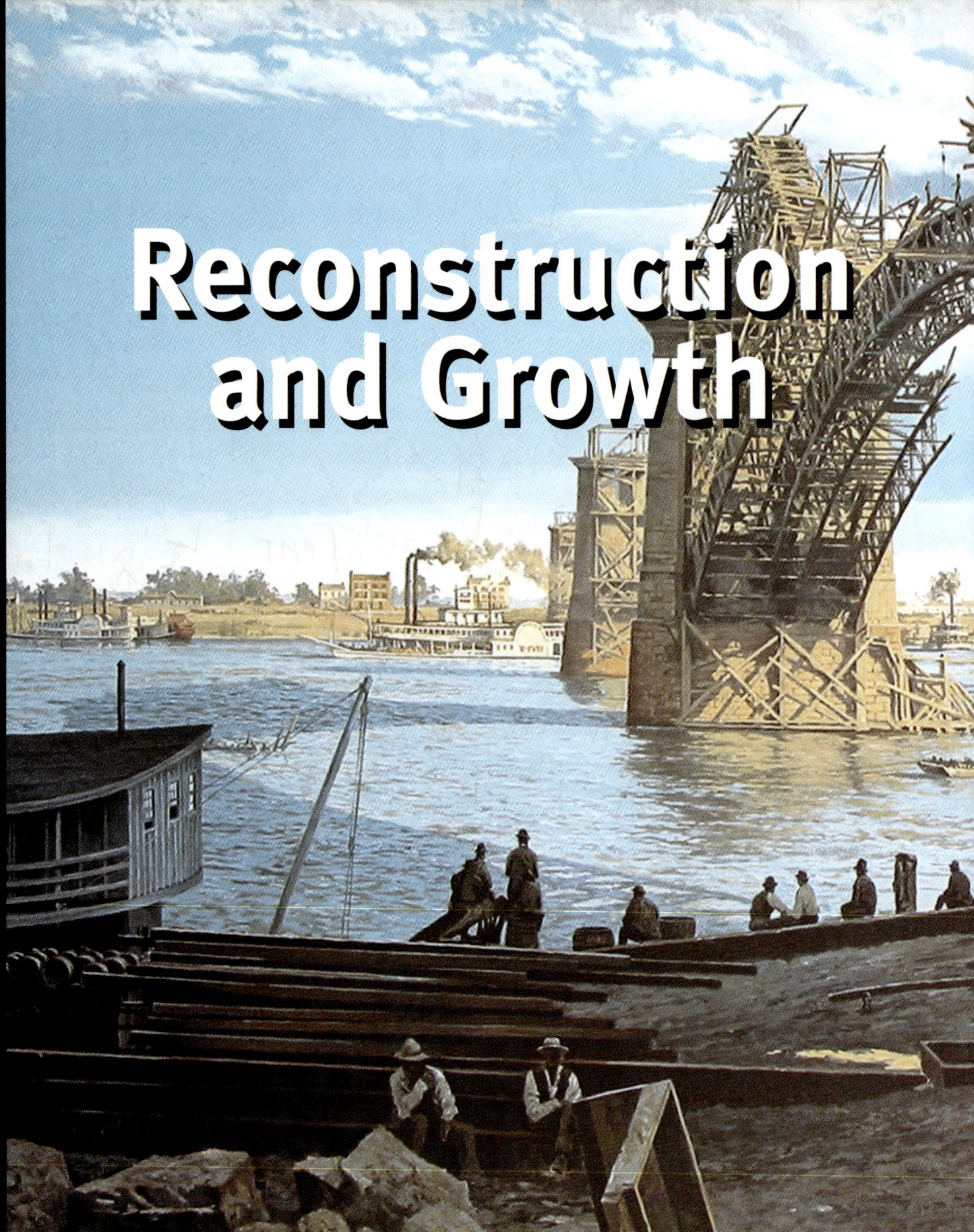

Timeline of Events

1835	1865	1866	1867	1868	186

1835 Samuel Clemens (Mark Twain) is born in Missouri.

1865 The Pacific Railroad connects St. Louis and Kansas City.

1865 A new Missouri constitution frees all slaves in Missouri.

1866 Jesse James and his gang rob their first bank in Liberty.

1867 Laura Ingalls is born in Wisconsin.

1868 The 14th Amendment to the U.S. Constitutio makes former slaves citizens of the U.S.

Chapter 9

Gary Lucy painted "The Eads Bridge Under Construction, 1873." Eads had little formal education, but he designed and built the largest bridge ever constructed at the time. It was the first bridge in the world to use steel instead of iron.

The bridge was tested by walking an elephant across it. Everyone cheered as the huge animal walked over the bridge to Illinois. Then 14 locomotives drove back and forth to test the strength of the huge arches.

The bridge opened on the 4th of July, 1874, and is still used today.

1870
The 15th Amendment to the U.S. Constitution gives former male slaves the right to vote.

1871
Kansas City stockyards open.

1873
The first public kindergarten opens in St. Louis.

1874
The Eads Bridge crosses the Mississippi River.

1875
Voters approve Missouri's third constitution.

1885
Mark Twain publishes *The Adventures of Huckleberry Finn*. Laura Ingalls marries Almonzo Wilder.

1899
Scott Joplin publishes the "Maple Leaf Rag."

1870 | 1871 | 1872 | 1873 | 1874 | 1875 | 1890 | 1900

LESSON 1

Black sharecroppers in 1879 raised crops on someone else's land. They were free, but still very poor.

PEOPLE TO KNOW

Susan Blow
Frank James
Jesse James
Younger brothers

PLACES TO LOCATE

Harrisonville
Kearney
St. Joseph
St. Louis

WORDS TO UNDERSTAND

outlaw
segregate
sharecropper

Reconstruction

After the painful years of the Civil War, it was very hard for life in Missouri to return to normal. Many families had lost fathers, brothers, and sons. Families who had owned slaves had to find a way to pay workers. Black families were free and had to find their own homes and food. Homes that had been destroyed had to be rebuilt. Farms had to be cared for once again. This was true all over the nation.

Reconstruction is the time when the country tried to put itself back together.

New Laws of Freedom

Right after the war, African Americans still did not have many rights. Then the Fourteenth and Fifteenth Amendments to the U.S. Constitution made them citizens and gave all men the right to vote.

Sharecroppers

The Reconstruction years first brought hope for African Americans. Since they were no longer slaves, they could move where they wanted to live. They were free to find a job and get paid for their work.

The new life of freedom was not easy. Most blacks worked in jobs that barely paid them enough to get by. Many became ***sharecroppers.*** They farmed land owned by white farmers. They lived in small cabins on the farm. They worked in the sun from morning until night, but they were still very poor.

At harvest time, the sharecropper had to give much of the crop to the farmer who owned the land. It was a very hard life.

A Boost to Education

During Reconstruction, government leaders opened schools for all children. For the first time, the children of former slaves could go to school and learn to read and write. There were separate schools for black children and for white children. Sadly, the schools for the black children were older and more run down. Black students had to use the old worn-out textbooks that white schools were getting rid of.

What do you think?

Why do you think white and black children had to go to separate schools? How do you think they felt about this?

This school in La Forge was attended by Missouri farm children.

Segregation

As the years went on, the white and black races in Missouri became more and more ***segregated.*** This means they lived separate lives. Blacks and whites in cities and towns lived in separate neighborhoods. They ate at separate restaurants. Hotels that served whites would not allow blacks to stay. This was the case in Missouri and other places.

MISSOURI PORTRAIT

Susan Elizabeth Blow
1843-1916

Susan Blow was born into a wealthy family in St. Louis. She went to the best schools and got a good education.

When she was a young woman, Susan traveled to Europe, where she learned about the schools there.

She saw that German schools started teaching children at a younger age than American schools did. They called their grade for young children "kindergarten." In German, "kinder" means "children." Kindergarten students learned letters, shapes, colors, and many other things.

When she returned to St. Louis, Susan Blow worked to bring kindergarten to the city. The first successful public kindergarten in the United States opened in St. Louis. After a while, all of the grade schools in St. Louis had kindergartens. Because of Blow's work, St. Louis was a model for the nation.

Susan Blow spent the rest of her life working with children and writing books on education.

THE RISE OF OUTLAWS

The pain of the Civil War went on during Reconstruction. Some Bushwhackers and Confederates did not return to their normal lives. They had grown used to a life of violence and living in hiding. These men became ***outlaws.***

The James and Younger Brothers

Even today, the name of Jesse James is known around the world. Who was Jesse James? The James and Younger brothers led a famous gang of outlaws. The men had been Bushwhackers during the war. After the war they stayed on the run and committed crimes across Missouri and in other states.

Jesse and Frank James grew up on a farm near Kearney. Frank, the older brother, fought in the war. Jesse was too young to fight. He stayed home. Union soldiers came to his farm and beat him up. They hanged his stepfather and left, but Jesse and his mother were able to get him down before he died.

When he was only a teenager, Jesse left the farm and joined the Bushwhackers. He rode with Quantrill and "Bloody Bill" Anderson. (You read about them in the last chapter.) Jesse saw much killing during those years.

After the war, Jesse and Frank did not return to their lives as farmers. Instead, they led a gang of outlaws. They robbed banks and trains. The Younger brothers sometimes rode with them. Cole, Bob, and Jim Younger were from Harrisonville. Their father had been killed by Union troops during the war.

"Hand Over the Money"

The James-Younger gang brought fear to many Missourians. During a robbery, they entered the bank, drew a gun on the scared clerk, and demanded money from the safe. They stopped trains and robbed all the passengers. During these robberies, innocent people were sometimes shot and killed.

Law and order eventually returned. The James-Younger gang broke up after a failed bank robbery. The Youngers were captured and put in prison. Frank and Jesse escaped, but life became difficult for them.

Jesse James Is Killed

Jesse was killed by one of his own gang members who wanted to collect the reward money. He shot Jesse in the back when he stood up on a chair to dust a picture.

After his brother's murder, Frank turned himself in. He spent very little time in jail. He spent the rest of his life obeying the law.

A New State Constitution

The anger caused by the Civil War started to fade. Voters adopted another new state constitution. This one tried to protect the rights of everyone. The people of the state began trying to live with one another in peace.

Farmers

During the Civil War, many Missouri farms had been left behind when their owners had to leave the state. After the war, farmers worked hard. The state once again became one of the nation's leaders in farm goods.

Hemp and tobacco were no longer important. Corn became Missouri's largest crop. Farmers also grew oats and wheat. They drained the swampland of the boot heel region and began to grow cotton.

Missouri became the nation's leading producer of mules. Fine saddle horses were also raised here. Farmers raised other animals, too.

Life remained hard for farmers. The railroads helped them get their goods to market. New machines helped them produce bigger crops. But now that they sold food to places all over the world, the prices were set in other states and countries. Sometimes farmers could not get much money for their crops.

Farmers also had to deal with nature. A drought or a hailstorm could destroy their entire crop. Sometimes grasshoppers ate entire fields of wheat and oats. Farming remained a very hard way of life.

Have you heard the saying: "stubborn as a mule"? What does the saying mean? Missouri mules used to pull heavy pioneer wagons and farmers' plows. They pulled carts of ore from mines. Sometimes the mules stopped and refused to work. They were stubborn! Today, you can ride a mule along trails in the Ozarks.

1 MEMORY MASTER

1. How did sharecroppers earn a living?
2. What did the government do to help all children of the state?
3. How did Susan Blow help children?
4. Who were some famous outlaws and what crimes did they commit?
5. How was life hard for farmers?

LESSON 2

PEOPLE TO KNOW

Tom Bass
James Eads

PLACES TO LOCATE

Carthage
Hannibal
Joplin
Kansas City
Springfield
St. Joseph
St. Louis
Abilene, Kansas
Ozarks

WORDS TO UNDERSTAND

locomotive

Chugging Across the State

Before the Civil War, the first railroad line to go across the state went from Hannibal to St. Joseph. Then the war came, and most railroad work came to a halt. Men and supplies were needed to help fight in the war.

After the Civil War, Missouri changed quickly. Railroads began to crisscross the state. Life seemed to zoom by. It was much faster to ship crops, goods, and people by train than by horse and wagon.

Working on the Railroad

Building the railroads was hard work. Many of the workers were new immigrants. They worked 10 hours every day in the heat or cold. All the work had to be done by hand. Railroad workers used picks, shovels, and plows to make a flat path.

Then they laid the ties. Ties were heavy beams of wood 8 feet long. Across these, the men placed heavy iron rails. Finally they pounded long thick nails called spikes into the rails to keep them on the ties.

Building railroads took many trees. The ties on tracks were made of wood. Steam ***locomotives*** that pulled the train cars burned wood for fuel. To provide all of this lumber, companies used Missouri's trees. After a while, the forests in the Ozarks were completely cut down. They took many years to grow back.

What do you think?

What energy sources do we use now? Why do we need to be careful about the energy we use?

Can you imagine what it was like to pound spikes with heavy hammers for many hours a day?

A train ride was fast, but it was not always comfortable. In the summer, trains were hot. With the windows open, cinders and smoke entered the cars and covered the passengers with black soot. Still, people at the time thought train travel was a miracle.

Riding the Railroads

Riding on trains was a new and exciting experience. People could ride on the train during the day and night and in all kinds of weather. People could travel on trains faster and farther than ever before. Trains could travel 20 miles an hour or faster. Wagons could only travel 15 to 20 miles in an entire day.

Railroad Towns

Every city and town in the state hoped to connect to the railroad. Being a stop on the line meant that farmers could bring their goods there to ship to distant cities. It meant people would come to town to buy the supplies brought by trains. Stores and hotels were quickly built around a new railroad station. The town grew.

Railroads Change Everything

Railroads led to big changes for the people of Missouri and the nation. While some towns boomed, others began to fade. River towns that had been stops for steamboats became smaller. With the coming of the railroad, the era of the steamboat was over.

Railroads led to other changes as well. Now Missouri farmers could ship their crops to distant markets in the East and then on to Europe on steamships. The railroads brought goods such as tools, clothes, glass, fruit, and furniture to Missouri. No longer did families need to make everything themselves.

Linking the Past to the Present

Do railroads still connect the cities of Missouri? What other forms of transportation connect cities today?

Growth of Cities

Railroad tracks crossed the land. Cities grew faster than ever before. Immigrants still came to Missouri. Germans and the Irish continued to come in large numbers. Italians also came. People from other states came, too.

Kansas City

The growth of Kansas City was amazing. Thousands of people moved there, year after year. What made the city grow? The railroad!

Kansas City became a major cattle center. Ranchers walked their cattle across the plains to places like Abilene, Kansas. From there, the cattle were put on trains and taken to Kansas City.

Kansas City had a large area called the stockyards. Cattle were penned up there and sold to meat companies. Then the cattle were killed and the meat was shipped all over the world.

Kansas City had miles of stockyards. How did all the cows get to the stockyards?

Flour milling was also crucial to Kansas City. Farmers on the Great Plains were starting to grow great crops of wheat. The wheat was shipped to Kansas City to be made into flour.

St. Louis

St. Louis was still Missouri's largest city. Factories made steel and furniture. City workers made more shoes than any other city in the country. Workers made streetcars that carried people around the cities. Streetcars were pulled by horses or mules along tracks. Later, they were powered by electric power lines.

Other Cities

The coming of the railroad helped other Missouri cities grow.

- St. Joseph also became a meatpacking center with its own stockyards.
- Springfield used its railroads to ship woolen goods and lumber products from the Ozarks.
- Joplin did not even exist before the war. But the discovery of lead and the coming of the railroad led to a fast-growing town.
- Carthage had limestone that the new railroads shipped all over the nation. Our State Capitol Building is made of limestone from Carthage.

Activity

Write a Poem About Your Town

C.L. Edson wrote this poem about Kansas City:

Hogs made Chicago with their dying squeal,
Up popped Pittsburgh at the birth of steel;
Come, Kansas City, make your story brief:
"Here stands a city built on bread and beef."

1. Talk with your teacher about the words that describe the cities in the poem.
2. Talk with your class about your town. Make a list of words you might use to describe it.
3. Now write a poem about your town!

MISSOURI PORTRAIT

Tom Bass
1850s–1934

Tom Bass, who was born a slave, was one of the greatest horse trainers who ever lived. He worked with cattle, but his true love was working with horses. He had amazing ways to train any horse.

After the Civil War, Bass was a free man. Businessmen in Kansas City asked Bass to move there to run their stables. He helped make Kansas City a center for fine horses.

Bass helped start the American Royal horse show in Kansas City. It became one of the finest horse shows in the country. You can still see the show there every November.

Over the years, Bass developed a horse bit that did not hurt the animals' mouths. He could have made a lot of money on it, but he said he just wanted to make life easier for the horses he loved. The Bass bit is still used today.

Born a slave, Tom Bass became a friend of presidents. Three different U.S. presidents asked him for advice on horses. But most of all, Tom Bass was a friend of the horses he loved.

This drawing shows that the Mississippi River was frozen over while part of the bridge was being built. What can you learn about bridge-building from the picture?

James Eads designed a bridge to cross the Mississippi River.

The Eads Bridge

How did the railroads cross rivers? Kansas City built a bridge over the Missouri River. But Missouri's largest city, St. Louis, still did not have a railroad bridge across the great Mississippi River.

Then St. Louis started to build a bridge. Its designer was a St. Louis engineer named James Eads. People told Eads a bridge could not be built at St. Louis. They said the river was too deep and wide there.

It took almost 4,000 men to build the steel bridge. Hundreds of men were injured, and 14 men died while building the bridge. One of the biggest problems was building the large limestone supports to hold up the bridge. The supports had to be built underwater.

The Eads Bridge is one of the greatest bridges in American history. Today, both cars and the St. Louis light rail system use the bridge.

2 MEMORY MASTER

1. How did the railroads affect Missouri towns and cities?
2. Why is Tom Bass important?

LESSON 3

Old Drum

History isn't always about people. Sometimes it is about animals! "A man's best friend is his dog." Have you ever heard someone say that? Did you know that saying comes from Missouri? It comes from the story of a dog named Old Drum.

Charles Burden lived near Warrensburg with his dog named Old Drum. Old Drum was a black-and-tan dog with floppy ears. He loved his master and was a great hunting dog.

Burden's neighbor swore to shoot any dog that came on his land. Stray dogs had killed some of his sheep. Sadly, Old Drum wandered onto the neighbor's land, and the neighbor's nephew shot him.

Burden took his neighbor to court. He sued him for killing his beloved pet. He won the case and received $50. What is remembered, however, is the speech Burden's lawyer gave to the jury. He told the jury why Old Drum meant so much to Mr. Burden. Here is part of what he said:

> Gentlemen of the Jury:
>
> The one absolutely unselfish friend that a man can have in this selfish world, the one that never deserts him, and the one that never proves ungrateful . . . is his dog. . . . A dog will sleep on the cold ground, where the wintry winds blow and the snow drives fiercely, if only he may be near his master's side. . . . He guards the sleep of his [poor] master as if he were a prince.

What do you think?

Do you have a dog? Do you agree with the lawyer that a dog is a man's (or a child's) best friend?

Today, if you visit Warrensburg, you will find a statue of Old Drum on the courthouse lawn. Dog lovers from all over the country come to see Old Drum.

PEOPLE TO KNOW

John Boone
Samuel Clemens (Mark Twain)
Scott Joplin
Laura Ingalls Wilder

WORDS TO UNDERSTAND

horrified
pen name

Missouri Culture

After the Civil War, Missouri's factories, railroads, and farms grew. This time in our state's history is also remembered as the time when Missouri gave the nation great writers and music composers.

MISSOURI PORTRAIT

Mark Twain

1835–1910

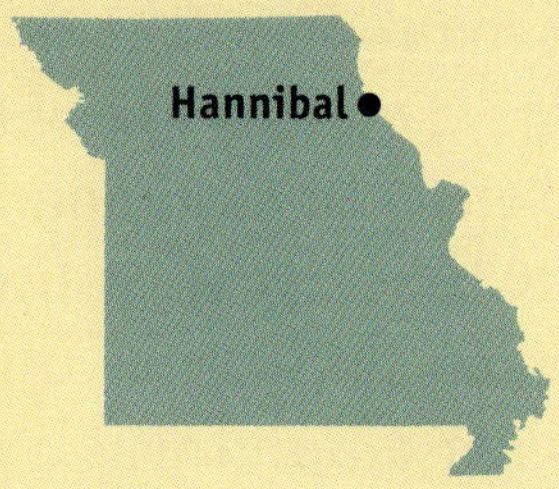

A Baby Boy and a Comet

Mark Twain is considered by many to be America's greatest writer. His name was actually Samuel Clemens. He was born in Florida, Missouri. When he was born, Halley's Comet was in the sky. As he grew up, Sam often wondered if he might die when Halley's Comet returned 75 years later.

When he was four, Sam's father moved the family to Hannibal, 30 miles away. Sam remembered his boyhood in Hannibal for the rest of his life. Those memories became a big part of his writing.

As a small child, Sam was sickly. His family often made medicines for him. No one knew for sure if they made him better. Sam just remembered how awful some of those medicines tasted. By the time he was nine or ten, Sam was as strong as the other boys in town.

Sam thought Hannibal was an exciting place to grow up. It sat right on the Mississippi River and was a port for steamboats. Three times a day, steamboats arrived. Sam and the other boys in town loved going to the docks to see this. Young boys saw gamblers, immigrants, fur traders, and farmers come and go. There were also new products and goods being loaded on and taken off the boats.

Sam loved seeing the boats. As a boy, he dreamed of being a riverboat pilot. The pilot was the person who stood at the wheel and steered the boat up and down the river. When they weren't watching the boats, Sam and his friends loved playing along the river. They swam, fished, explored caves, and pretended they were pirates.

Hannibal could be a rough and tumble frontier town. As a boy, Sam saw some scary things. He saw fights in the street and even a murder. Another time he saw a friend drown.

One other memory of childhood had a great impact on Sam. He grew up around slaves. His own father owned a few slaves. As a young boy Sam saw his father beat a slave. This ***horrified*** him.

After moving to Hannibal, Sam still spent a few months a year on his Uncle John's farm. His uncle owned 20 slaves. Sam loved going to the slave cabins and listening to their music and stories. He loved the stories of one slave, a man people called "Uncle Dan." Some of the stories were funny, while others were sad. Sam loved the way Uncle Dan talked.

Becoming a Writer

Sam's boyhood ended when he was a teenager. His father died, and Sam had to go to work to support the family. He first worked helping his brother print a newspaper. He helped set the type in the old printing presses. The best part was that he got to read all of the exciting stories. He loved writing and began to print his own stories in the paper.

As he grew up, Sam Clemens lived an exciting life. For a few years, he even lived his boyhood dream and became a riverboat pilot on the Mississippi. When the Civil War began, he was a soldier in Missouri. After two weeks he left the war and went west. He lived in Nevada, California, and even Hawaii. All along the way he wrote for magazines and newspapers. People across America loved his writing. Sam made them both laugh and think about the problems of society.

When he wrote, Sam used a ***pen name.*** The name he chose was Mark Twain. It was a riverboat term. When riverboats moved upriver, one of the sailors would throw a rope overboard to see how deep the water was. The rope had marks on it to test the water's depth. If the water was 12 feet deep, the sailor would shout, "by the mark twain," meaning all was safe for the boat to move on. As a man, many people only knew Samuel Clemens by the name Mark Twain.

Worldwide Fame

Mark Twain, as he was then called, traveled throughout America and Europe giving speeches. People loved his stories. Over the years, these stories found their way into his books. He wrote many famous books that are still read by millions today. His most famous books are *The Adventures of Tom Sawyer* and *The Adventures of Huckleberry Finn*. Even though the books are fiction, everyone knew that many of the people in the books were people Sam knew as a boy.

Before he became famous, Twain had married and had children. The family lived in New York and Connecticut and rarely made it back to Missouri.

Mark Twain lived to be an old man. Sure enough, just as he had always suspected, Halley's Comet was in the sky on the night he died.

Many people think *Huckleberry Finn* is the greatest novel in American history.

MISSOURI PORTRAIT

Laura Ingalls Wilder

1867–1957

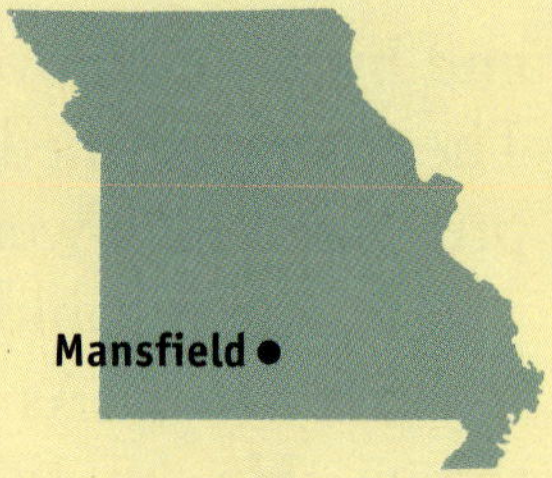

Laura Ingalls Wilder did not publish her first book until she was 65 years old. She lived 63 of her 90 years in the Missouri Ozarks. Laura was born to Charles and Caroline Ingalls. Her books tell the story of her family's life, joys, and hard times as they moved from place to place, trying to live on the land.

Have you read these books?

- *Little House in the Big Woods* tells of Laura's early days in Wisconsin.
- *Little House on the Prairie* follows the family to the Kansas Plains.
- *On the Banks of Plum Creek* tells the story of Laura and her family in Minnesota.
- *By the Shores of Silver Lake* is about the time Pa got work on the railroad in South Dakota.
- *The Long Winter* is about the time the family almost starved during a terrible winter.
- *Little Town on the Prairie* is filled with stories of how Laura's sister Mary goes to the school for the blind. Laura starts teaching school.

Along the way, the family faced many hardships. There were hot summers when grasshoppers filled the sky and ate all of the crops. There were cold winters when the family faced starvation. Laura also tells the story of her sister Mary getting scarlet fever, which left her blind.

When Laura was 16, she became a teacher in a one-room school in South Dakota. She met a farmer named Almanzo Wilder and married him when she was 18. He was 28. They lived on the Great Plains. Then they moved to the Ozarks of Missouri with their daughter Rose. Rose grew up hearing her mother's stories of life on the frontier. She finally convinced Laura to write down those stories in books.

Through all of the hard times Laura's family faced while she grew up, they stayed close and loved one another.

At the end of *Little House in the Big Woods*, Laura describes a memory of her childhood. She tells of going to sleep in a warm cabin listening to Pa play his fiddle by the light of the fire.

> Laura lay awake a little while, listening to Pa's fiddle softly playing and to the lonely sound of the wind in the Big Woods. She looked at Pa on the bench by the hearth, the firelight gleaming on his brown hair and beard. . . . She looked at Ma, gently rocking and knitting.
>
> She thought to herself, "This is now."
>
> She was glad that the cozy house and Pa and Ma and the firelight and the music were now. They could not be forgotten, she thought, because now is now. It can never be a long time ago.

Scott Joplin

"The King of Ragtime"

1868–1917

A Piano-Playing Genius

Scott Joplin was born in Texas after the Civil War ended. His parents had been slaves on a plantation. When he was a boy, Scott's mother worked in a home where the people had a piano. Both of Scott's parents loved music. They showed him how to play a little, but he mostly taught himself. Scott was a genius on the piano. He played for hours every day.

Ragtime!

As a young man, Scott traveled the country, playing the piano for anyone who would listen. Then he went to the World's Fair in Chicago and played for weeks in cafes at the fair. People loved to hear his music.

Then Joplin moved to Sedalia, Missouri. Sedalia was a booming railroad town. All day, men worked hard on the rail lines. At night, they went to clubs to relax. The clubs always had a piano player or small band playing music for people to enjoy. Joplin played at the Maple Leaf Club. He became famous in Sedalia. The music he wrote was unlike anything anyone had ever heard. People called it "ragtime." Ragtime was American music.

Then Scott Joplin wrote his most famous song, the "Maple Leaf Rag." Its lively melody swept the nation, then the world.

Joplin moved from Sedalia to St. Louis. He played at the 1904 World's Fair. At that time, most of the United States was still very segregated. Blacks could not go to many places, including the fair. It bothered Scott that white people loved to come to the fair and hear his music, but African Americans were not allowed to visit the fair.

Scott moved to New York and kept writing music. Even after he died, Scott Joplin's music lived on and on. People still love to hear the "Maple Leaf Rag."

MISSOURI PORTRAIT

John “Blind” Boone

1864–1927

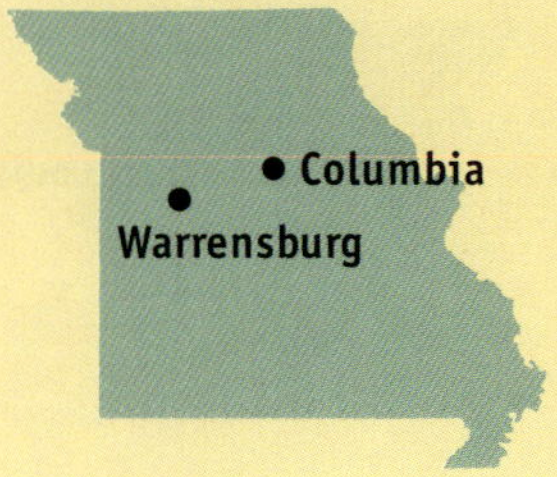

Another great African American musician was John Boone. John was born during the Civil War. His mother was an escaped slave. When he was born, she was serving as a cook for the Union army.

After the war, John and his mother lived in Warrensburg. As a small boy, John got very sick. Doctors said he had “brain fever.” They told his mother that the only way to save his life was to remove his eyes. This would take pressure off the brain. They performed the operation, and John was blind for the rest of his life.

When he was nine years old, friends in Warrensburg paid for John to attend the Missouri School for the Blind in St. Louis. John discovered the music room. He listened to other students play the piano. When a teacher tried to give him lessons, John refused and taught himself. It seemed almost a miracle that he could listen to any music and then play it. We call this kind of talent “playing by ear.”

John later ran away from school and traveled across the Midwest, going from town to town playing in theaters and churches. He thrilled both black and white audiences. He played hymns, classical music, African American music, and ragtime. Everyone came to know him as “Blind Boone.”

John wrote a famous piece called the “Marshfield Tornado.” It told the story of a storm that hit the Missouri town one Sunday evening while people were at church. The sounds in this song helped the audience “see and feel” the terror of the tornado.

John and his wife made their home in Columbia, but he was rarely home. He spent most of his years traveling. He amazed everyone with his music.

3 MEMORY MASTER

1. What are two books Mark Twain is famous for?
2. Why is Laura Ingalls Wilder still important today?
3. What new kind of music did Scott Joplin play?
4. What handicap did John “Blind” Boone have to overcome?

Chapter 9 Review

From There to Here

When this chapter began, the people in Missouri were happy that the terrible long Civil War was finally over. Many people were sad, however. Thousands of soldiers had been killed in battle. Others had died from disease. Thousands had lost an arm or a leg.

In the years after the war, great changes came to the United States of America. People were no longer enslaved. Reconstruction began. It was a time of rebuilding Missouri's transportation, cities, farms, and schools. It was a time of rebuilding lives.

Activity

Trends Help Us Learn From Numbers

Charts and graphs are useful tools. They help us see **trends**. A trend is when you see numbers going steadily up or steadily down. After you see a trend, you should ask, "What was going on that caused the trend?"

Population Trends in Missouri

Year	1810	1830	1850	1870	1890	1900
Total Population	19,783	140,455	682,044	1,721,295	2,679,184	3,106,665
White People	16,303	114,795	592,004	1,603,146	2,528,458	2,944,843
Free Colored People	605	569	2,618	118,071	150,184	161,234
Enslaved People	2,875	25,091	87,422	0	0	0

Source: U.S. Census Bureau, released 2002

1. What trends do you see on the chart?
2. Talk with your class about the history that might explain the trend.
3. On a separate piece of paper, make a bar graph or a line graph that shows the information.
4. Which is easiest to understand—this chart or your graph?

THE TIME
1900–1940

Meet me in St. Louie, Louie,
Meet me at the fair,
Don't tell me the lights are shining
Any place but there,
We will dance the hoochee koochee,
I will be your tootsie wootsie,
If you'll meet me in St. Louie, Louie,
Meet me at the fair!

—Chorus to famous song about the St. Louis World's Fair of 1904.

Into a New Century

Timeline of Events

1904
The World's Fair and Olympics are held in St. Louis.

1914-1918
World War I

1917
The U.S. enter World War I.

1905 — 1910 — 1915

Chapter 10

St. Louis hosted a World's Fair in 1904. This busy street shows some of the buildings built for the fair. Each building held exciting exhibits of new inventions. There were shops to buy things from all over the world.

1920-1929
The Roaring Twenties

1929-1939
The Great Depression

1920
For the first time, women vote for president of the U.S.

1923
J.C. Penney opens his 500th store in Hamilton.

1924
The Kansas City Monarchs win the first Negro Leagues World Series.

1926
The St. Louis Cardinals win their first World Series.

1926
The Liberty Memorial opens in Kansas City.

1927
Charles Lindbergh flies solo over the Atlantic Ocean.

1928
Walt Disney's first Mickey Mouse cartoon opens.

1934
Harry Truman is elected to the United States Senate.

1936
Helen Stephens wins a gold medal at the Olympics.

1920 — 1925 — 1930 — 1935 — 1940

LESSON 1

PEOPLE TO KNOW

George Washington Carver
J.C. Penney
George Poage

PLACES TO LOCATE

Alabama
Iowa
Diamond
Kansas City
Neosho
St. Louis
The Hill
Caldwell County

WORDS TO UNDERSTAND

fascination
inventor

A New Century and Amazing Changes

Think about an imaginary person who was born in 1900 and lived to an old age. Maybe your great-great-grandmother lived during that time. If so, she saw the world change before her very eyes.

When she was born, very few people believed that a person would ever fly in an airplane. Before she died, people could fly across oceans in large jets. Astronauts went to the moon and back. As a young girl, she probably had not seen a telephone. By the time she died, people had phones in nearly every room of their houses.

As a girl, your great-great-grandmother would never think that voices, music, and pictures could travel through the air. Then radios were invented. Later, the miracle of television came to people's homes.

The 20th century began in 1900. A century is 100 years. People looked forward to the new century when it arrived. They had no idea how much the world around them would change.

Linking the Past to the Present

What changes do you think will take place in your lifetime?

Electricity

In the late 1800s, if you wanted to cook food or heat your house, you had to fill a stove with wood or coal. Then you lit a fire. Today, you only have to push a button or turn a knob to cook on the stove or get heat from the furnace.

To get light in the late 1800s, you filled a lamp with oil and trimmed a wick every day. Today, you flip a switch, and a light comes on. There are lights in every room of your house.

Bringing electricity to homes and businesses was one of the most important changes in the early 1900s. Electricity changed the way people in many parts of the United States worked, played, and lived. Streets and homes were lit with electric lights for the first time. There were electric washing machines, irons, stoves, and vacuum cleaners. Factories could run machines with electricity.

Electricity became common for people in the larger cities such as St. Louis and Kansas City. Other towns also started to get "wired" for electricity. But most Missourians still lived on farms. Electric lines did not reach many farm families until the 1940s and 1950s.

On this early pay telephone, the caller spoke the phone number to an operator instead of dialing or pushing buttons. Before the caller could make the call he had to put money in the phone.

The Telephone

In the late 1800s, if you wanted to talk to someone across town, you had to go and see him. Then the telephone made it easier for people to talk to each other. Telephone lines were strung from business to business and from home to home. Later, people could call from town to town.

When phone lines came to farms, several families on one road often shared the same phone line. The telephone in each farmhouse had a different ring. One house might have two short rings. Another house would have a short and a long ring. That way, when the phone rang, you knew if the call was for you or your neighbor. This was called a "party line." When you talked on the phone, you had to be careful about what you said because your neighbors might be listening!

Fourth Street from Market Street in St. Louis had electricity to run lights, trolley cars, and even elevators.

The first streetcar in Kansas City was pulled by a mule in 1912. How could one mule pull a streetcar full of people?

More Immigrants

In the new century, more immigrants came across the ocean. Most of Missouri's immigrants had come from Ireland and Germany. Then, in the 20th century, they came from places like Greece, Russia, and Italy.

Kansas City and St. Louis had large Italian communities. In St. Louis, Italian families lived around an area known as "The Hill." To this day, you can still visit The Hill and find Italian stores and restaurants.

New Ways to Get Around

In the new century, railroads were still being built across the state. You could ride a train to almost any town in Missouri.

As cities grew, it was no longer easy to walk from one end to the other. In large cities, streetcars carried people from place to place. Each streetcar held many people.

Streetcars were first pulled by horses or mules along tracks. The tracks were placed down the middle of the street. Then steam engines replaced the horse-drawn cars. Horses, however, still pulled carriages, carts, and wagons around the cities and farms.

By the turn of the new century, electric streetcars replaced the steam-powered cars. They got power from electric wires that ran above the tracks. Kansas City and St. Louis had electric streetcars for many, many years. In the 1960s they were finally replaced by buses.

Automobiles

Automobiles did not become a common sight in Missouri until the early 1900s. At first, only wealthy people could afford one. They drove their shiny black cars mostly for fun. The cars often stopped working and needed to be fixed.

Most roads outside of towns were still dirt roads. If it rained, the roads turned to mud. A car easily got stuck in the mud.

MISSOURI PORTRAIT

George Washington Carver

1864–1943

Science Helps Farmers

During the new century, scientists and *inventors* solved many problems. They invented new products that made life easier. One of the greatest scientists of the new century was from Missouri.

George Washington Carver was born near Diamond at the end of the Civil War. His parents had been slaves. He never knew his father. When George was a baby, Confederate Bushwhackers kidnapped George and his mother. Moses Carver, the master, went searching for them. He found only little George.

The Carver family raised George. As he grew, he was often sick. He did not have the strength to work in the fields. Instead, he helped Mrs. Carver in the house and in the garden. He spent his free time outdoors.

George was *fascinated* with plants. He wondered why wildflowers had different-colored blossoms. He studied insects. He took care of the roses around the house. Once a visitor asked him what she might do to make her flowers prettier. "Love them," George said.

Going to School

Mrs. Carver taught George to read and write because there was no school in Diamond for black children. Then, one day when George was 11 years old, he visited the nearby town of Neosho and saw black children lining up to enter a school. He got so excited that he went back and told the Carvers.

When he got a little older, George left the Carvers and walked, arms swinging, down the dirt road. He got to Neosho and slept the first night outside, frightened and alone. The next morning he saw a black woman at a water pump. She invited him to sleep at her home in exchange for work. He could go to school during the day.

George was very smart and did very well in school. After school he washed dishes, scrubbed clothes, and ironed for his new family. Finally he graduated from the small school. Then it was time to move on.

George spent his teenage years traveling all over the Midwest. He worked and went to school when he could. It was a hard life. Finally, George ended up in Iowa. He became the first African American student in that state to graduate from college. Then he was the first African American to teach at that same college. Later, he taught at Tuskegee Institute in Alabama. It was a famous school for former slaves and their children.

Carver, second from the right, is teaching in a chemistry laboratory at Tuskegee Institute about 1906.

A Famous Professor

George Washington Carver taught at Tuskegee for almost 50 years. He became one of the most famous scientists in the world. He found better ways to grow plants such as peanuts. He found over 300 uses for peanuts and hundreds of uses for pecans, soybeans, and sweet potatoes.

George Washington Carver also helped people in the South to be better farmers. For decades, southern farmers had grown only cotton. This was bad for the soil. It left the soil with few minerals. Carver said farmers should plant cotton one year and peanuts, peas, or soybeans the next year. These crops put minerals back into the soil. His advice saved many farms.

After he became famous, Professor Carver spoke all across the nation. He told young people that all races could get along.

What do you think?

Do you know anyone who gives great service to others the way George Washington Carver did?

Department stores were larger than the old general stores. Different departments sold cloth, shoes, tools, dishes, and toys. Some of these buildings on High Street in Jefferson City were stores. Others were offices for workers. What kind of transportation do you see in this old photograph?

New Ways of Shopping

With the new century came a new way for Americans to shop. Before 1900, each town across America had stores and restaurants that were owned by a person or a family. All the stores looked different from the others.

Each town had a general store. Farmers came to town to buy food, hardware, clothes, and supplies at the store. Children loved to go to the store to see all the bins of coffee, grain, rice, and sugar. They loved the counter where colorful candy sticks were kept behind the glass. Once a year they could buy a new pair of shoes. People went to the store not just to buy things. It was a gathering place to see friends and catch up on the news.

The 1900s saw the birth of chain stores. Chain stores are all owned by one company. The stores look almost the same from town to town. They sell the same kinds of things.

The first chain stores were grocery stores, such as A&P and Piggly Wiggly. Later came chain clothing stores and chain restaurants. Today, chain stores of all kinds reach every corner of America. You can travel across the country, and even in other countries, and eat at your favorite places. You might buy shoes at your favorite store no matter where you travel.

Linking the Past to the Present

Are there chain stores in your town? What do they sell? What other stores are in your community?

"Do unto others as you would have others do unto you."

—the Golden Rule

J.C. Penney
1875–1971

MISSOURI PORTRAIT

One of the first great chain stores started in Missouri. James Cash Penney was born on a farm in Caldwell County. He graduated from Hamilton High School and then became a clerk in the town's store.

As a young man, Penney went west, hoping to make his fortune. He worked as a clerk in stores in Colorado and Wyoming. He always saved his money. Over the years he joined with some other men and opened first one, then more stores. Then he began to start clothing stores of his own. At first he owned just a few stores. Then he owned over 20 stores. Later, he owned hundreds of stores.

Penney and his business partners called their stores the "Golden Rule Stores." He taught his store managers that the keys to success were hard work, honesty, and always treating customers by the Golden Rule.

In 1912, the name on the stores changed to J.C. Penney. He opened his 500th store in Hamilton. It was the same store where he had worked as a clerk many years before. He had waited until his former boss retired, and then he bought the store. He made it part of his chain. Over the years, towns all across America had their own J.C. Penney store.

J.C. Penney's first store was the Golden Rule Store in Wyoming.

ST. LOUIS WORLD'S FAIR 1904

It was the 100-year anniversary of the Louisiana Purchase. To celebrate, St. Louis welcomed the world to a great fair. The fair was a place to focus on the future. It opened in the spring of 1904. For one wonderful summer and fall, people from all over the world came to St. Louis to see the fair. Over 20 million people made the trip!

The fair was at Forest Park, where the famous St. Louis Zoo is today. Nations from all over the world had their own buildings and showed off their own cultures. There was a Chinese village, an Eskimo village, a Wild West Show, and streets made to look like the streets of Paris, Cairo, and Tokyo. People could "see the world" in a day. Every state also had a building.

There were buildings for inventions, too. People jammed the Palace of Electricity to see new inventions like air brakes, telephones, and x-ray machines. There was a Moving Picture Theater, where many Americans saw a movie for the first time.

The Palace of Machinery had many new inventions for women to use in their homes. They saw electric stoves, vacuum cleaners, and machines to wash clothes.

People flocked to a long road with carnival rides. A huge Ferris wheel had 36 cars that could each hold 60 people.

People remember the St. Louis World's Fair for famous inventions. On a hot day, a man who sold ice cream ran out of dishes. The booth next door sold waffles. The two men worked together to make waffles to hold ice cream. Ice cream cones were born!

Many people also had their first hot dog at the fair. It was German sausage sold on a bun. The weather was too warm to sell hot tea at the

Up, up, it goes! Don't drop it! A man lifts a very heavy weight during the 1904 Olympic Games. The games were part of the fair.

Japanese exhibit. So they began to sell tea with ice cubes. Iced tea became popular! Finally, children loved eating spun sugar called "fairy floss." Today, we call it cotton candy.

The Pike was a long road through exhibits. Look at how the people were dressed. Styles have changed!

Olympic Games

Another highlight of the fair was the Olympic Games. For the first time ever, the Olympics came to America. Only 12 countries sent athletes. It was the first time the Olympics gave gold, silver, and bronze medals for first, second, and third places. Americans won 80 of the 100 gold medals. George Poage, from Hannibal, became the first African American to win an Olympic medal. He ran the hurdles.

The Fair Ends

Over 100 years later, there is little left of the St. Louis World's Fair. The Palace of Fine Arts is now the St. Louis Arts Museum. A large birdcage became part of the St. Louis Zoo. It is still visited by thousands of people each month. Mostly, the fair disappeared. But people remembered its excitement for years and years.

1 MEMORY MASTER

1. How did new inventions help people?
2. How did George Washington Carver overcome problems to help the world?
3. How did the J.C. Penney stores begin?
4. What were some of the things people could see and do at the St. Louis World's Fair?

LESSON 2

PEOPLE TO KNOW

John J. Pershing
Harry S. Truman

PLACES TO LOCATE

Europe
Germany
New York
Grandview
Independence
Kansas City
Laclede
Lamar
Pershing

WORDS TO UNDERSTAND

submarine

The Great War

The 20th century is remembered as a century of wars. World War I began in Europe. It lasted about four years. For many years it was known as The Great War. Today we call it World War I. The United States did not enter the war until about a year before it ended.

The countries of Europe divided into two sides. England, France, and Russia were on one side. Germany, Austria-Hungary, and Turkey were on the other.

New weapons made war deadlier than ever. Such weapons included machine guns, tanks, airplanes, ***submarines,*** and poison gas. Millions of soldiers died on both sides in the horrible war. Thousands of people who lived in the towns of Europe also died when bombs hit their homes and apartment buildings.

Over 150,000 men from Missouri went overseas. When the war ended, over 1,300 Missourians had died.

War Brings Hatred

You will remember that many Missourians came from Germany. Since we were at war with Germany, some Missourians became hateful toward their German neighbors.

Cass County made it against the law to speak German on the telephone. Schools could not teach the German language. German newspapers were closed. The town of Potsdam had been named after a German city. During the war, the people who lived there changed the name of their town to Pershing. Pershing was an American general in the war.

The Liberty Memorial

In downtown Kansas City there stands a large tower with an eternal flame. This tower is the Liberty Memorial. It honors all of the people from many nations who died in World War I.

The people of Kansas City raised millions of dollars to build the memorial. When it was finished, the top generals of the war came and spoke. One was Missouri hero John J. Pershing. The president of the United States came, too. The memorial's flame still burns to remind us of that painful war so long ago.

Thousands of people watched the dedication of the future site of the Liberty Memorial in Kansas City.

MISSOURI PORTRAIT

John J. Pershing
1860–1948

John J. Pershing was a great American hero during World War I. Pershing was born on a farm near tiny Laclede. He was a baby during the Civil War. Bushwhackers attacked his family, but they survived. As a young man, Pershing grew strong working on farms. Then he taught school in a one-room schoolhouse.

The turning point in his life came when Pershing went to the United States Military Academy at West Point in New York. He became an officer in the army. Over the years, he led U.S. troops in many battles.

For part of his career, Pershing commanded African American troops. At that time, the army was segregated. Black troops had to serve separately under white officers. He was a fair commander and earned the nickname, "Black Jack."

When the United States entered World War I, President Wilson made Pershing commander of all U.S. troops. Pershing led the troops to victory against the German army.

Germany surrendered. Both sides agreed to stop fighting. People in Missouri and across the country celebrated in the streets. Pershing led his army home and marched in victory parades as people cheered.

After Pershing died, he was honored as a national hero and buried in Arlington National Cemetery near our nation's capital.

MISSOURI PORTRAIT

Harry S. Truman

1884–1972

World War I was a turning point in the life of Harry S. Truman, a future president from Missouri. He was born in Lamar, but his family moved to Independence. When he was young, his mother noticed his poor vision. Harry became one of the few boys in his school to wear glasses. Because glasses were expensive, the family could not afford for Harry to break them. When other boys played games in the streets, Harry had to stay safely in the house. He read books and played the piano. He later said that he had read every book in the city library.

Harry loved to read about history. He knew all of the stories of great generals and the wars they fought. He dreamed of being a general himself. When he finished high school, he hoped to attend West Point and train to be an army officer. His poor vision made that impossible, but he did join the Missouri National Guard.

As a young man, Truman worked at jobs in Independence and Kansas City. He never did very well at those jobs. When his father and mother moved to Grandview to farm, they needed Harry's help. He became a farmer. Had it not been for World War I, he probably would have been a farmer all of his life.

When the war broke out, Harry Truman was 33 years old. He quit farming and went to Europe. As an officer, he led his men through heavy combat.

After the war, Truman returned to Missouri, but he decided not to farm anymore. He married Bess Wallace. Bess and Harry had gone to school together from the fifth grade through high school.

Truman opened a men's clothing store in Kansas City, but the store went broke. He ran for judge in Jackson County. All of his army friends worked to help him get elected.

Truman later became a U.S. senator. Then he became President Franklin Roosevelt's vice president. When the president died after only a few months, Harry S. Truman became our 33rd president.

2 MEMORY MASTER

1. Who was the great leader of the U.S. army during the war?
2. Which military leader from Missouri became president of the United States?

LESSON 3

The Roaring Twenties

After World War I, new industries created new jobs for people. Most of the jobs were in cities. People had enough money to take care of their families.

Families in small towns got electricity for the first time. A family could keep their food cold in a new refrigerator. They could put away their oil lamps and use electric lights that hung down from a cord in the middle of the room. Many families also bought their first car.

It was a special treat for people in cities to see movies in a theater. The first movies had no sound. A piano player played along with the movie while people read words on the screen.

A new invention families really loved was the radio. Families on farms with no electricity put small windmills on their roofs to charge the batteries that ran radios. The radio brought music and news to people. KMOX was an early radio station in St. Louis that can still be heard today.

PEOPLE TO KNOW

Walt Disney
Charles Lindbergh

PLACES TO LOCATE

Paris, France
California
Florida
Chicago, Illinois
Marceline

WORDS TO UNDERSTAND

animated

All that Jazz

After World War I, people wanted to forget the war and just have fun. They went to ball games. They went to movies. They held dance contests. Sometimes they danced all night! People often danced to a new kind of music—jazz.

Jazz is an American form of music. African Americans first started playing jazz, then people everywhere started playing it.

Missouri was home to some of the world's greatest jazz in the 1920s and 1930s. During that time, Kansas City and St. Louis had dozens of jazz clubs. People also listened to jazz on the radio.

Families all around the country gathered to listen to radio programs. Radio brought them stories, music, and news they had never had before.

MISSOURI PORTRAIT

Walt Disney

1901–1966

Do you like movies? Movies became popular in the 1920s, and they are still popular today. One of the great moviemakers of all time was Walt Disney. Walt grew up in Missouri. He even met his famous mouse here!

Walt was born in Chicago, Illinois. When he was a small boy, the family moved to Missouri. They lived on a small farm near Marceline. Life was hard, but Walt always remembered being very happy on the farm.

When he was only seven, Walt began to draw. He drew everything—people, plants, and a lot of animals. His family was amazed at his natural talent.

When Walt was nine, the farm failed. The family moved to Kansas City. There he helped his dad deliver newspapers. He also took classes at the Kansas City Art Institute. He still loved to draw.

Disney began his career as a cartoonist in Kansas City. He started a company called Laugh-O-Gram and made short cartoons for movie theaters. Then his business failed. Walt Disney moved to California to start over.

The artist created a rabbit named Oswald. He hoped Oswald would be popular with children. But the creation that really became famous was a mouse. Walt always said that he got the idea for his mouse from his poor days as a cartoonist in Kansas City. When he sat drawing at his desk late one night, a mouse appeared. Walt fed him crumbs of bread.

The cartoon mouse was named Mortimer. But Lillian, Walt's wife, suggested another name, "Mickey." Mickey Mouse is still one of the most famous cartoon characters ever. In his early films, Walt was the voice of Mickey.

Walt went on to hire many cartoonists. They made the first full-length ***animated*** movie, *Snow White and the Seven Dwarfs*. Since that time, his company has made many movies people love.

Later in life, Walt created Disneyland in California. Years later, Disney World was built in Florida. If you go to one of these parks, walk down Main Street USA. Walt said he created Main Street USA to look like Marceline, Missouri—the town of his boyhood.

A Family Man

Walt Disney gave love to adults and children everywhere. He was always there for his family and friends. Walt's daughter, Diane Disney Miller, said her father always came to watch programs she was in. She said:

> I'd say, "Oh, Daddy, you don't need to come. It's just some stupid thing." But he'd always be there, on time.

The Spirit of St. Louis

One of the greatest heroes during the 1920s was Charles Lindbergh. He lived in Missouri only a few years, but his famous plane still reminds people of our state.

Charles did not like school very much. He wanted to be outdoors in the woods. When he got older he loved taking apart cars and farm machines. Then he discovered flying. It was his greatest joy. He moved to St. Louis to work at a job making airplanes. He also flew the mail between St. Louis and Chicago.

There was a contest to see who could be the first pilot to fly solo (alone) across the Atlantic Ocean. The prize was $25,000. Other pilots had died trying to make the trip. Lindbergh got the help of some St. Louis men to build a special plane that could hold enough gas for the long trip. He named the plane the *Spirit of St. Louis*.

Lindbergh left New York and flew toward Europe. He had to stay awake all night to guide the plane and keep it from crashing into the ocean. There was a storm. It got very cold. Would the fuel last? Over 33 hours later, Lindbergh landed the plane in Paris, France. He was mobbed by an excited crowd. Never before had a person flown solo across the ocean.

Charles Lindbergh is shown with his famous plane in this photograph. After the flight across the Atlantic Ocean, everyone knew the name of the Spirit of St. Louis. *You can see the plane today at the Smithsonian in Washington, D.C.*

Women Win the Right to Vote, 1920

For many years, women had worked hard for the right to vote. They had put up posters and given speeches. Finally, a new amendment to the U.S. Constitution gave women the important right. For the first time, millions of women voted for the president of the country.

Then two women were elected to the Missouri General Assembly to help make laws for our state. They were the first women to be elected to our state government.

Women changed in other ways, too. For the first time, young women cut their hair short and wore shorter dresses. They danced to the new jazz music. Some women even learned to drive a car!

Linking the Past to the Present

Do people today still do difficult things? Who are they? What do they do?

3 MEMORY MASTER

1. How did life change during the 1920s?
2. What made Charles Lindbergh famous?
3. Tell about two events in Walt Disney's life.

LESSON 4

PEOPLE TO KNOW

Cool Papa Bell
Thomas Hart Benton
Jay and Paul Dean
Yogi Berra
Joe Garagiola
Josh Gibson
Satchel Paige
Franklin Roosevelt
Helen Stephens
Sam Van Arsdale

PLACES TO LOCATE

Italy
Germany
France
New York
Fulton
Independence
Jefferson City
Joplin
Marshall
Neosho

WORDS TO UNDERSTAND

mural
racism
veterinary

The Great Depression

A depression is a time when many people can't make enough money to care for their families. They want to work, but they can't find jobs. The depression of the 1930s was the worst depression the United States has ever known. That is why it is called the Great Depression.

The Stock Market Crash

People knew that businesses were in trouble on one terrible day. It happened in New York City at a place called Wall Street. People traded stock there. If you own stock, then you own part of a company. When business is good, stock prices go up. When business is bad, stock prices go down.

One day in 1929, people agreed that business was bad. They all started selling their stock. Stock prices fell. By the end of the day, most stocks were worthless. People said the stock market had "crashed."

Many banks had invested their money in stocks. When the stocks became worthless, the banks lost all their money. When people went to the banks to get their money, it wasn't there. Many people lost every penny they had saved.

People could only afford the most necessary things. They stopped buying washing machines, radios, cars, and refrigerators. This meant that factories did not need to make many of these things, so they sent their workers home. Without paychecks, workers could no longer buy things. More businesses slowed down.

How People Survived

Many families lost their homes. Many moved in with relatives. Some people lived under bridges or made shelters out of scrap wood or metal.

The depression was very hard on African American families. Their incomes had been low even before the depression. Often black workers were fired before white workers were. This was not fair, but it happened anyway.

Missouri's farmers suffered greatly during these years. They got less and less money when they sold their crops. Many farmers could not pay the bank what they owed for loans. These farmers had to watch as the bank sold their farms to pay their debts.

One out of every four workers in the country was out of work. Even more people were jobless in Missouri.

People tried to help each other as much as they could. They opened soup kitchens to serve meals to hungry people. They collected food and gave it to families who had no money. The Salvation Army, Red Cross, and many churches all pitched in.

The New Deal

People began to wonder if the depression would ever end. Then President Franklin Roosevelt had a plan. He called his plan the New Deal. The government hired people to do all sorts of work. Then people would have more money.

In Missouri, workers closed up mines that were no longer being used. They built new schools and fixed up state parks. They planted trees and fought forest fires. They built swimming pools, bus stops, and ball fields. The New Deal helped thousands of Missourians. It didn't end the Great Depression, but it did help.

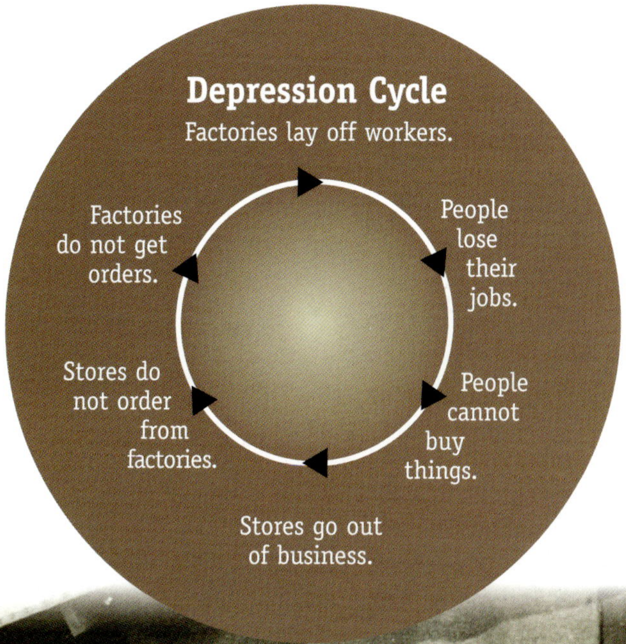

Men were paid by the government to raise chickens and other animals for food.

MISSOURI PORTRAIT

Yogi Berra

1925–

One of the greatest catchers in baseball history was Yogi Berra. Yogi's real name is Larry, but his friends said he looked like a snake charmer from India they had seen in a movie. So they called him Yogi after the man in the movie.

Yogi was born in St. Louis. He grew up on The Hill, the Italian area of St. Louis. Yogi's best friend was his neighbor, Joe Garagiola. Their dads had both come from Italy to find work in St. Louis. Yogi and Joe played stickball in the streets and then on baseball teams around the city.

Both Yogi and Joe became major league catchers. The Cardinals gave Joe $500 to play, but they offered Yogi only $250. So Yogi joined the New York Yankees to make more money.

When Yogi turned 18 he joined the navy. World War II was in full swing, and Yogi went to war. After the war, Yogi returned to baseball. Today, he is in the Baseball Hall of Fame.

Gathered in the clubhouse after their win over the Detroit Tigers in 1934, Dizzy Dean, his brother Paul, their manager, and catcher Bill DeLancey pose for a photograph.

Baseball

Even during the worst times of the Great Depression, people still played baseball. Missourians loved their St. Louis Cardinals. Even if they could not afford to go to the games, they could listen to the Cards on the radio.

St. Louis won the World Series over the New York Yankees in 1926. They won the Series again in 1934. Two of the most popular Cardinals were brothers, Jay and Paul Dean, who both pitched. But everyone knew these two as "Dizzy" and "Daffy."

Negro Leagues

The Cardinals were not the only great team in Missouri. The greatest team may have been the Kansas City Monarchs. All the players were African American.

Since blacks were not allowed to join any of the Major League teams, African Americans formed their own leagues. They became known as the Negro Leagues. Some of the best players were in the Negro Leagues.

The great pitcher Satchel Paige played for the Monarchs. The fastest player in the league was Cool Papa Bell. Bell was from St. Louis. Satchel once said Cool Papa Bell was so fast, he could turn off the lights in his bedroom and be in bed before the room got dark! Another great player in the league was Josh Gibson, one of the greatest home run hitters of all time.

No one knows what would have happened if the Kansas City Monarchs had played the Cardinals. Black teams did not play against white teams. You can learn about all of these great African American players at the Negro Leagues Museum in Kansas City.

Prejudice in Baseball

During this time, only white players could play for the Cardinals or any other major league team. Prejudice ruled. Prejudice is judging people by their race, religion, whether they are male or female, or whether they are rich or poor.

Racism is a form of prejudice. Many white people discriminated against black people and people of other races. Some blacks also discriminated against other races. Racism was not fair to anyone.

Baseball began allowing African American players to play in the major leagues in 1947. Jackie Robinson, a man from Georgia who played for the Kansas City Monarchs and the Brooklyn Dodgers, led the way.

MISSOURI PORTRAIT

Helen Stephens

1918–1994

A poor farm girl from Fulton was an American hero at the 1936 Olympic Games in Berlin, Germany. Many people remember that Jesse Owens, the great African American runner, won the 100-meter dash. But a teenager from Missouri won the 100-meter women's race.

Helen Stephens set a world record that would stand for 24 years. She became known across the United States as "The Fulton Flash!"

Helen spent the rest of her life helping girls to play sports. In her day, many people thought sports should be only for boys. Helen did not think so. She played many sports, including track, bowling, baseball, softball, and basketball. She was the first woman to own and play on her own basketball team. It was a women's team that traveled across the nation playing against men's teams.

Helen kept running races until she was over 70 years old. When she died, she held the record for the longest career of any athlete.

MISSOURI PORTRAIT

Thomas Hart Benton

1889–1975

Missouri was home to one of our country's greatest artists, Thomas Hart Benton. Benton became famous during the 1930s. He was born in Neosho. He was named for his great-uncle, Thomas Hart Benton, the famous senator from Missouri.

As a boy, Tom had a talent for drawing and said he wanted to be an artist. His father was against this. He wanted Tom to be a lawyer. When his father was elected to Congress, Tom moved to Washington, D.C., where he saw great works of art.

When the family moved back to Missouri, Tom got a job drawing cartoons for a newspaper in Joplin. Tom's dad finally gave up trying to get Tom to become a lawyer. He agreed to send Tom to art school in Chicago and then in Paris. Tom later painted in New York.

During the 1920s and 1930s, Thomas Benton came back to Missouri. He began to paint people and places. He crossed the Missouri Ozarks, watching people and drawing. He drew common people such as workers and farmers.

Benton became famous for his ***murals.*** Murals are large paintings that cover entire walls. Murals usually tell a story. Benton's murals told stories of America's history and showed common people working. His murals even included painful things, such as slaves at work and criminals such as Jesse James. You can see some of Benton's murals in museums and in the Missouri State Capitol Building in Jefferson City.

Benton lived and painted in Kansas City until he died. You can visit his home there. You can see his paintbrushes just like he left them.

"Field Workers" shows blacks picking cotton. The painting was done in 1945 by Thomas Hart Benton. Notice the small child sleeping in the shade.

Jim the Wonder Dog

Perhaps Missouri's most famous dog lived in Marshall. His name was Jim the Wonder Dog. He was the runt of a litter of setters. Sam Van Arsdale bought him for $5. The other puppies sold for $25.

One day Van Arsdale took Jim out hunting for quail and said innocently, "Jim, let's go sit down by that hickory tree and rest." Jim went immediately to the hickory tree. Amused, Sam asked Jim to go find an oak—and he did. A cedar, a hazel bush, a stump—Jim found them all. Over the next few years Jim became the wonder of central Missouri. According to witnesses:

- On the streets of Marshall he could find any car by its license plate.
- Once Van Arsdale was surprised when a visitor asked if he could give Jim a command in French. He did, and Jim went and put his paw on the town preacher. When asked what the French words were, the man said he had asked Jim to find a Bible. The preacher had one in his pocket.
- Jim could tell whether an unborn baby would be a boy or a girl. He would put his paw on a piece of paper saying "boy" or "girl" to show his choice. People claimed he was never wrong.
- Van Arsdale took Jim to the University of Missouri, where doctors from the **veterinary** school studied him. They talked to Jim in different languages that the dog had never heard before. Jim found an oak tree when asked in Italian. He found a car with a certain license number when asked in French. He found a girl in a blue dress when asked in German.

One day Van Arsdale and Jim took a trip to the Lake of the Ozarks. Jim jumped out of the car as usual. But a few steps later he fell to the ground. He died soon after Van Arsdale got him to a vet.

In 1999, Jim the Wonder Dog Memorial Garden opened in Marshall. It is on the site of the hotel that Van Arsdale owned and where Missouri's most famous dog lived. There you can see a statue of Jim and read all about his many wonders.

What do you think?

To this day, no one really knows if all of these stories about Jim are true. What do you think?

4 MEMORY MASTER

1. What are some of the ways the depression was hard on people?
2. What two famous teams played baseball in Missouri?
3. How did Thomas Hart Benton help us remember American life?

Chapter 10 Review

From There to Here

The 20th century was a time of great change. Children who lived at the beginning of the 1900s saw many exciting changes. They rode into town in a carriage behind a clopping horse. Then they jumped onto the red leather seats of a yellow streetcar and rode through town. After they got home, they dialed the number of a friend on a new telephone.

On a cold evening, children looked forward to sitting indoors around the new radio. It was a large piece of furniture. What programs would they hear tonight? If it was their birthday, boys and girls might be lucky enough to go into Kansas City, Independence, or St. Louis and watch a movie! And best of all, the father of a family may have bought a shiny black automobile! What a great time to be alive.

Then World War I came. It was a terrible time. The Great Depression was also very hard for everyone. There were still good things, though. People played baseball and other sports. They played music. They found things to be happy about.

Activity

Meeting Our Needs

What are people's needs? Think about how needs are met. Sometimes they can be met by family. Other times your needs are met by friends. Schools, churches, businesses, and the government can also help meet needs. Sometimes you can help yourself! Talk with your class about how needs are met.

Now choose a person from this chapter and write down his or her name. Get clues about the person's needs. Write down two or three. Did the person get what they needed? Why or why not? Who or what helped?

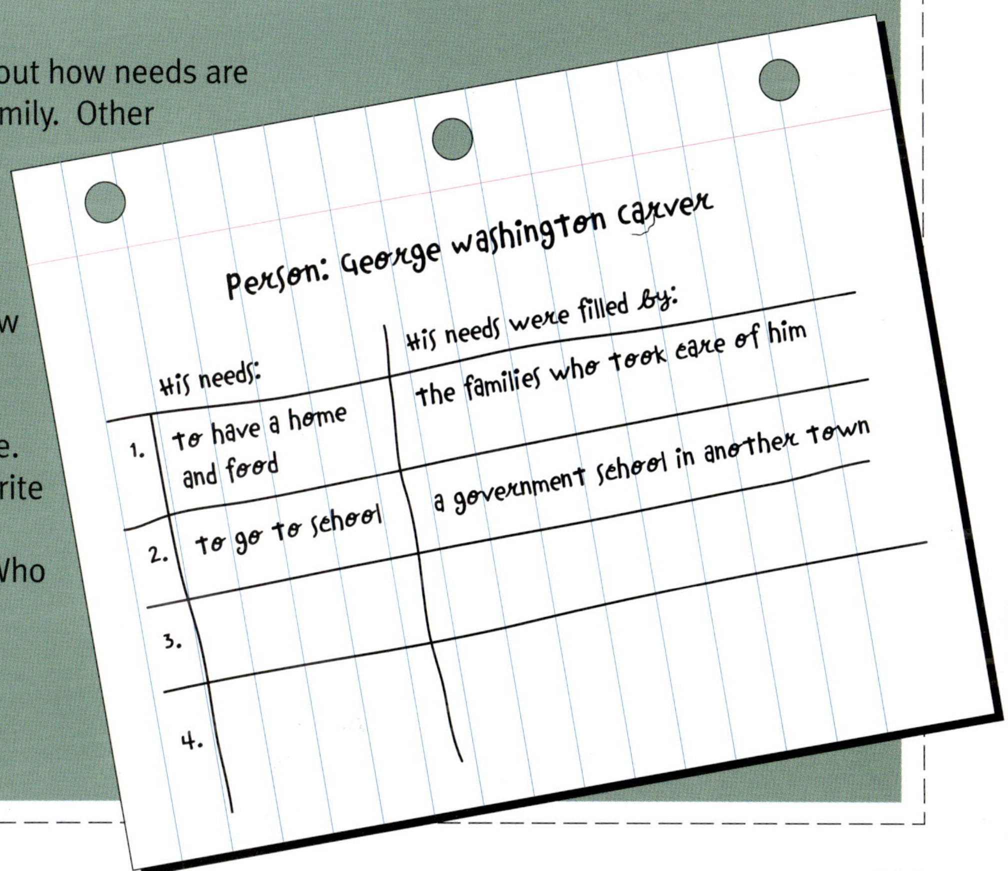

THE TIME
1939–PRESENT

"We know more about war than we know about peace, more about killing than we know about living."

— Omar Bradley

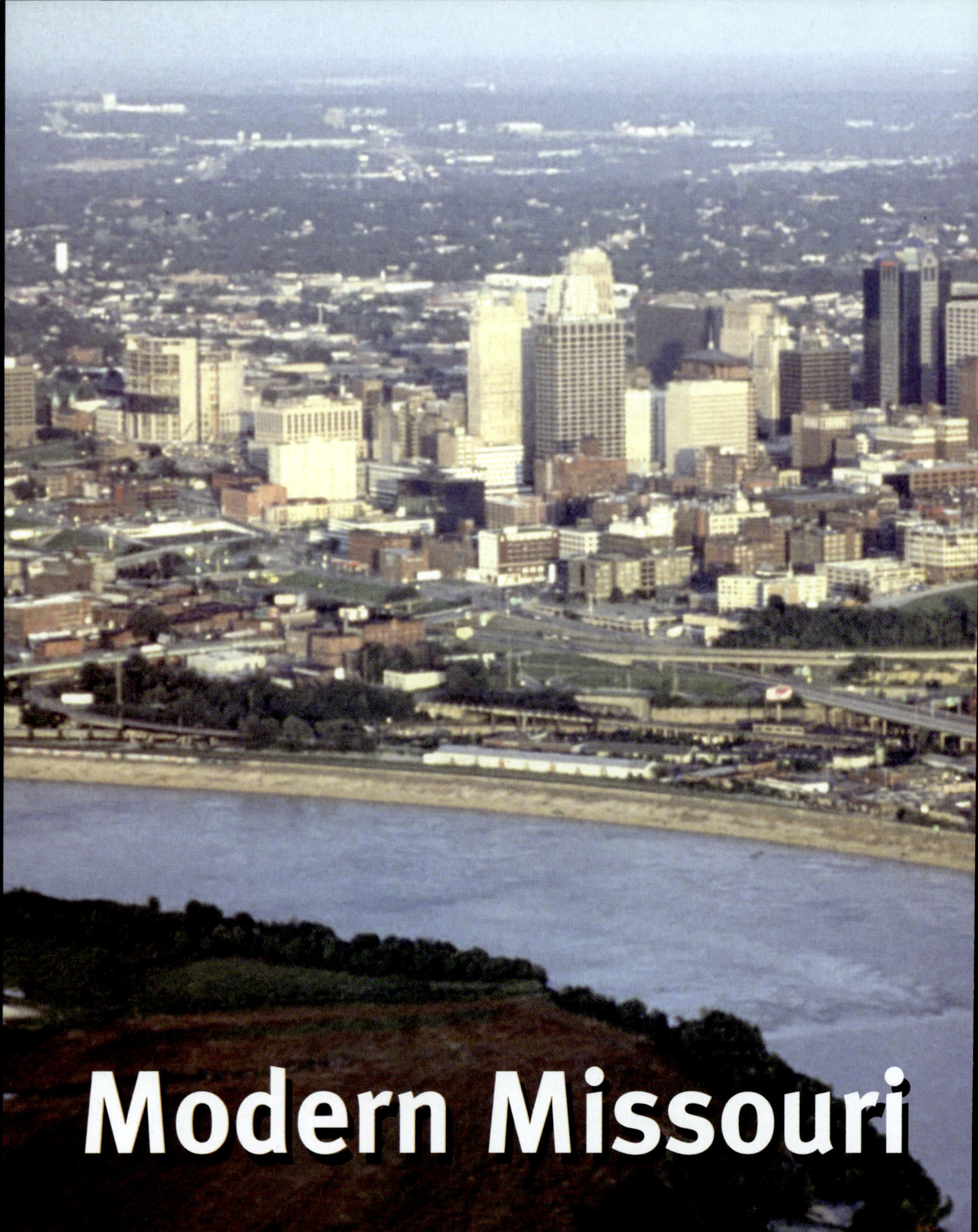

Modern Missouri

Timeline of Events

1939-1945
World War II

1941
The U.S. enters the war.

1945
President Roosevelt dies, and Harry Truman becomes president.

1948
Harry Truman wins election for president.

1950-1953
Korean War

1954
The U.S. Supreme Court says school segregation must end.

1940 1945 1950 1955

Chapter 11

Kansas City started as a small trading post on the Missouri River. Today it has grown into a major U.S. city.

1960s
Civil Rights Movement

1964
The Civil Rights Act states there can be no segregation in public places.

1963-1975
Vietnam War

2000
Americans celebrate the beginning of a new century.

September 11, 2001
Terrorists attack the United States.

2003
War on Iraq begins.

1960 · 1965 · 1970 · 1975 · 2000 · 2005

LESSON 1

PEOPLE TO KNOW

Omar Bradley
Franklin Roosevelt
Harry S. Truman

PLACES TO LOCATE

Asia
Europe
Germany
Japan
Korea
Pearl Harbor, Hawaii

WORDS TO UNDERSTAND

ammunition
surrender

A Second World War

In the 20th century, millions of people died or were injured in wars. Why do countries go to war? Sometimes country leaders think they can't solve problems any other way. Sometimes they want more power, land, or wealth and try to get it from other countries. Sometimes leaders feel it is important to free people from dangerous leaders or governments. There were many wars in the 20th century. They happened for all of these reasons, and more.

World War II was fought in Europe and Asia. The leader of Germany tried to take over other countries. Japan also tried to take over other countries. The United States did not join the war at first. No one wanted to fight in another war.

Then something terrible happened. Early one Sunday morning, Japanese airplanes dropped bombs on Pearl Harbor, Hawaii. The bombs blew up ships and killed many people. Pearl Harbor was a U.S. naval base. Once again, our country was at war.

Missourians Helped Win the War

Thousands of Missouri men joined the armed forces during the war. Women worked as nurses, drivers, and pilots. At home, the people of Missouri all pulled together. Children collected rubber and scrap metal to be used to make weapons. Women took factory jobs to replace men who were fighting around the world. Farmers worked hard to produce crops to feed our troops. Missouri lowered the speed limit on state highways to 35 miles per hour. This saved gasoline.

St. Louis and Kansas City factories made things needed in the war. Auto factories made bombers instead of cars. Shoe factories made boots for soldiers. St. Louis produced more ***ammunition*** than any other city in the country. Missouri factories also made helmets and uniforms. Factories were buzzing 24 hours a day. Soldiers from all over the nation trained at four major army bases in the state.

Prisoners of War

Missouri was also the home to some unusual visitors. Enemy soldiers who had been captured by our army were shipped to the United States. Thousands of German and Italian prisoners lived in camps surrounded by guard towers and barbed wire.

During the day, our government paid the prisoners a small wage to go out and work on farms. Some prisoners and farmers became good friends. The prisoners were happy when the war ended and they could go home.

Making Things Last

One way to be sure that our soldiers had everything they needed was to limit what people at home could buy. People could only buy small amounts of sugar, meat, butter, coffee, gas, tires, and other things.

Each family was given stamps to buy these items every month. When the stamps ran out, the family had to wait until the next month to buy more.

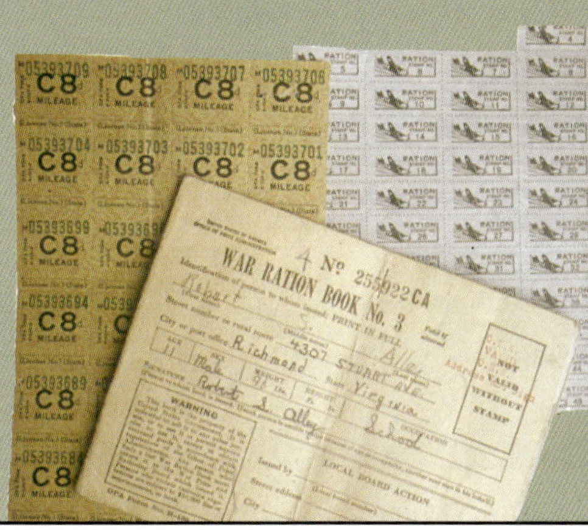

The "C" stamps were for gasoline. The others were for food and other items.

MISSOURI PORTRAIT

Omar Bradley
1893–1981

Omar Bradley was born in the small Missouri town of Clark. After high school, he wanted to go to college, but he could not afford it. Instead, he worked for the railroad.

Then Bradley learned that he could be paid to go to college at the U.S. Military Academy at West Point in New York. His friends and family urged him to go to St. Louis to take the test to get into West Point. Omar was earning 17 cents an hour at his job. He hated to lose the money if he took time off to take the test.

Bradley finally traveled to St. Louis and passed the test. He went to West Point and later became a great general. During World War II, the man who almost spent his life working for the railroad commanded over a million men. During another war in Korea, he served as the nation's highest general.

General Bradley was known as a quiet, polite, leader. He was loved by his soldiers. They called him "The G.I. General." (G.I. is a term for soldier.)

Harry S. Truman Becomes President

President Franklin Roosevelt was not in good health when he was elected for the fourth time. A few months after taking office, Roosevelt died. Suddenly, the nation had a new president. Vice President Harry S. Truman became the new leader of the United States. Could President Truman help the country end the war?

What Does the "S" Stand for?

Harry Truman's middle name is S. Just S! It does not stand for any name. When he was born, his parents gave him the middle name S because both of his grandfathers had a name beginning with an S. Each grandfather could claim then that Harry's middle name honored him!

"The Buck Stops Here"

When Truman became president, he put a famous sign on his desk. It said: "The Buck Stops Here." It came from the saying, "Pass the buck," which means to let someone else do the job. Truman wanted the world to know that HE would take care of his job, even when things went wrong. People loved this about him. They liked a president who was a man of "plain talk."

President Truman takes an oath to become president. His wife, Bess, and his daughter, Margaret, look on.

The Instrument of Surrender is signed on board the USS Missouri *2 September, 1945. The war was over.*

The War Ends

When President Truman took charge, the war was almost over in Europe. The Japanese were still fighting in Asia and on islands of the Pacific Ocean.

Countries on both sides tried to build a super bomb so they could beat the other side. The United States and England finally did it. Our scientists built the first atomic bomb. The bomb was so secret that Truman was told about it only after he became president. He knew it would kill thousands of people. But he believed it would also bring the war to an end. No more people would die fighting in the war.

The United States first dropped the atomic bomb on a large city in Japan. It destroyed the entire city with one terrible explosion. But Japan did not ***surrender.*** After U.S. planes dropped another bomb, the Japanese agreed to stop fighting. They signed the papers on the deck of a battleship named the *USS Missouri*.

1 MEMORY MASTER

1. How did the people of Missouri help win the war?
2. How did Omar Bradley help his country?
3. What man from Missouri became president of the United States?

LESSON 2

PEOPLE TO KNOW

George W. Bush
John Dewey
Martin Luther King Jr.
Harry S. Truman

PLACES TO LOCATE

Iraq
Korea
Persian Gulf
Vietnam
Georgia
Pennsylvania
Kansas City
St. Louis
Washington, D.C.
New York City

WORDS TO UNDERSTAND

character
civil rights
desegregate
interstate
protest
suburbs
terrorism

After the War

When the war was over, thousands of men and women came home to Missouri. They had served their country in many parts of the world. Now they could be with their families again. They wanted jobs and homes, and many wanted to go to college.

The government passed a law that helped men who had been soldiers pay for college. The men could also get loans to buy homes and start businesses.

Jobs for Everyone

When World War II ended, there were plenty of jobs for people who wanted to work. Factories all over the country went back to making goods. They made washing machines, dryers, stoves, refrigerators, furniture, cars, and toys.

Many people bought their first television in the years after the war. All the shows were in black and white. People also spent money on music. They bought record players and records. The most popular music was something new called "rock and roll."

Roads and Highways

People spent money on new cars and trucks. With all the new cars and trucks came new roads and highways. A new kind of highway connected one state with another. It was called an ***interstate,*** or a freeway. The new interstates were important. They would help our country grow.

The Suburbs

Cars, new roads, and highways let people live farther away from where they worked. They could drive to work, park their cars or trucks, and then drive home after work.

People began to build their homes away from the cities. The areas outside the cities, with rows of houses and yards, are called ***suburbs.*** Suburbs grew outside of Kansas City and St. Louis.

A Very Close Election

Harry Truman had become president when Franklin Roosevelt died. Then Truman ran for re-election. Running against him was Thomas Dewey, the governor of New York. A news magazine asked 20 "experts" who they thought would win the election. All of them said Dewey would win.

Truman refused to believe this. He took a train out of Washington, D.C., and crossed the country, giving speeches in large cities and small towns. The train even stopped in towns so small they were called "whistle stops." Trains only stopped there if a passenger pulled a cord to let the engineer know he wanted to get off. Then the engineer blew the train's whistle to let everyone know the train was stopping. Truman's trip became known as the "Whistle Stop Tour."

Truman gave speech after speech, day after day. Most of his speeches were from the back of the train. Truman's wife and daughter also rode on the train and greeted the people. As the Whistle Stop Tour kept going, the crowds around the train got bigger and bigger.

On election night, people went to bed thinking Truman had lost the election. Some newspapers even printed stories saying Dewey had won. It took all night to count the votes, but by the next morning the country learned Truman was right. He had won!

Thousands of people gathered in Washington, D.C., to hear Dr. Martin Luther King Jr. speak about equal rights.

The Civil Rights Movement

Civil rights are the basic rights of every person in our country. But not all citizens in Missouri have always been able to enjoy those rights. Missouri and other states had a system of segregation.

In Missouri, black students and white students went to separate schools. The schools for black children were nearly always old and run-down. They had very few books or supplies. Black students often had to walk farther to go to school, even if a white school was close by.

Hotels in St. Louis and Kansas City would not allow black people to stay. Restaurants would not serve black customers. At the movie theaters, African Americans had to sit in the balcony. Many people began to say this was unfair. They called for an end of segregation.

President Truman ordered an end to segregation in the armed forces. From then on, black soldiers and white soldiers would serve side by side. Then the United States Supreme Court said it was against the U.S. Constitution to keep students in separate schools. Schools began to ***desegregate.*** That means they ended segregation.

In many parts of Missouri, this happened without a problem. But it took many years for the schools in St. Louis and Kansas City to desegregate. People there fought to keep schools separate, just like they had been for many years.

Linking the Past to the Present

What progress still needs to be made in relations between different races?

Dr. Martin Luther King Jr.

Young black leaders worked hard to end segregation. One leader was Dr. Martin Luther King Jr., a minister from Georgia. He led peaceful marches and ***protests.*** He reminded everyone that our nation was founded on the belief that "all men are created equal."

Both white people and black people joined his marches. In Washington, D.C., Dr. King gave his famous "I Have a Dream" speech. Sadly, Dr. King was murdered a few years later.

Some people were so upset after the murder that they burned buildings and smashed windows in cities. In Kansas City, many buildings in the city were burned, and six people died. Other people were hurt. This would have made Dr. King very sad. He always spoke for peaceful change.

The struggle for civil rights grew stronger and stronger. Finally, things changed. Laws said people of all races could live or work wherever they chose. As Martin Luther King had said, only a person's ***character,*** not his or her color, should count.

The third Monday in January is Martin Luther King Jr. Day. The holiday helps us remember what he did for all Americans.

Fighting Overseas

Our country has fought in other wars since World War II. Our soldiers fought a long war in Vietnam. They fought in Korea, the Persian Gulf, and Iraq. Not everyone agreed about fighting these wars. Many used their right to protest. Others were grateful that the United States was working for freedom around the world.

In cities across the state, people held memorial services.

"America was targeted for attack because we're the brightest beacon for freedom and opportunity in the world. And no one will keep that light from shining."

—President George W. Bush

A New Kind of War—September 11, 2001

On the morning of September 11, 2001, something happened that changed our country. Americans learned that terrorists had taken control of four airplanes. The terrorists flew two of them into the World Trade Center Towers in New York City. Another plane flew into the Pentagon in Washington, D.C. Americans also learned that another plane crashed into a field in Pennsylvania.

Over 3,000 people died in the attacks. Nearly 350 firefighters died trying to save the lives of people trapped in the explosion of the Towers. The first war of the 21st century in America began when President George W. Bush declared a war on ***terrorism.*** It was a new kind of war.

Far away from New York City, Washington, D.C., and Pennsylvania, the people of Missouri gathered in parks, churches, and homes to express their anger and sorrow. In Jefferson City and in other cities, people held memorial services to grieve with the country. Missourians also hung flags to show support for America.

Americans raised millions of dollars to help families that had lost loved ones in the terrorist attacks. The government increased security all over America. It sent soldiers to the Middle East and other places to fight terrorism.

2 MEMORY MASTER

1. Why did Harry S. Truman go on a "Whistle Stop Tour"?
2. Give three examples of discrimination in Missouri during this time period.
3. How did Martin Luther King Jr. want people to work for change?
4. What happened on September 11, 2001?

Great People in a Great State

The people in our state are very busy. Children, teens, and many adults go to school. They know that education is very important. Adults work at many different kinds of jobs. They earn money for themselves and for their families. They give money to people who need help. They work to keep their homes and yards clean.

You can have a good time in Missouri. You can learn to play music and practice sports. You can walk, hike, bike, camp, and explore.

Our state has one of the finest state park systems in the nation. Katy Trail State Park is a hiking and biking trail that runs for 225 miles along the Missouri River. Is there a state park near you? What state parks have you visited?

Sports

Missourians are great sports fans. St. Louis has the Cardinals, the Blues, and the Rams. Kansas City has the Royals and Chiefs. Missourians also cheer for college teams like the Missouri State Bears, the Missouri Tigers, and the Billikens of St. Louis University. Our people also run, bike, bowl, or play team sports such as basketball, baseball, or soccer. What sports do you play?

Missouri has many professional sports teams such as the Kansas City Royals.

For years and years, farmers have looked forward to county fairs. In late summer, they come together and show off their best animals and crops. Almost every county in the state still has a county fair. The biggest fair of all is the Missouri State Fair. You can visit the fair in Sedalia every August.

Holidays and Celebrations

Missouri has many different festivals and celebrations. There are music festivals where you can listen to jazz and bluegrass. Missouri is famous for its barbeque, so people have cooking contests.

There are many other events, too. Here are some of them:

- Kansas City and St. Louis both have free outdoor Shakespeare festivals every summer. Families watch plays under the stars.
- Every May there is a German festival in Hermann.
- In October, Italian Americans celebrate on the Hill in St. Louis.
- Every Labor Day, Independence holds Santa-Cali-Gon Days to celebrate the three trails that left Missouri and headed west.
- In November, the American Royal horse show is in Kansas City.
- Every Thanksgiving, thousands of people crowd the Country Club Plaza in Kansas City to see the Christmas lights come on.
- Every July 4th, the Fair St. Louis attracts millions of people who gather near the Arch to watch fireworks. Fair St. Louis is called "America's Biggest Birthday Party."

Linking the Past to the Present

Families also have special celebrations and traditions. What are some of your family traditions?

3 MEMORY MASTER

1. List three ways the people of Missouri keep busy.
2. Describe a celebration or festival in our state.

Chapter 11 Review

From There to Here

The 20th century was a time of war. It was also a time to work for racial equality. African Americans worked for many years to get equal rights. Laws in the country and the state changed to end segregation. It took more time for change to happen in the hearts of the people.

People moved to Missouri from many states and countries. They went to school. They worked and played. They helped each other and tried to solve problems. They made a good life in beautiful Missouri.

Activity

The Census: It Counts!

Missouri is home to people from many different places in the world. Who lives here? Let's find out.

Every 10 years, the government has a census. It is a way of seeing who lives in our country and our state. The adults in each house or apartment must fill out a special form. Census forms ask people what race they are.

Look at the graph to see what the census said about Missouri for the year 2000. Then answer the questions:

1. Where did your ancestors come from?
2. What group do you think you belong to?
3. If your ancestors lived here before Columbus came, what group would you belong to?
4. If you or your ancestors moved here from China, Japan, or Vietnam, what group would you belong to?
5. If you moved here from Mexico, what group would you belong to?
6. If your ancestors came from a country in Africa, what group would you belong to?

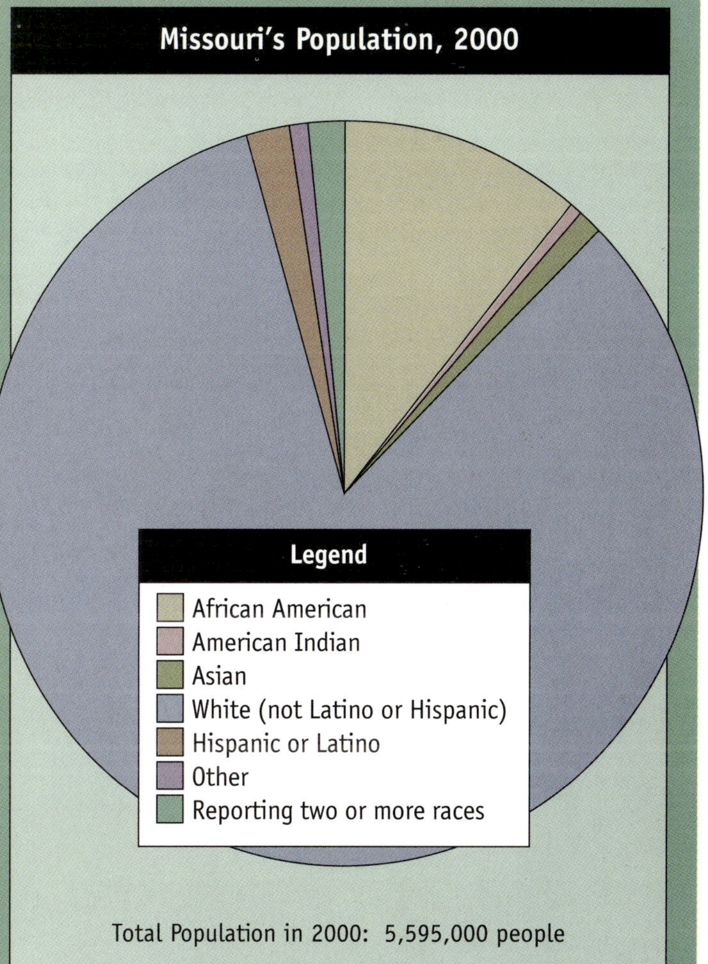

"The strength of America is in the hearts and souls of our citizens, people who are willing to feed the hungry, provide shelter for the homeless, love a neighbor in need."

—President George W. Bush praising volunteers in Springfield, Missouri, 2004

Government for Missouri

Chapter 12

Our state government offices are in our State Capitol Building in Jefferson City. The General Assembly meets there to make the laws. Have you ever visited the State Capitol Building?

LESSON 1

PEOPLE TO KNOW

Thomas Jefferson
James Madison
George Washington

PLACES TO LOCATE

England
United States of America
Washington, D.C.

WORDS TO UNDERSTAND

campaign
checks and balances
jury
legislator
political party
representative

Our Government

Government is all around us. There is national government for our whole country, state government, and local government. Your school may even have a student government that decides certain things. Governments provide many things for us. They make laws and rules, provide protection, and offer many services.

The Declaration of Independence, 1776

On July 4, 1776, men from the 13 colonies approved a document called the Declaration of Independence. It was a letter to the king of England explaining why the colonists wanted to form a new and independent country. The Declaration listed all the unfair things the king had done to the colonists. The first battles of the American Revolution had already begun. After a long war, we became a separate country. We became the United States of America.

The Constitution, 1787

About four years after the war ended, our nation organized a new, stronger government. George Washington, James Madison, and other leaders gathered to write a new Constitution. Our national government is based on our Constitution. The Constitution is one of the most important documents in the United States.

The Constitution says the power to rule the nation comes from the people, not from a king or queen. The people can vote for their leaders. The Constitution also splits the government into three branches. The three branches divide the power. This is a very important part of our government.

The Bill of Rights, 1791

The first leaders of our country did another important thing. Several years after the Constitution became the law of the land, the leaders added a Bill of Rights. It lists rights the government cannot take away from people.

One of these rights is the freedom to belong to any religion. People can speak freely. They can write and print what they think is important. These are rights people in some other countries do not have.

The leaders of our country signed the Declaration of Independence. They wanted to be a free country. They wanted to elect their own leaders. These words from the Declaration are in the Jefferson Memorial in Washington, D.C. Thomas Jefferson wrote the famous words. What do the words mean?

...s of ...ment

...tution gives power ...ches of government. ...n has its own powers. ...ch also limits the ... the other two. That ...o single branch can ...me too powerful. ...one branch can make ...ws. This is called ***checks and balances.***

Look at this giant government tree to see all the important things that go on in each branch.

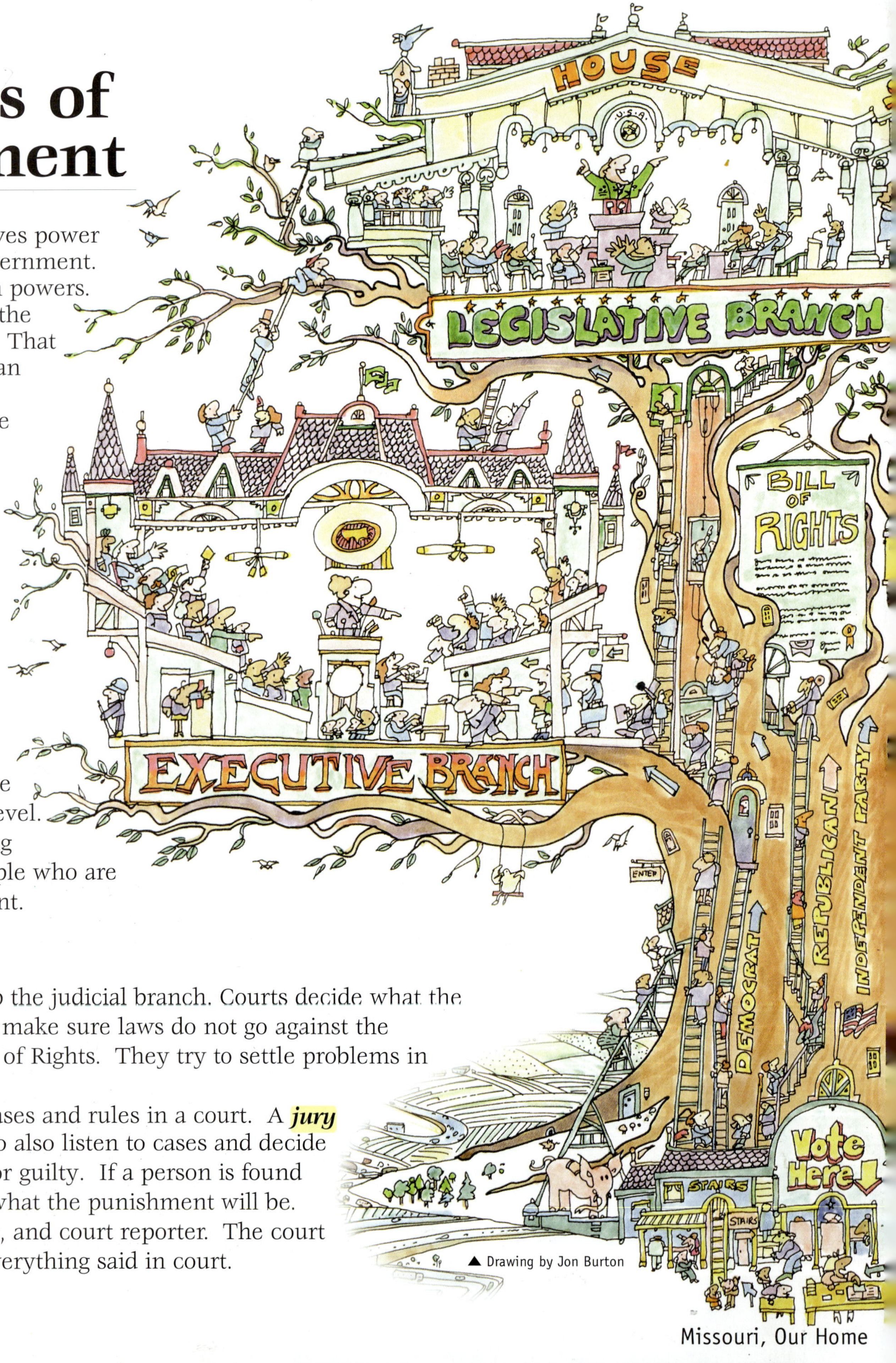

▲ Drawing by Jon Burton

Executive Branch

The executive branch carries out the laws. The president is the head of the executive branch at the national level. Find the reporters asking questions. Find the people who are talking with the president.

Judicial Branch

The courts make up the judicial branch. Courts decide what the laws mean. They must make sure laws do not go against the Constitution and its Bill of Rights. They try to settle problems in a peaceful way.

A judge listens to cases and rules in a court. A ***jury*** is a group of people who also listen to cases and decide if a person is innocent or guilty. If a person is found guilty, a judge decides what the punishment will be.

Find the judge, jury, and court reporter. The court reporter writes down everything said in court.

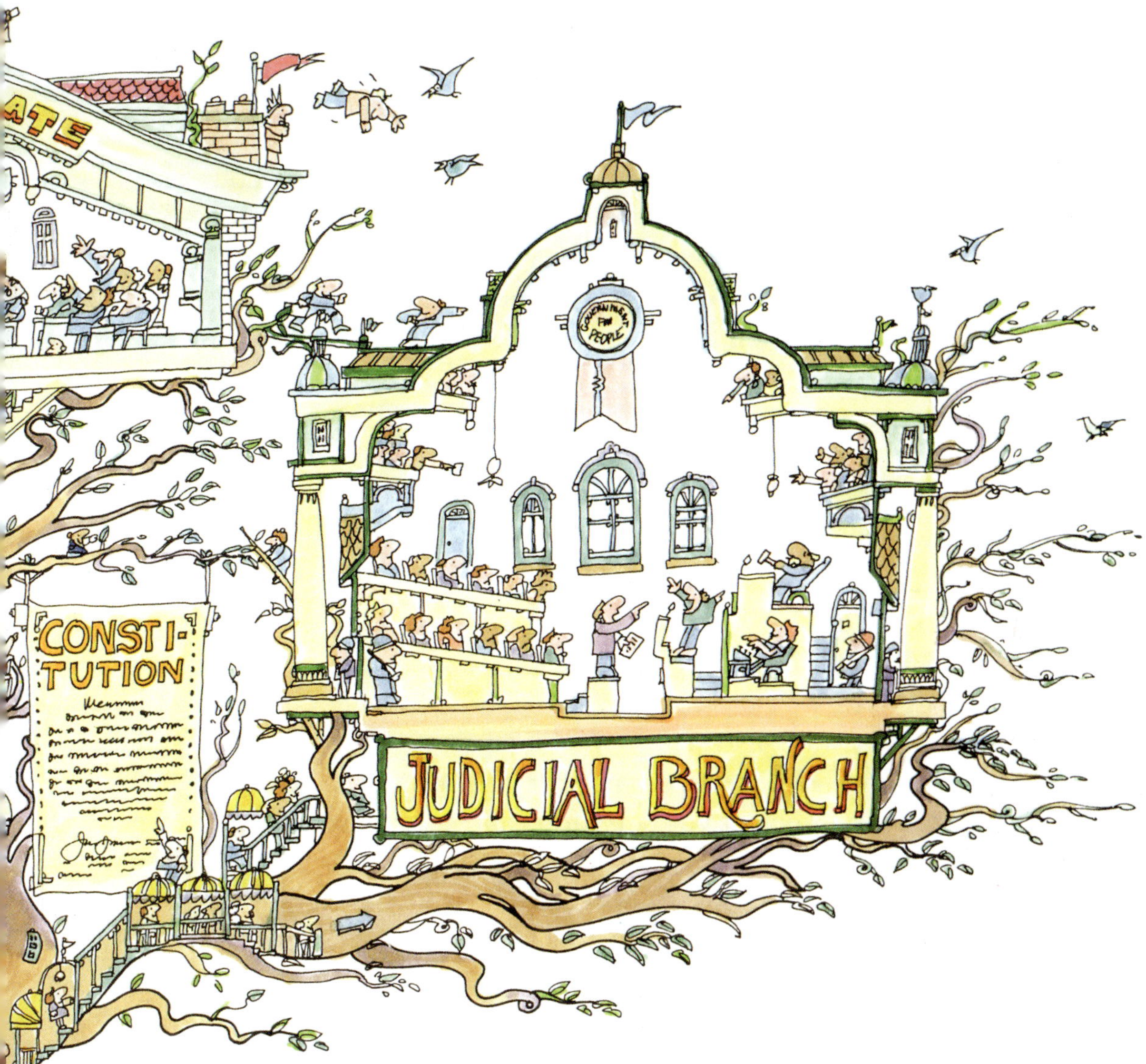

Legislative Branch

The men and women who make our laws are our representatives. They are also called ***legislators.*** On the legislative branch, find the people who are giving speeches about the laws they want passed in the House and the Senate.

Voting

It is important to remember that the people choose their leaders. Most people who are citizens of the United States and are at least 18 years old can vote for their leaders.

If representatives don't make laws the people want, the people might vote for someone else in the next election. Find the people voting. Then find the leaders climbing up the tree to serve in one of the branches of government.

Representatives of the People

Has your class ever elected someone to be on a student council? Student council members from all of the classes vote for changes in the whole school. They are ***representatives.***

When there is a law to be made for our state or our country, each person does not vote on the law. Instead, adults vote for representatives to make our laws.

Representatives from Missouri and all of the 50 states go to Washington, D.C., the capital of the United States, to make laws for the whole country. They serve in Congress. Congress is made of two parts— the Senate and the House of Representatives.

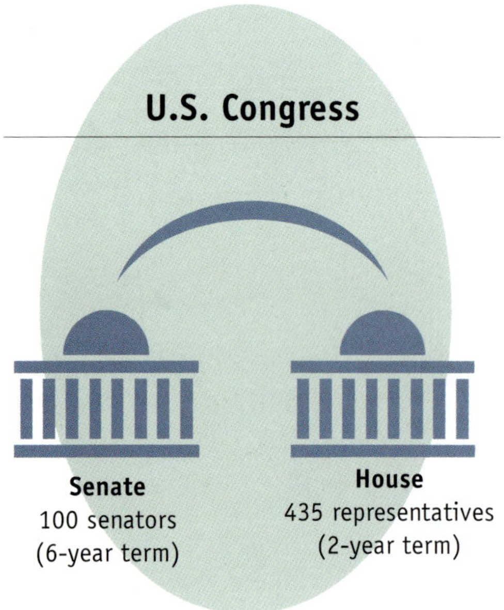

The main job of Congress is to make laws for the whole country.

The U.S. Senate

Missouri sends two people to serve in the U.S. Senate. Senators serve for six years. They can serve longer if people elect them again.

Every other state also sends two representatives to the Senate. This means all states have the same number of votes in the Senate. Missouri gets the same number of votes as large states such as California, Texas, and New York.

Activity

Write to Your Representatives

Who are your senators and representatives? Is there something important you would like them to do for our state or for the nation?

Discuss this with your class. Write a letter to your representatives about an issue. You can find their names and addresses in the phone book under "Government" or from this website: **www.congress.org**

The U.S. House of Representatives

Unlike the Senate, the number of people a state sends to the House of Representatives is based on its population. This means states with more people, like California, Texas, and New York, have many representatives. States with fewer people have a smaller number of representatives.

Missouri sends nine people to the U.S. House of Representatives. They serve for two years unless we elect them more than once. If our population grows large enough, someday we might be able to send more people to represent us.

Political Parties

Adults vote for representatives who come from different ***political parties.*** A political party is a group of people who have the same ideas about how to run the government.

The two main parties in the United States are the Democrats and the Republicans. There are other parties, too. People who don't belong to any party are called Independents. You can find these words on the tree trunk on pages 252-253.

Campaigning for Office

Candidates and people in a political party ***campaign*** to win the election. They raise money, print signs, buy TV and radio advertising, and give speeches. After the campaigning is over, citizens vote for the person they think will do the best job.

1 MEMORY MASTER

1. Name the important document that is the basis for our national government.
2. List the three branches of government.
3. Who chooses the representatives who make our laws?
4. Name the two parts of Congress.
5. What are the two main political parties in the United States?

LESSON 2

WORDS TO UNDERSTAND

local
responsibility
veto

State Government

The 50 states of our country are not all alike. They have different land, people, and industries. Each state has different problems. Each state has its own state government to solve these problems.

In the West, Arizona and Utah make laws about how water can be used. They are desert states, so water is very important. California's government inspects crops. It doesn't want insects to get into the fruit and vegetable plants. Wisconsin makes laws about fishing in its many lakes and rivers. Louisiana has laws about shipping to and from its docks. Virginia makes laws to prevent pollution of its coastline. West Virginia has laws to keep workers in coal mines safe. In Missouri we have laws to see that our highways are safe and that all children go to good schools.

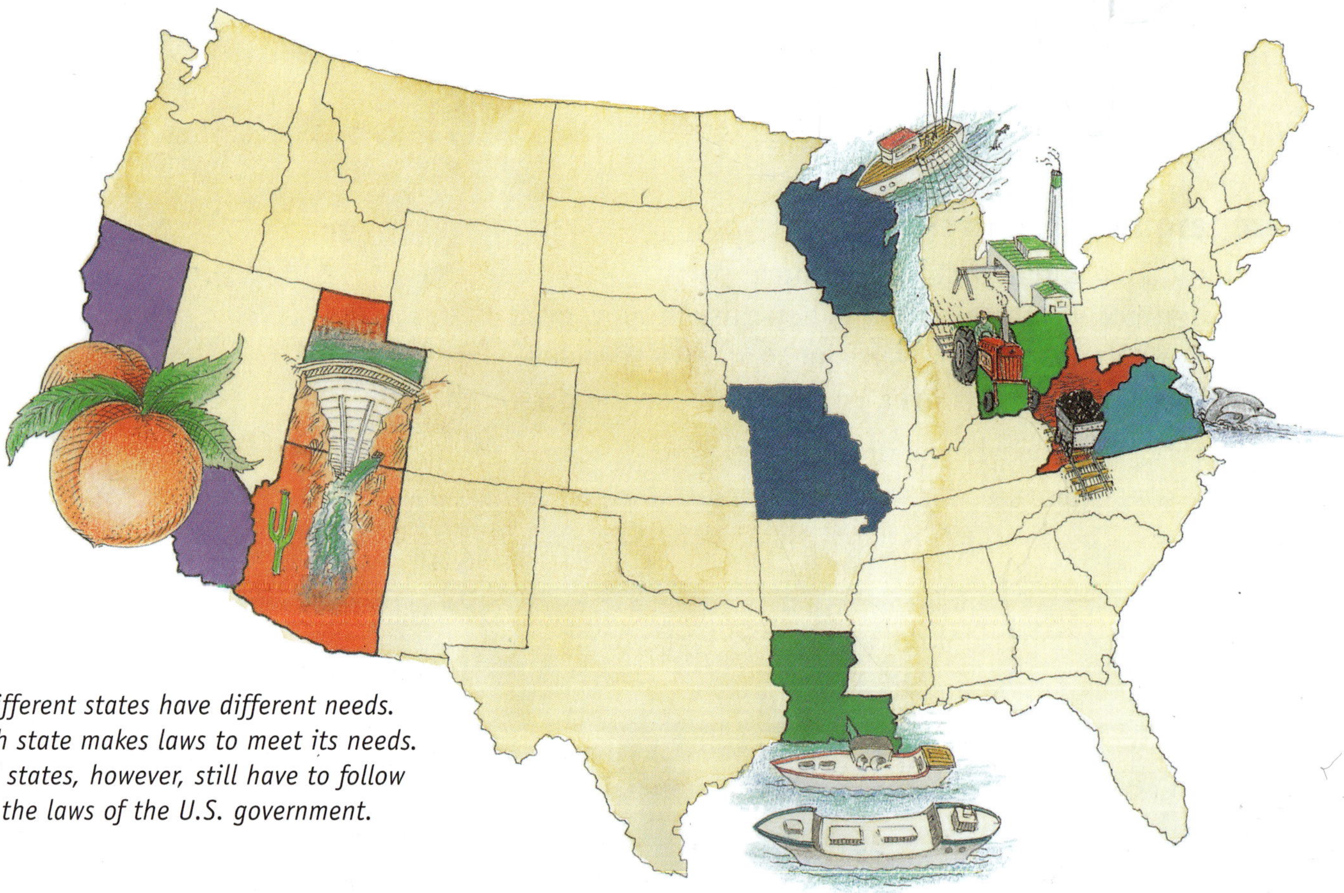

Different states have different needs. Each state makes laws to meet its needs. All states, however, still have to follow the laws of the U.S. government.

Our State Constitution

Each state has its own state constitution. Missouri has had four state constitutions. The constitution we have today was written in 1945. It meets the needs of a modern Missouri.

Since 1945, there have been many amendments. Amendments are changes or additions to a constitution.

Missouri's Branches of Government

Like the national government, the state has three branches of government. Each branch has certain jobs.

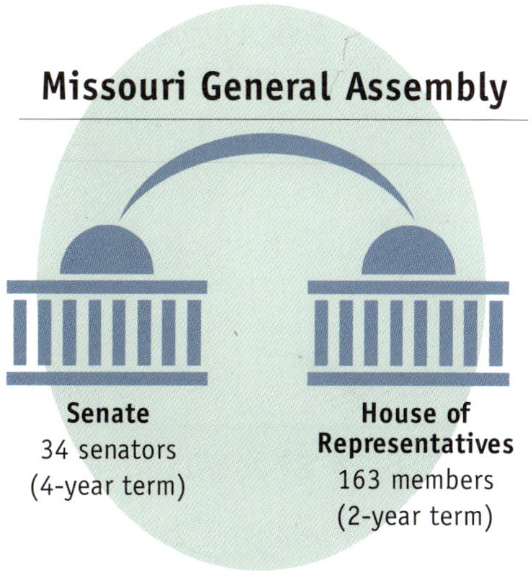

Legislative Branch

Our state legislature is called the Missouri General Assembly. It is made up of a Senate and a House of Representatives. Together they make the laws for Missouri.

Executive Branch

The main task of the executive branch is to carry out the laws of the state. The governor is head of the executive branch. Here are some of the jobs the governor does:

- Sees that state laws are carried out.
- Signs or ***vetoes*** new laws.
- Makes a budget of how state money will be spent.
- Commands state military forces.
- Oversees state offices and agencies.

Many people help the governor by working in state agencies. Some agencies help farmers sell their crops or inspect farm animals. Other agencies give driver's licenses, run state parks, work on state roads and highways, collect taxes, and help run the state's schools and colleges.

Judicial Branch

The courts are another branch of our state government. Judges and juries are part of the courts. Courts decide who is right when people disagree about what a law means. Courts also decide if a person has broken the law.

There are different kinds of courts. Your parents might go to one kind of court if they get a traffic ticket for driving too fast. A person would go to another court if he or she were caught stealing from a store or robbing a bank.

Each county has a courthouse. The Old Courthouse in St. Louis has many offices. You can get a copy of your birth certificate there. Adults can find property records and health records. A judge hears court cases.

Levels of Government

There are different levels of government. You must obey the laws of all the levels. Study the chart to see how this works.

- What level includes the president of the United States?
- What level includes our governor?
- What level includes the mayor of your town or city?

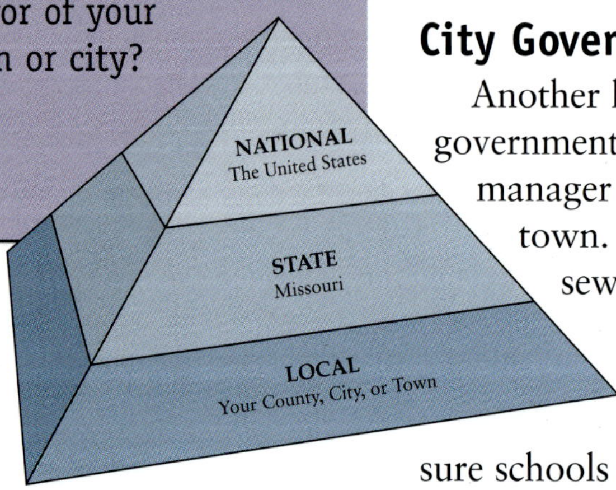

Local Government

In some places in Missouri, there are factories. In other places, there are farms. In large towns, you can see many buildings. City roads and sidewalks are crowded with cars and people. Other places are quieter, with very few people.

Because different places have different needs, ***local*** governments are important. Local governments are governments close to home. County and city governments are both types of local governments. These levels of government help take care of our needs.

City Government

Another kind of local government even closer to home is city government. Missouri has cities and towns. A mayor or a city manager is in charge of departments that provide services for the town. Some of the services are clean water, garbage removal, sewage systems, health care, and fire and police workers.

Cities and towns make rules about what kinds of buildings can be built in different parts of town. They often keep houses separate from businesses. They make sure schools are in safe places. They make laws about speed limits on the roads. Cities also have city courts.

Missouri Counties and County Seats

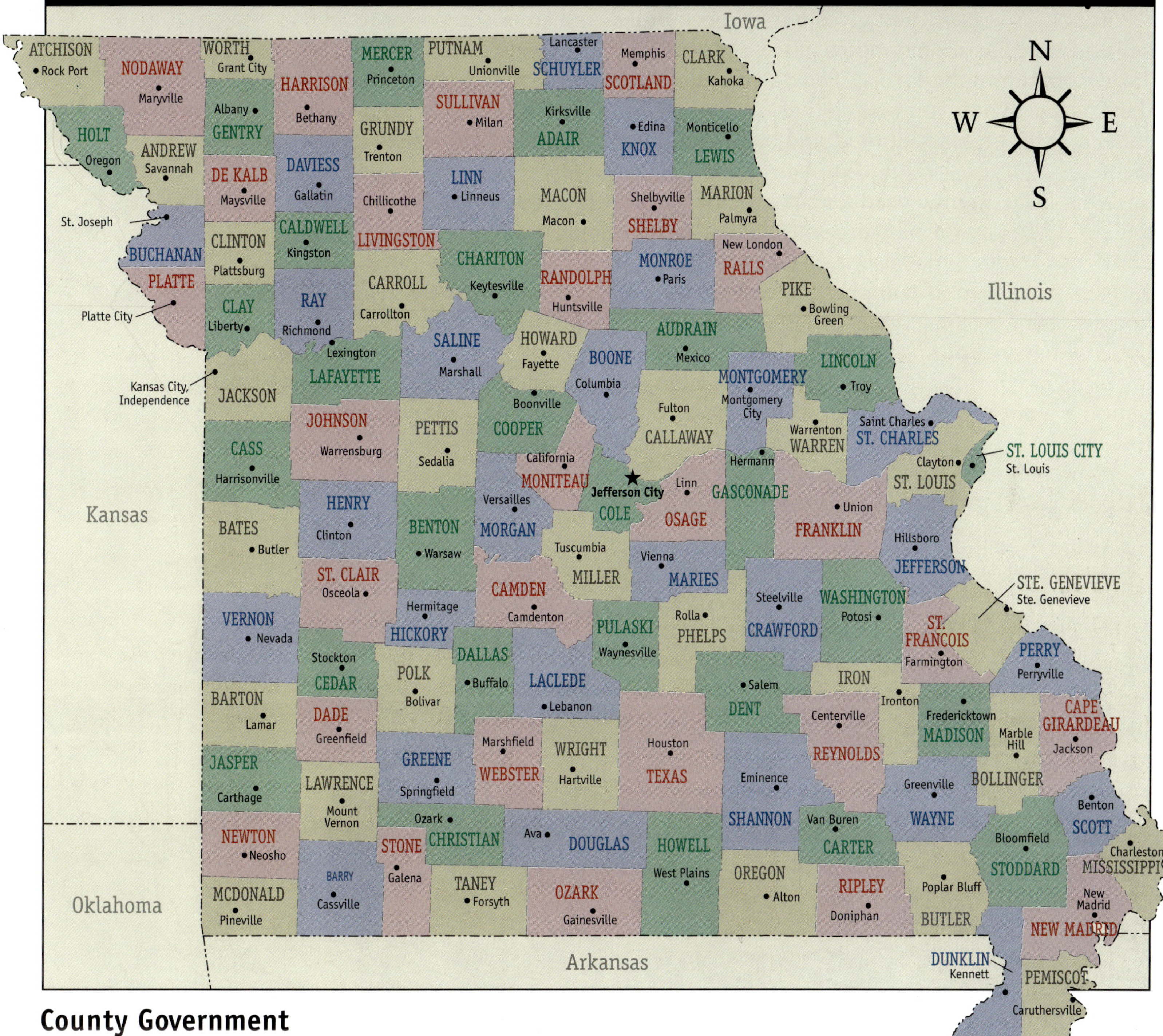

What county do you live in?
What is your county seat?

County Government

Missouri is divided into 114 counties. Citizens elect the people who run the county government. Each county has a county seat. That is the town or city where the government offices are located. In the county seat, there is a county courthouse.

Judges and juries hear cases at the county courthouse. Births, deaths, and marriages are recorded there. If your family owns land, a map of your land is recorded in your courthouse.

Taxes Pay for Services

Missouri's constitution gives our state, counties, and cities the power to collect taxes. Tax money helps pay for services all of the people can use. Taxes come in many forms. People and businesses pay taxes on the money they make. When you buy clothes or toys, you pay a sales tax. Each county collects taxes on land, homes, and buildings. These are called property taxes.

What is tax money used for? Taxes pay for making and fixing local streets. They pay for plowing snow. Taxes pay for libraries where you can check out books. Cities use tax money to pay for clean water. They have garbage picked up. If you play soccer on a city team or swim in a city pool, you are using a city service. Cities also pay for parks where you can play ball and have picnics.

Taxes pay for public education. If you go to a public school, your building, your books, and your teachers are paid with tax money. If you go to a private school, your parents pay for most of these things.

Some public services are provided by volunteers who also have other jobs. In Missouri, many of our fire fighters and rescue workers are volunteers.

How many public services can you find in this town?

Our Responsibilities

Our government does many things to make life better for all of us. It protects our rights and provides many services.

We, the people who live in our state and our country, should also do our part. We have ***responsibilities.*** We should:

- obey the laws our elected leaders have made.
- respect the rights of others.
- be kind.
- get an education.
- learn to take care of ourselves and help others.
- keep our homes and our yards clean.
- keep Missouri beautiful and safe.
- pay taxes.
- vote when we are old enough.

Vote for Me!

Adults have the responsibility to vote and take part in government. This is what "government by the people" means. A person has to be at least 18 years old before he or she can vote.

Voters choose leaders for their city, their county, their state, and their country. It is an important responsibility!

Voters mark ballots to choose their leaders. Voting is private. No one can see who a person votes for.

I'll Do It!

All of us can help our community. We can volunteer to help others without being paid. Adult volunteers help raise money for good causes. They help people learn to read. They help people take care of their homes or their children. They work in hospitals, take food to older people, read to people who can't see well, and give tours in famous places.

How can you be a volunteer? You can start by volunteering to help out in your own home and your neighborhood. You can pick up trash. You can walk the dog. You can bring in garbage cans if they aren't too large. You can help water flowers, bring in the mail, and feed the cat for a neighbor who is on vacation or is sick. You can read a story or play a game with younger children. What else can you do?

Be a good citizen! Start volunteering!

Activity

Volunteer in Your Community

Community leaders have the job of solving problems in their cities or towns. But each citizen can do his or her part to help solve local problems.

Some things leaders might be working on are:

- helping poor people
- protecting the environment
- making sure people have jobs
- teaching kids and adults to read and write
- improving and building roads
- helping their community grow

1. What are some problems in your community? Make a list of them. Ask your leaders which problems they are working to solve.
2. As a class, choose one problem and think about how you might help solve it. List your ideas on the chalkboard. How do you propose to solve the problem?
3. See if you can volunteer to help solve the problem. Volunteers are people who give their time to help others.

2 MEMORY MASTER

1. Why do we need state and local governments?
2. What do taxes help pay for?
3. How can you help your community?

Chapter 12 Review

From There to Here

The 13 colonies declared their independence from England. After fighting a war for their freedom, the leaders of the new United States of America set up their own government. They wrote the Constitution. Later, leaders wrote the Bill of Rights. These important documents are still the basis of our government today.

In the United States, citizens vote for representatives. The representatives listen to the ideas of the people. They make laws for all of us.

We have three levels of government: national, state, and local. Each level of government is divided into three branches: legislative, executive, and judicial. Each level and branch of government has a different job. That way, the power is balanced.

Activity

Your Fair Share of Taxes

Kids! It's time to pay your taxes again! Did you know that every time you buy something you are giving money to the government? You are a citizen paying a sales tax. Thanks for your money. It helps keep Missouri running!

On what kinds of things does Missouri charge sales tax? Do some research to find out. Find out what the rate of sales tax is. Then figure out how much sales tax you would have to pay if you bought something that cost $1, $10, or $500.

Activity

Local Laws

Can you think of local laws that affect you? They might have to do with speed limits, crosswalks, or rules for your park.

- Why do you think these laws were passed?
- Which laws do you agree with?
- Which ones would you like to change, and why?
- What can you do when you think a law should be changed?

Most cities have a rule that says dogs must have a license and cannot run loose.

Activity

Make a Book About Government

Why is government important? Make a book about some of the things you have learned in the chapter.

1. Choose the topics you would like to include in your book and make a page for each one.
2. At the top of each page, write the name of the topic. Draw a picture and write some things about it so others can learn about it.

Here are some examples:

- **Laws**
  Government leaders make laws. Laws tell people how they must behave. For example, today's laws say children must go to school. They say cars must stop at stop signs. Laws help protect us and the things we own.

- **Services**
  The government provides services our towns need—from schools, to streetlights, to clearing snow off our streets and roads in the winter. Services are paid for with tax money.

Activity

The Pledge of Allegiance

School children all across the country say this pledge every morning. They have been doing this since 1892! The words have been changed several times. They may change again. Even so, the words show our respect for our country and our flag.

When you say the Pledge of Allegiance you must stop, stand, face the flag, and put your right hand over your heart. If you are a scout or soldier in uniform, you must salute the flag instead.

Do you know what these words in the pledge mean? Discuss them with your class.

I pledge allegiance to the Flag
of the United States of America,
and to the Republic for which it stands:
one Nation under God, indivisible,
With Liberty and Justice for all.

I Pledge Allegiance to the flag	I promise my loyalty to the flag of the United States of America.
And to the Republic for which it stands	I pledge my loyalty to our government, where the people elect their own leaders to make laws.
Indivisible	The country cannot be divided up. All states join together in unity.
with Liberty	The people of this nation have freedoms guaranteed in the Bill of Rights.
and Justice for all.	Everyone is entitled by law to be treated justly and fairly.

"Far and away the best prize that life has to offer is the chance to work hard at work worth doing."

—*Theodore Roosevelt*

"Nothing will work unless you do."

—*Maya Angelou*

Making a Living in Missouri

Chapter 13

Do you like apple cider made in Missouri? This worker at Centennial Farms in Augusta, Missouri, dumps apples into a tub of bleach water to clean them. Then the apples are ground up and pressed to get the juice out. Apple cider is just one of our state's products.

LESSON 1

WORDS TO UNDERSTAND

capital
capital resources
consumer
economics
goods
human resources
products
services
scarcity
supply and demand

Goods and Services

We all need food, clothing, and shelter. We want things like books, bicycles, beds, games, and radios. All of these things are called ***goods*** or ***products.***

We also need things workers do for us. We need care from doctors and dentists. We need to go to school and learn from teachers. We need pilots to fly planes and bus drivers to take us to school. These things are called ***services.*** Bankers, policemen, store clerks, and people who collect the garbage also provide services.

When we are children, adults usually make sure our needs are met. When we grow up, we will work to earn money so we can pay for the goods and services we need and want.

Economics

Economics is the study of how people make money and spend it. It is also the study of how people produce, buy, and sell the goods and services they need and want. In this chapter, we will see how people in our state earn money to meet their needs and wants. We will see how goods made in Missouri are used all over the world.

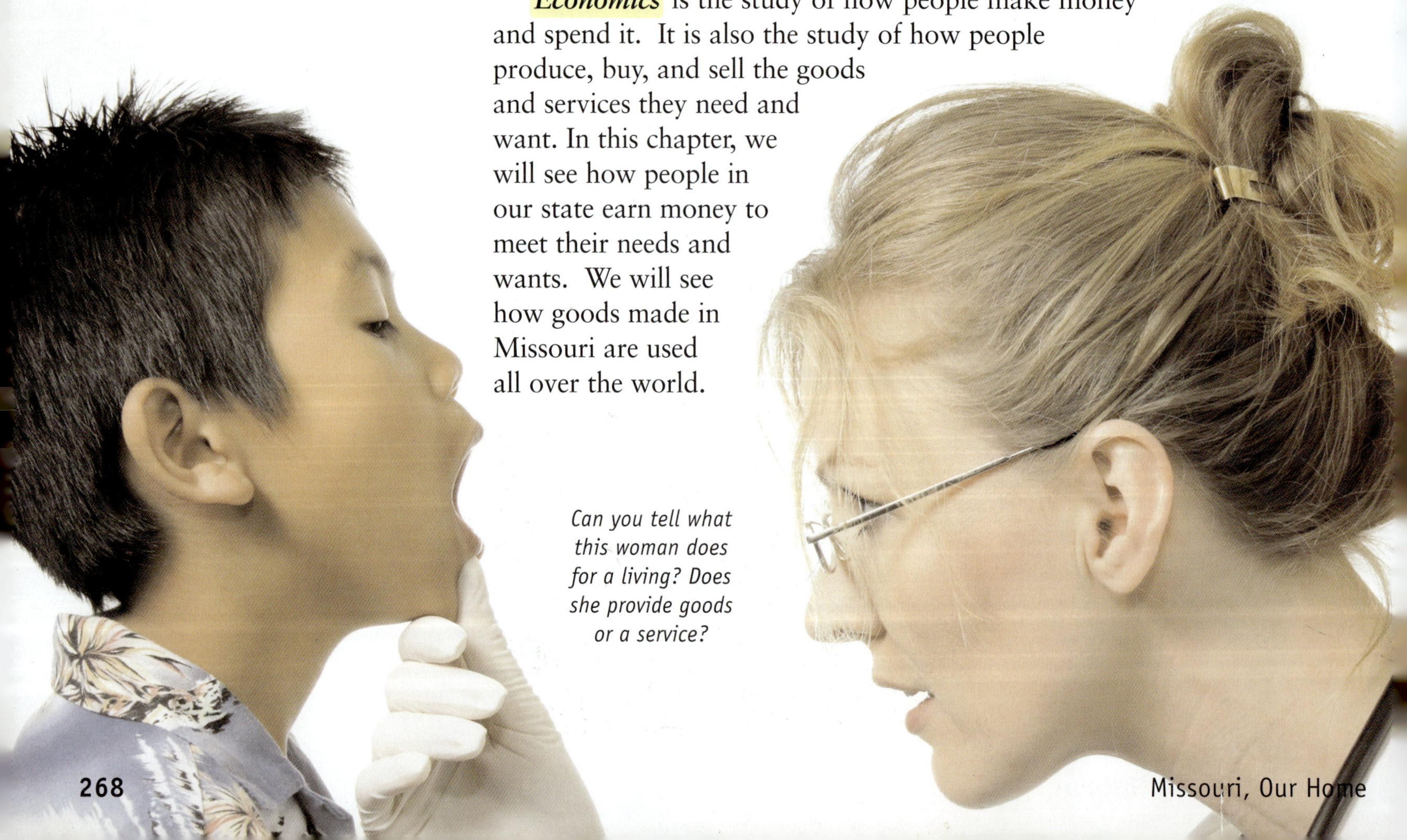

Can you tell what this woman does for a living? Does she provide goods or a service?

Supply and Demand

How do business owners decide how much to charge for their products? The selling price depends on a lot of things.

For coats, it might depend on how much the cloth costs. The price may also depend on how many coats there are for sale. For example, if a certain kind of coat becomes so popular that a company cannot make enough for everyone who wants one, the company can sell the coats for a higher price. People will be willing to pay more for them. This is called ***supply and demand.***

When there is a large supply of something, the cost is lower. When there is a small supply of something, the cost is higher. For example, if a store has too many basketballs, the balls might go on sale.

What Is Scarcity?

Scarcity is part of supply and demand. A scarcity is when there is not enough of something that people want. Think of the gasoline you use in your family car. Gasoline is made from oil. A lot of the oil we use in the United States comes from other countries. Sometimes there are problems with buying enough oil from these countries. Sometimes there are also problems in our own country in shipping the oil to refineries. A refinery makes oil into gasoline. What if the refinery was hit by a terrible storm and had to shut down? There would be a scarcity of gasoline.

Scarcity really affects our choices. People may decide to drive less and walk more to save gas. They may carpool to work or to school. They will also have to pay a lot more for gas.

In some small towns there is a scarcity of services. The town may be too small to have a dentist or a doctor. Maybe there is no hospital or airport in the town. No matter how much you are willing to pay a dentist or a doctor, there is not one in town.

What happens to the price of gasoline if the supply is low?

Producers and Consumers

Who makes all the goods you use? Workers "produce" goods by making or growing them. Study this bicycle factory to see how bicycles might be produced.

Natural Resources

Sand, gravel, trees, water, soil, metal, and wood are natural resources. If you are making chairs, you might use wood. Machines need energy. This energy can come from coal, oil, the sun, and even the wind. These are natural resources, too. What natural resources are needed to make bicycles?

Capital Resources

When you use products to make other products, you are using ***capital resources.*** The hammer and nails a carpenter uses are capital resources. The tools used to make bicycles are also capital resources. The money you need to run a business is also called ***capital.***

Human Resources

To provide goods and services, people must work. Even when a machine does the work, it takes people to build the machine and run it. The people in a bicycle factory all work. That is how they make money. These workers are sometimes called ***human resources.***

Consumers

Both adults and children are ***consumers.*** They buy and use the goods and services that other people produce. If you drink milk, wear shoes, or ride a bike, you are a consumer. You are part of the economy. Where is the consumer in this picture?

1 MEMORY MASTER

1. What is the difference between goods and services?
2. If there is a lot of something, the price is usually ______. If there is not much of something, the price is usually ______.
3. Compare and contrast a producer and a consumer.

LESSON 2

WORDS TO UNDERSTAND

agriculture
barter
export
import
tourist

Money, Money, Money

Today, we use money to buy what we need, but things were different a long time ago. People used to trade, or ***barter*** for what they wanted. Native Americans and the early settlers made their own clothes and homes and grew their own food. Then they traded for better tools or different food than they already had. White settlers came to Indian villages and traded cloth, metal tools and pots, and other things in exchange for animal furs.

After a while, governments printed money and made coins. The money was easier to carry than wheat, furs, or other goods. People produced goods and sold them for money. Some people worked on the railroad or steamboats to earn money. People worked hard, but most people still had very little money. They had to be very careful to use their money wisely.

Activity

How Much Money Does It Cost?

What can you buy with a dollar? You can probably buy ice cream, paper, or crayons. Look at this list of things adults spend their money on.

Do some research to find out how much money these things cost. You can go to a store, look in newspaper ads, or search the Internet. List the lowest and highest prices you find.

1. a pound of hamburger
2. a pound of oranges
3. a pair of shoes
4. a large pizza
5. a bike

Making Choices

Whenever you buy something, you are making a choice. Sometimes, you have to make a trade-off. A trade-off is choosing not to buy one thing in order to have enough money to buy something else. Imagine that you have $25 to spend. You want to buy a book and a new video game, but you don't have enough money for both. What would you choose to buy? What trade-off would you make?

A New Bike

If you wanted a new bike, how would you choose what kind to buy? There are many kinds to choose from. Comparing products is an important part of choosing how to spend money.

First you have to figure out what you want. Do you want a road bike or a mountain bike? Do you want a green bike or a red one? Then search for bikes at different stores. You can make a chart to compare the bikes. Then choose the bike that fits your needs and wants and has the best price.

Look at this chart. Decide what kind of bike you would buy.

Brand	Price	Color	Extras
Brand A	$80	blue	bell
Brand B	$75	red	basket, 3 speeds
Brand C	$100	silver	flashing lights, 10 speeds, soft seat

Activity

Make a Product Chart

Think of something you want to buy. Find out as much as you can about it. Would a chart help you decide how to make the best choice?

Saving and Planning

Money is important to people. It helps them get the things they need and want. Money also gives us a way to plan ahead for things we will want later. Suppose you get an allowance from your family. Or, you might walk dogs or do other jobs. Suppose you earn $10 each week, and you want to buy a scooter that costs $100. You could save your money until you have enough for the scooter.

- How long would it take if you saved all of the $10 each week?
- How long would it take if you saved $5 and spent $5 each week?

Earning a Living

Not long ago almost everyone in our state worked in agriculture. That is how they earned money for their families. There were jobs on farms, in food packing plants, and in grocery stores. These and other businesses depended on growing food or raising animals.

How do the adults in your home earn money? What work would you like to do when you get older?

Today, people in our state do many different kinds of jobs. They design, build, and sell homes and other buildings. They work in factories and at department stores. They sell and repair cars. They work in offices on computers. They write stories and take photographs for newspapers. These are some of the ways people earn a living.

Many people work for our state or local government. They are police officers, gardeners in parks, teachers in schools, and workers in museums. They are street cleaners, secretaries, and city planners. Some government workers help other people find jobs.

Activity

Where Do Missourians Work?

Look at this pie chart to see where Missouri people work. People who work in hotels or hospitals are part of the service industry. What other service jobs can you think of? What jobs are part of transportation or manufacturing?

Use the chart to answer these questions:

1. What industry employs the largest number of people? What kind of jobs does this include?
2. How many people work for the government? What kind of jobs does this include?
3. How many people work in agriculture?
4. What industry employs 401,000 people?

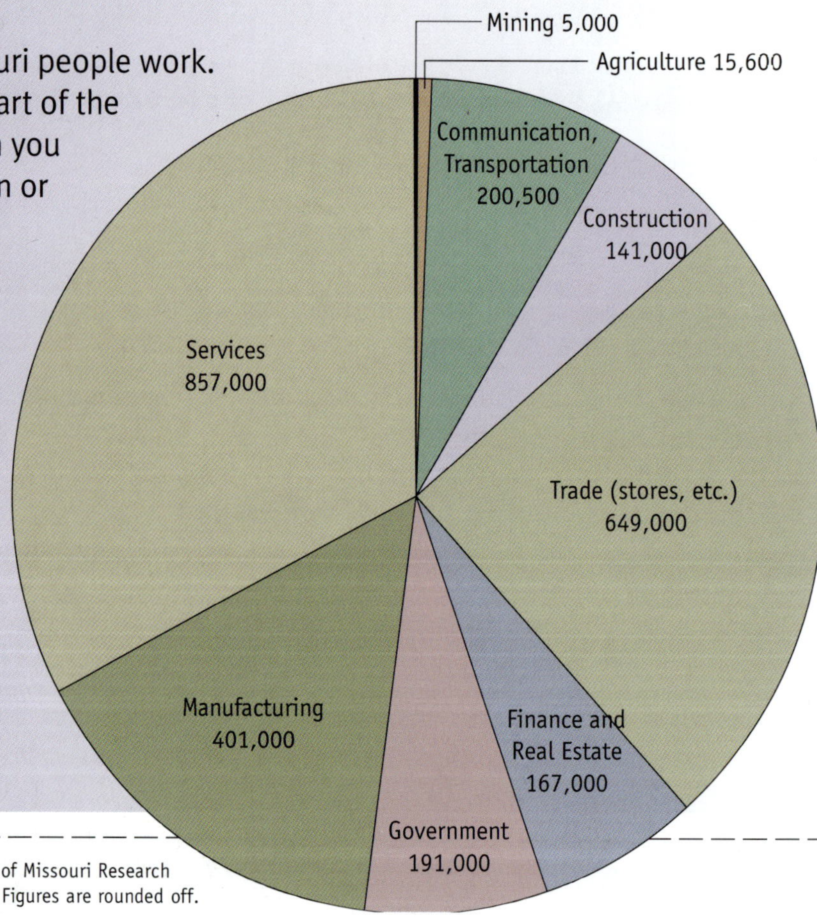

Source: Dept. of Missouri Research and Planning. Figures are rounded off.

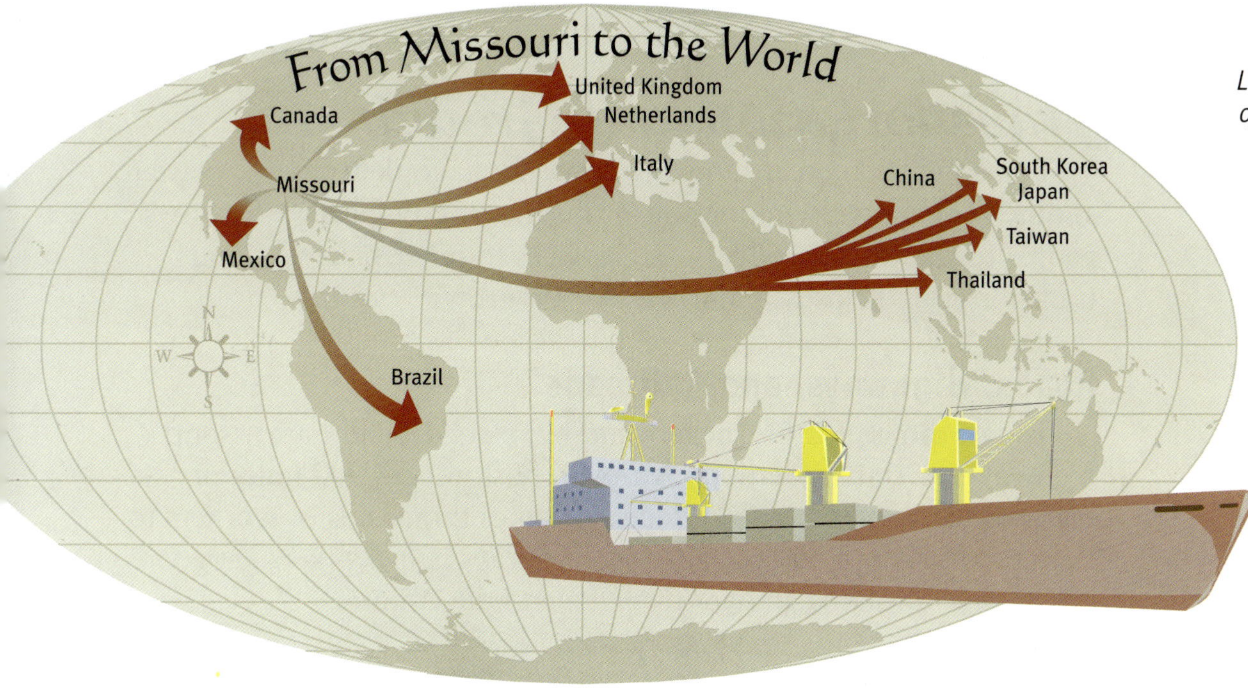

Look at this map to see some of the top countries that buy Missouri's products.

All Over the World

Roads, airports, railroads, and rivers link Missouri to other states and countries around the globe. These things help people ***import*** and ***export*** many products. Imports are goods we bring INTO our state from other places. Exports are goods we send OUT of the state. Many Missourians make a living by selling their products to places all over the world.

The cattle in this photo are beef cattle. Many kinds of cattle are raised in our state. Some cows are raised for their milk, which can be made into cheese, ice cream, or other dairy products. Some are raised for their meat, which we call beef.

Agriculture

Agriculture is still one of the most important businesses in Missouri. Missouri farmers and ranchers provide food for many other states and countries.

Companies that make tractors, grain bins, and barns are part of agriculture, too. Feed and seed stores that sell to farmers are part of agriculture. So are grocery stores that buy from farmers. Banks that make loans to help farmers buy farm land, and stores that sell trucks, trailers, tires, and other farm machines are all part of the agriculture business.

Transportation and Growth

Transportation means moving goods and people from one place to another. This is very important for business and industry. It allows people to ship their products and services to other places. Good transportation helps Missouri's economy grow.

Roads, Highways, and Railroads

Today, thousands of truckers and travelers depend on Missouri's highways for transportation. Missouri has over 32,000 miles of highways and over 10,000 bridges. It takes thousands of workers to keep the roads in good repair. The highways help workers get goods and people to places all over the state and the country.

An Amtrak train carries passengers on a scenic trip.

Railroads are still important. Coal trains bring coal to help run our power plants. The power plants produce electricity. Other trains take crops and cattle from Missouri farms to other places around the nation. There are still a few trains that take people between St. Louis and Kansas City every day.

Waterways

In early Missouri, our two big rivers provided the most important way for people to travel and ship goods. Rivers are still important today. Both the Mississippi and Missouri Rivers are deep and wide enough for ships and barges. Large barges leave Kansas City and St. Louis every day and move down to the Gulf of Mexico. From there, products from Missouri travel all over the world.

Airports

Airplanes help people move across our state and on to other places. Airplanes also carry goods and mail. St. Louis and Kansas City have large airports. Many other Missouri cities and towns have smaller airports.

Tourism

People come from other states and countries to visit Missouri. They come to see a Chiefs or Cardinals game. They come to Branson to visit Silver Dollar City and see live music shows. They come and canoe on our rivers or fish and water ski on our lakes. They come to visit the homes of famous people. Visitors come for music festivals and horse shows.

Visitors are called ***tourists.*** A person can be a tourist in their own state if they "tour" or visit places away from their homes. When was the last time you were a tourist?

How do tourists help our state? Tourists spend money on food, gas, and hotels. They spend money on fun things to do and see. Tourists help many businesses earn money.

Tugboats pull long, flat barges up and down the Mississippi River. The barges are loaded with goods going to market. Why is water transportation better in many ways than truck or train transportation?

A Sample of Missouri Products

Missouri makes products that are used here and around the world. Which products have you seen? Which products have you used?

Harley Davidson

A little over 100 years ago William Harley, age 21, and his friend Arthur Davidson, age 20, wrote the words "Harley-Davidson Motor Company" on the door of a small wooden shed. Inside the shed they built a bicycle with an engine on it. They wanted the bike to be a racer. Later, Arthur's brother Walter helped with the work. Today, thousands of workers in Kansas City and other towns make motorcycles and sell them all over the world.

KC Masterpiece

A Kansas City doctor named Rich Davis loved to cook in his backyard. He made his own barbeque sauce. His friends and family loved it. In the 1980s he began to sell it. Today, people all over the country buy KC Masterpiece barbeque sauce. It has helped make people aware that Missouri is one of the best places in the world to eat barbeque.

Hallmark

J.C. Hall started selling postcards in Kansas City in 1910. He only had two shoeboxes full of cards to sell. Today, Hallmark Cards is the largest seller of greeting cards in the world. You have probably seen cards for birthdays, Mother's Day, Father's Day, Christmas, and Halloween. The artists and writers at Hallmark try to make just the right card to say what you would like to say if you were making the card yourself.

IBC and Fitz's Root Beer

Do you love to drink cold root beer on a hot day? Do you like root beer floats? Two famous brands of root beer are bottled in St. Louis. During the 1920s, Americans made it against the law to drink real beer, so IBC started making a soda they called root beer. People still love to drink it. Over 20 years later, another company made and sold the fizzy drink. Families loved to drive up, order a burger and root beer at Fitz's, and wait for a "car hop" to bring their order. The root beer was always served in a cold glass mug.

Bass Pro Outdoor World

A few decades ago, Bass Pro started as an eight-foot display of fishing goods. Today, Bass Pro Outdoor World in Springfield is the world's largest sporting goods store. It sells fishing and hunting equipment, camping gear, and things people need for any sport.

Guber Burgers

For years, people have driven to the Wheel Inn drive-in restaurant in Sedalia for a "Guber Burger." This is a hamburger with peanut butter on it. Why do they call it by that name? Peanuts used to be called "guber peas." Don't knock it until you've tried it!

Monsanto

For over 100 years, Monsanto has been a St. Louis company that helps farmers. Scientists and other workers at Monsanto make products that protect crops from weeds and insects. They also develop seeds that produce bigger crops. Monsanto workers help farmers in Missouri and around the world grow food to feed us all.

2 MEMORY MASTER

1. List five kinds of jobs Missouri people do to make money.
2. How does transportation help people make money?
3. Choose one of the products made in Missouri and tell what natural resources, capital, and human resources were used.

Chapter 13 Review

Activity

Big Business

There are many businesses in our state. Look at some businesses on pages 278-279 of this chapter. Ask your teacher to help you find businesses in your town or city. You can look in the yellow pages of a telephone book.

Now choose one business or company to study. Work by yourself or with a team. The business may have a website that will help you. You can also write to the business to get information. Some of the things to research are:

1. Does the company provide goods, services, or both? What are they?
2. Does the company export any of its products?
3. What kinds of jobs do workers do?
4. How have changes in technology helped the company grow?

Now make a poster about the company or business. Use words and pictures.

Activity

Technology Changes Agriculture

Things have really changed on many of the farms in our state! In the old days, work was most often done on foot or on horseback. Now many farmers and ranchers ride the range on a four-wheeler or a motorcycle. Tractors, combines, and other machines are big. Machinery now does the work that people and animals once did.

Animals and crops are bought and sold online with the use of computers and the Internet. In what other ways is technology a part of agriculture today? Try to find at least three examples.

Activity

Understand a Budget

People make budgets to know where they can spend their money. Look at this example of a family budget and then answer the questions.

1. How much money is spent on the house payment?
2. Can you think of other expenses that should be in the budget?
3. How much money is left over after all the expenses are subtracted?
4. What do you think the family will do with their extra money?

Monthly Budget

Income:	$3,000

Expenses

House payment:	$1,200
Food:	$500
Clothes:	$150
Savings:	$100
Electricity/Gas:	$200
Car payment:	$250
Gas for the car:	$50

Activity

Make a Map of Places to Visit

The Internet makes it easy to tour Missouri with a computer. The Missouri Division of Travel and Tourism has information on many things to do here. Go to its website at: **www.missouritourism.org**. Search the site for things to see and do in our state.

1. Make a list of five places you would like to visit in Missouri.
2. Draw a map of Missouri.
3. On your map, write the names of the places you want to visit.
4. On a piece of paper, write two reasons why you want to visit each place you chose.

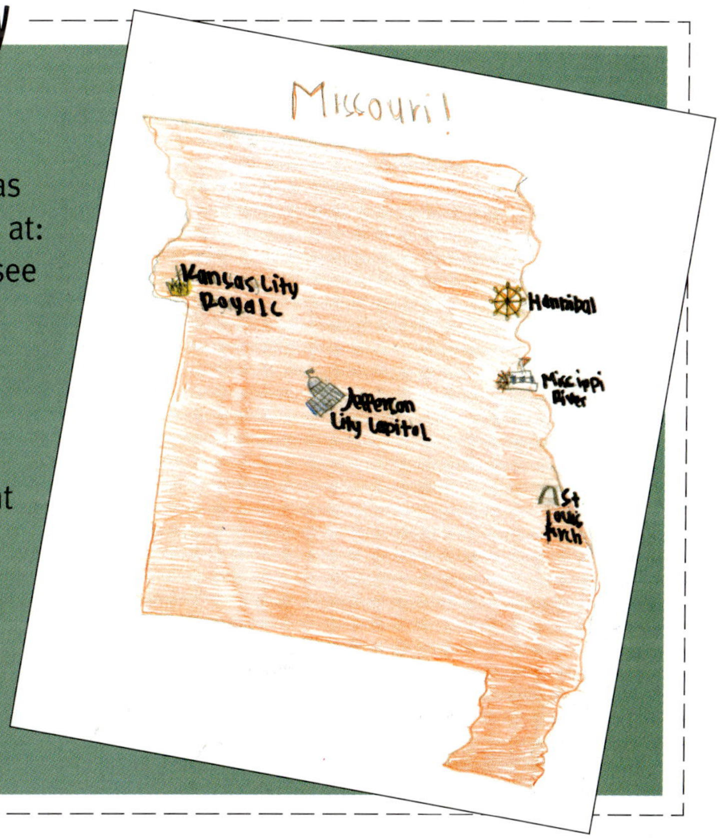

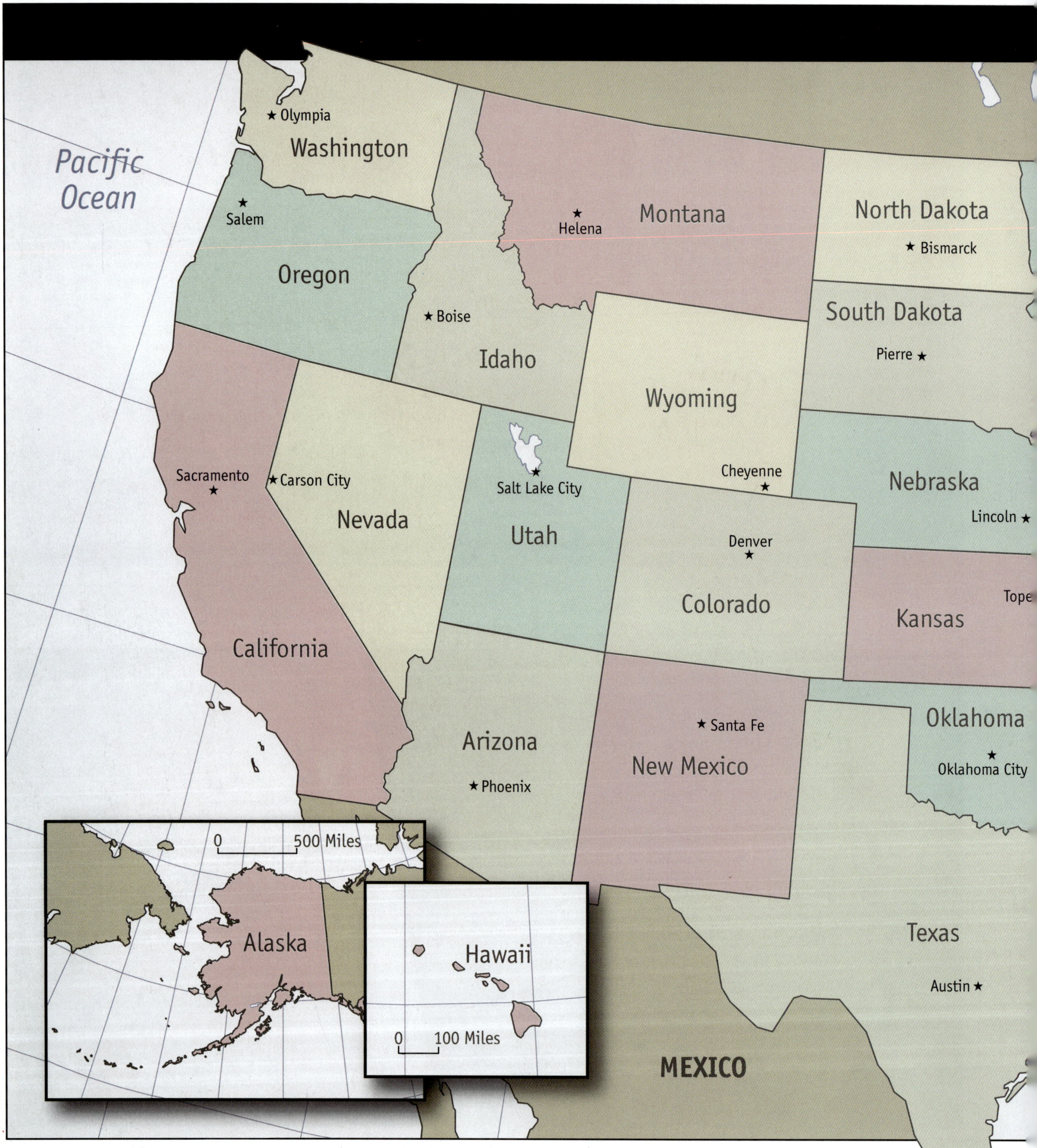
Pacific Ocean
Olympia
Washington
Salem
Oregon
Helena
Montana
North Dakota
Bismarck
Boise
Idaho
South Dakota
Pierre
Wyoming
Sacramento
Carson City
Nevada
Salt Lake City
Utah
Cheyenne
Nebraska
Lincoln
Denver
Colorado
Kansas
California
Santa Fe
New Mexico
Arizona
Phoenix
Oklahoma
Oklahoma City
Texas
Austin
MEXICO
0
500 Miles
Alaska
Hawaii
0
100 Miles

The United States of America

The World

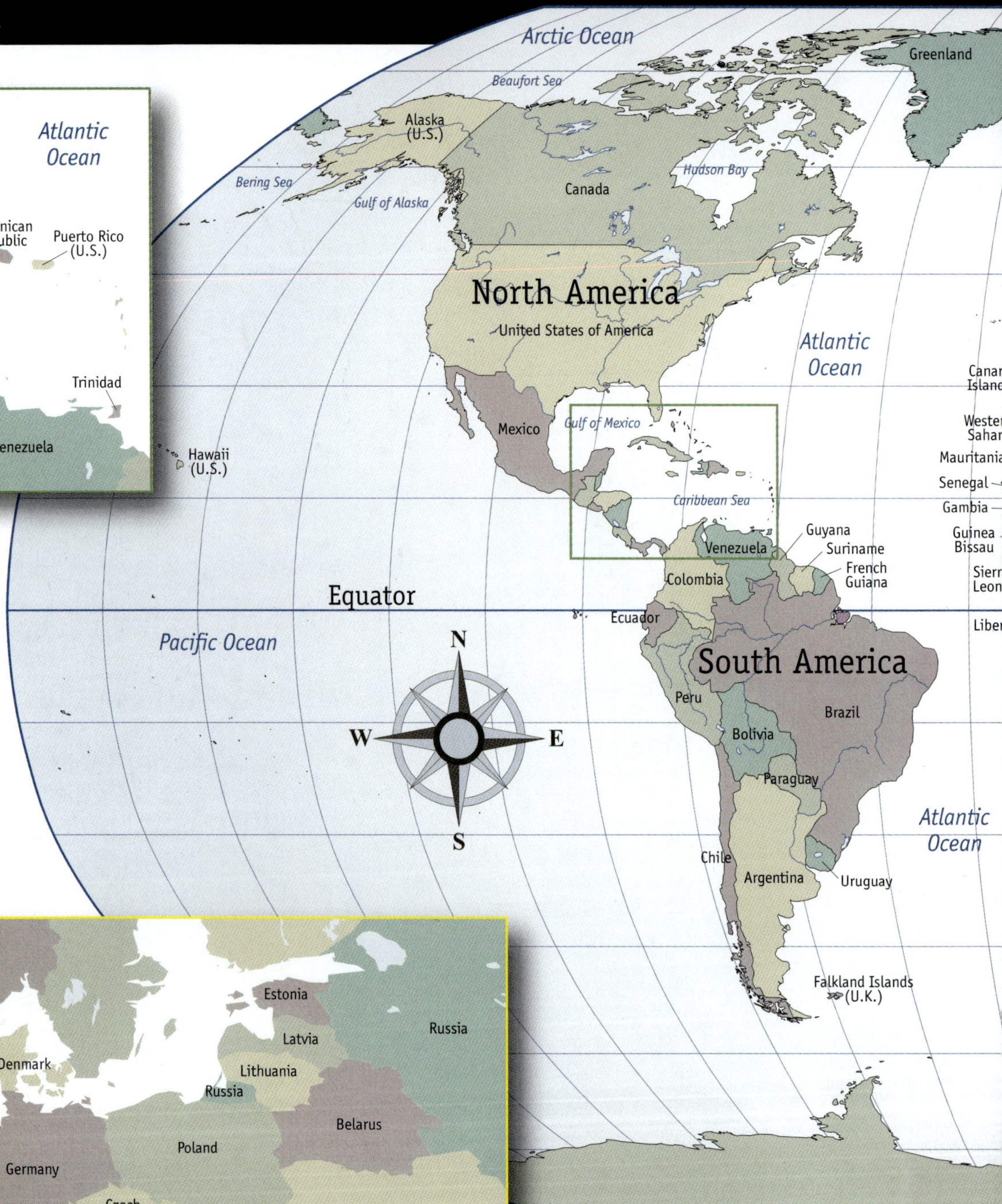

Country Abbreviations	
Fr.	France
It.	Italy
Sp.	Spain
U.E.A.	United Arab Emirates
U.K.	United Kingdom
U.S.	United States

Arctic Ocean
Iceland
Norway
Sweden
Finland
Russia
North Sea
Europe
Asia
Sea of Okhotsk
Kazakhstan
Mongolia
Black Sea
Uzbekistan
Kyrgyzstan
Turkmenistan
Tajikistan
North Korea
South Korea
Japan
China
Tunisia
Morocco
Mediterranean Sea
Iran
Afghanistan
Nepal
Bhutan
Algeria
Libya
Egypt
Qatar
Pakistan
Saudi Arabia
U.A.E.
India
Taiwan
Pacific Ocean
Mali
Niger
Chad
Red Sea
Oman
Myanmar
Laos
Africa
Sudan
Eritrea
Yemen
Bangladesh
Thailand
Philippine Sea
Philippines
Burkina
Djibouti
Vietnam
Cote d'Ivoire
Nigeria
Central African Republic
Ethiopia
Sri Lanka
Cambodia
Brunei
Malaysia
Togo
Cameroon
Somalia
Ghana
Benin
Uganda
Kenya
Singapore
Zaire
Equatorial Guinea
Rwanda
Burundi
Gabon
Indian Ocean
Java Sea
Indonesia
Papua New Guinea
Congo
Tanzania
Malawi
Timor Sea
Angola
Zambia
Mozambique
Coral Sea
Fiji
Zimbabwe
Namibia
Madagascar
Botswana
Australia
New Caledonia (Fr.)
Swaziland
South Africa
Lesotho
Great Australian Bight
Tasman Sea
New Zealand
Prime Meridian
Antarctica
Russia
Black Sea
Georgia
Caspian Sea
Armenia
Azerbaijan
Turkey
Cyprus
Syria
Iran
Lebanon
Mediterranean Sea
Iraq
Israel
Gazzah
Jordan
Egypt
Kuwait
Saudi Arabia

Glossary

The definitions given here are for the **Words to Understand** as they are used in this textbook. The words are highlighted in yellow where they first appear in the book.

A

abolish: to do away with; to end
adobe: bricks made of mud and straw and baked in the sun
agriculture: raising crops and animals for sale
ammunition: bullets and other explosives such as grenades and bombs
ancestor: a relative who lived before you
animated: a movie made by photographing a series of drawings to make the pictures seem to move
apology: a statement of sorrow for past actions
archaeologist: a scientist who learns about people of the past by studying their artifacts and ruins
argument: a verbal disagreement
artifact: something made or used by people and left behind
atlatl: a tool that helped early people throw a spear farther and faster
auction: a sale in which the person who bids the most money gets the item

B

barter: to trade without using money
boarding school: a school where children live
buckskin: soft leather

C

calico: cotton cloth printed with colored patterns
campaign: the work of running for office, including making speeches and putting up signs
capital resources: in business, things used to make something else
capital: the money needed to run a business
cardinal directions: north, south, east, west
character: the qualities that make one person different from another; moral excellence
checks and balances: a system in which each of the branches of government has only certain powers
civil rights: the rights that belong to every citizen
civil war: a war in which groups in the same country fight against each other
climate: the weather pattern of a place year after year
colony: a settlement or land region under the control of another country
compromise: to settle an argument by each side giving up part of what they want
consumer: a person who buys goods and services
convert: to persuade a person into changing his or her religion
courageous: showing lack of fear
criminal: a person who has broken the law
culture: the way a group of people live

D

decision: the act of deciding
desegregate: to end segregation
disease: sickness
disloyal: not loyal or supporting
document: an official paper, such as a letter, form, or certificate

E

economics: the study of how people make, transport, buy, and sell goods and services
ecosystem: a community of living things that interact and depend upon each other
elders: elderly Indian men and women
emigrant: a person who leaves a country to live in another country
epidemic: a disease that affects many people at the same time
exaggerate: to stretch the truth
expedition: a journey for a specific purpose
export: to send goods out of a place
extinct: no longer living anywhere

F

fact: information that can be proven to be true
famine: a time when crops fail so there is little or no food
fascination: an extreme interest
ferry: a boat or raft that carries people across a river
fiction: stories that people make up
folktale: a story without a real time, place, or author
fossil: an imprint or remains of a plant or animal in rock
freight: a load of goods to be transported
frontier: land at the edge of settled places

G

geography: the study of the land, water, and living things of a place and their locations
glacier: a large, thick, heavy sheet of ice and snow
glossary: a list of words and their meanings
goods: products; things that are made, bought, and sold
guerrilla warfare: unorganized attack

H

hemisphere: half of the earth
historian: a person who studies history
horrified: terrified; filled with horror
human feature: things on the land made by people, such as buildings, bridges, and roads
human resources: people whose work produces goods and services
hunter-gatherer: a person who survives by hunting animals and gathering wild foods

I

identify: to establish identity
import: to bring goods into a place from another place
impressive: having the power to excite attention or awe
index: an alphabetical list of items in a book with page numbers where they can be found
intermediate directions: directions halfway between cardinal directions, such as southeast
interpreter: a person who translates languages
interstate: between states
inventor: a person who creates something never made before
isolated: to be separated or away from others

J-K-L

jury: a group of people who listen to a case to decide if a person is innocent of a crime
landform: a natural land feature such as a mountain, hill, plain, plateau, valley, etc.
latitude: imaginary lines that run east and west on a globe or map
legal: according to the law
legend: a story that tells how things came to be
legislator: a person elected to help make the laws
local: close to home
locomotive: the train car that pulls the other railroad cars

longhouse: a large, long, Indian home made of saplings, brush, and bark
longitude: imaginary lines that run north and south on a globe or map

M

manufacturing: the process of making things from raw materials
merchant: a person who buys and sells for a living; the owner of a store
missionary: one who tries to convert others to his or her religion
mural: a large painting on a wall

N

natural feature: part of the land that was formed by nature, such as mountains, hills, rivers, and rocks
natural resources: things found in nature that people use, such as trees, water, minerals

O-P-Q

opinion: a belief or judgment
oral history: history told out loud
outlaw: a person who hides from the law
pen name: a name an author uses instead of his or her real name
permission: formal consent
persecute: to cause people to suffer because of their beliefs
petrified: turned into stone
pioneer: one of the first to settle a place
plains: a large region of flat land with few trees
political party: a group with about the same ideas about government
pollution: a condition of dirty and unsafe air, water, or land
portage: the carrying of boats and goods from one body of water to another
precipitation: water that falls to the earth in the form of rain, snow, sleet, or hail
primary source: something made or written by someone who was there at the time
products: goods; things that are made or grown
protest: to work for change by marching, carrying signs, giving speeches, etc.

R

racism: making decisions of worth based only on race
rebel: to fight against those with power
reference book: a book of information, such as an atlas, encyclopedia, or almanac
refuge: a place where animals can live without being harmed
region: a place that has features that are alike in some way, such as landforms or economic activity
rendezvous: a place where mountain men gathered to trade for furs and supplies and to celebrate
renewable: a resource that comes back again
representative: someone who has been elected to speak, act, or vote for other people
reservoir: a man-made lake formed behind a dam
resist: to go against
responsibility: job or duty
revenge: the act of punishing someone in return for something bad done to you
robust: strong and healthy
ruins: remains of buildings
rural: having to do with the country instead of the city

S

scarcity: a situation when the demand for something is greater than the supply
secede: to break away from a country
secondary source: something made or written by people who were not there at the time
segregate: to separate by race
services: in economics, work done for money

sharecropper: a farmer who works on land owned by another person in exchange for part of the crop
sinew: a tendon that connects muscles and bones
squatter: a person who lives on land without buying it
stockade: a heavy log fence built for protection
submarine: a boat that moves under the water
suburbs: communities of houses, stores, and schools next to large cities
supply and demand: the idea that cost is affected by the amount of something available for sale and by the number of people who want to buy it
surrender: to give up completely and yield to the power of the other side

T

table of contents: a list of chapter titles and the page numbers they start on
tattoo: a permanent colored mark on skin
terrorism: acts of violence and force
tourist: a person who takes a tour or visits for pleasure
tragic: terrible and sad
tributary: a small river that flows into a larger river or lake

U-V-W

urban: having to do with the city rather than the country
veterinary: a doctor who heals animals
veto: to say "no" to a bill so it will not become a law
volunteer: a person who gives service without pay
voyageur: a man employed by a fur company to transport furs and other goods
warrior: a man who fought in war
wigwam: a small, rounded Indian home covered with bark, brush, or animal hides
wilderness: unsettled land
will: a document that states what to do with a person's possessions after they die

Index

A

Adventures of Huckleberry Finn, The, 30, 163, 203
Adventures of Tom Sawyer, The, 30, 203
African Americans, 8, 80-81, 160-168, 183, 192, 206, 214, 219, 221, 223, 226, 228, 229, 243
Agriculture, 274, 275, 280 *See also* farming
American Indians, *See* Native Americans and specific tribes
American Revolution, 90, 92, 250
American Royal, 199, 246
Anderson, "Bloody Bill", 181, 186, 194
Appalachian Mountains, 56, 89, 92
Arabia, 139
Archaeology, 50
Archaic Indians, 49
Asia, 236, 239
Atlantic Ocean, 52, 70, 225
Augusta, 266-267
Austin, Moses, 91
Automobiles, 212

B

Bagnell Dam, 28
Baseball, 228-229
Bass Pro Outdoor World, 279
Bass, Tom, 199
Battle at Wilson's Creek, 179
Battle of Pilot Knob, 186
Battle of the Hemp Bales, 179
Beaver, 72-73, 86-88, 117
Becknell, William, 127
Beckwourth, James, 120
Bell, "Cool Papa", 228
Benton, Thomas Hart, 230-231
Berra, Yogi, 228
Bible, 162, 175, 232
Big Soldier, 107
Big Spring, 33
Bill of Rights, 137, 180, 250
Blacks, *See* African Americans
Blanchette, Louis, 89
Blow, Susan Elizabeth, 193
Boggs, Lilburn, 135
Bond, Kit, 135
Boone, Daniel, 91, 92-93, 106
Boone, John "Blind", 206
Boone, Nathan, 92
Boonslick Region, 109
Boonville, 109, 139, 161
Bradley, Omar, 237
Branches of Government, 252-253, 257
Branson, 33, 277
Bridger, Jim, 119
Brown, John, 167
Brown, William Wells, 166
Buffalo, 60, 88
Burden, Charles, 201
Burnett, Peter, 131
Bush, George W., 244, 248
Bushwhackers, 181, 182, 184, 194, 214
Butterfield Overland Mail Company, 140

C

Cahokia, 54-57
Caldwell County, 135
California Trail, 132-133
California, 105, 120, 121, 122, 132, 141, 224
Canada, 39, 72, 82, 89, 129, 165
Cape Girardeau, 34, 89
Carson, Kit, 119
Carver, George Washington, 214-215
Cass County, 221
Castor River, 41
Catholic Church/Catholics, 72, 82, 89, 129, 183
Census, U.S., 247
Centennial Farms, 266-267
Charbonneau, 102
Chariton River, 146
Chief White Hair, 59
Chillicothe, 164
Chouteau, Auguste, 78
Chouteau, Francois, 79
Chouteau, Therese, 78
Chouteau's Landing, 79
Christians, 70, 128-129, 134 *See also* specific religions
Church of Jesus Christ of Latter-day Saints, 134-135
Citizenship (responsibilities), 262-263
Civil Rights Movement, 243
Civil War, 170-188, 203
Clarence, 126
Clark, 237
Clark, William, 100-104, 113, 128
Clay County, 135
Clay, Henry, 110
Clemens, Samuel, *See* Mark Twain
Colorado, 31, 105
Columbia, 30, 35, 206
Community of Christ, 137

Congress (U.S.), 254-255
Constitution (Missouri), 109, 111, 195, 257
Constitution (U.S.), 243, 250, 252
Copper, 43
Corps of Discovery, 100-104
Courts, 252, 257
Couzins, Adaline, 183
Current River, 27, 32, 33, 146

D

Davis, Rich, 278
De Smet, Father Jean, 129
De Soto, Hernando, 71
Dean, Jay, 228
Dean, Paul, 228
Declaration of Independence, 250-251
Defiance, 92
Democratic Party, 255
Diamond, 214
Disney, Walt, 224

E

Eads Bridge, 200
Eads, James, 200
Education, *See* schools
Electricity, 210, 223
Eleven Point River, 27
Emigrants, *See* immigrants
England/English, 90, 250
Europe/Europeans, 70, 71, 135, 193, 220, 236

F

Fair St. Louis, 246
Fantastic Caverns, 41
Far West, 135
Farming, 30, 31, 33, 34, 35, 43, 56, 82, 84, 91, 155, 158, 195, 199, 214, 215
Fink, Mike, 12
First African Baptist Church, 166
Fitz's Root Beer, 279
Florida, 202
Florissant, 89
Fort Chartres, 78
Fort Osage, 106
Fort Sumter, 176
Fourchet, Jeanette, 81
France/French, 27, 62, 72-78, 94, 101, 220, 225
Franklin, 109, 121
Fremont, John C., 130
French and Indian War, 92
Fulton, 229
Fulton, Robert, 138
Fur trade, 62, 72, 86-88, 117-120, 138

G

Gall, John Henry, 157
Garagiola, Joe, 228
Gasconade River, 27, 142, 146
Gateway Arch, 35, 116
Germany/Germans, 156-157, 193, 212, 220, 221, 236, 237, 246
Gibson, Josh, 229
Glacial Plains Region, 30
"Golden Rule Stores", 217
Government, Federal, 250-255
Government, Missouri, 256-262
Graham Cave State Park, 50
Grand River, 27, 146
Grand View, 222
Grant, Ulysses S., 187
Great Depression, 226-227, 228
Great Lakes, 24, 53, 56, 72
Great Plains, 31, 52, 105
Gulf of Mexico, 27, 38, 53, 56

H

Hall, J.C., 278
Hallmark Cards, 278
Hamilton, 217
Hannibal, 30, 142, 155, 163, 202
Harley Davidson, 278
Harley, William, 278
Harrisonville, 194
Hermann, 142, 158, 246
Hopewell Indians, 53
House of Representatives, 255

I

IBC Root Beer, 279
Ice Age, 24, 30, 48
Illinois, 137, 164, 224
Immigrants, 156-159, 212 *See also* specific groups
Independence, 30, 121, 122, 134, 137, 222
Indians, *See* Native Americans and specific tribes
Iowa, 165, 214
Iraq, *See* War in Iraq
Ireland/Irish, 159, 212
Italy/Italian, 237

J

Jackson County, 134, 222
Jackson, Claiborne Fox, 178
James, Frank, 194
James, Jesse, 194, 230
Japan/Japanese, 236, 239
Jayhawkers, 180, 181
Jefferson City, 30, 35, 111, 178, 230, 244, 249
Jefferson, Thomas, 59, 98, 99, 100, 104, 251
Jim the Wonder Dog, 232
Jolliet, Louis, 74
Joplin, 31, 205, 230

K

Kansas City Art Institute, 224
Kansas City Chiefs, 245, 277

Kansas City Monarchs, 228
Kansas City Royals, 245
Kansas City, 29, 30, 35, 36, 53, 79, 139, 142, 155, 198, 199, 211, 221, 222, 224, 230, 234-235, 243
Kansas, 31, 66, 105, 165, 172-173, 180, 182, 184
Katy Trail State Park, 25
Kelsey, Nancy, 122
Kennett, 34
Kentucky, 92, 93, 110, 167
King, Martin Luther Jr., 242, 243
Kirksville, 30
KMOX, 223
Korean War, 244

L

La Forge, 193
La Salle, Robert de, 75
Laclede, Pierre, 78
Lake of the Ozarks, 28, 29, 232
Lamar, 222
Lathrop, 126
Lawrence, 173, 182, 184
Lead, 43, 76, 199
Lewis and Clark Expedition, 100-104
Lewis, Meriwether, 100-104
Lexington, 138, 139, 140, 179
Liberty, 161
Liberty Memorial, 221
Limestone, 43, 199
Lincoln, Abraham, 10, 175, 178, 188
Lindbergh, Charles, 225
Lindenwood University, 106
Long, Stephen, 105
Louisiana Purchase/Territory, 75, 89, 89, 94, 98
Loutre River, 50
Lovejoy, Elijah, 164
Lyon, Nathaniel, 170-171

M

Manufacturing, 155
Marceline, 224
Marquette, Father Jacques, 74-75
Marshall, 232
Marshfield, 206
Masterpiece Barbeque Sauce, 278
Mastodon State Park, 25
McNair, Alexander, 111
Meachum, John Berry, 166
Middle East, 244
Mining/minerals, 43, 76 *See also* specific minerals
Mississippi Lowlands Region, 34
Mississippi River, 24, 27, 34, 71, 74-76, 84, 86, 89, 200, 277
Mississippians, 53-57
Missouri Compromise, 110
Missouri Counties, 259
Missouri General Assembly, 225, 257
Missouri Indians, 58
Missouri Mule, 126, 195
Missouri River, 24, 58, 86, 101, 138, 160
Missouri State Bears, 245
Missouri State Capitol Building, 230, 248-249
Missouri State Fair, 246
Missouri Tigers, 245
Monsanto, 279
Montreal, 86
Mormon Trail, 134
Mormons, *See* Church of Jesus Christ of Latter-day Saints
Mound Builders, 53-57
Mountain men, *See* fur trade

N

National Parks *See* specific parks
Native Americans, 8, 17, 27, 46-67, 70, 98, 99, 100, 102, 103, 104 *See also* specific tribes
Natural resources, 44, 270-271 *See also* specific resources
Nebraska, 72, 105
Negro Leagues, 228
Neosho, 214, 230
New Deal, 227
New Madrid Earthquake, 34, 108
New Orleans, 77, 86, 98
New York Yankees, 228
Niangua River, 33

O

Ohio River, 27
Oklahoma, 31, 66
Old Courthouse, 258
Old Drum, 201
Olympic Games, 219
Oregon Trail, 128-129
Oregon, 105, 121, 129, 130
Osage Indians, 59-66, 106
Osage Plains Region, 31, 60
Osage River, 27, 146
Ozark Highlands Region, 33, 60
Ozark Mountains, 33, 60, 195, 196, 204, 230

P-Q

Pacific Ocean, 102
Pacific Railroad, 142
Paige, Satchel Paige, 228
Paleo Indians, 48
Pearl Harbor, 236
Penney, James Cash, 217
Pershing, 221
Pershing, John J., 221
Persian Gulf War, 244
Phelps, Mary Whitney, 183
Pike, Zebulon, 105
Pioneers, 121-137
Plains Indians, 58
Platte City, 164
Platte River, 137
Pledge of Allegiance, 265

Poage, George, 219
Political parties, 255
Pollution, 44
Pony Express, 141
Potosi, 91
Potsdam, 221
Prairie State Park, 31
Price, Sterling, 178-179, 186
Quantrill, William, 181, 182, 184, 186, 194

R

Railroads, 196-200
Reconstruction, 192-193
Red Cross, 227
Republican Party, 255
Rivers, 26-28, 55, 79 *See also* specific rivers
Roaring Twenties, 223
Robinson, Jackie, 229
Rocky Mountain Fur Co., 117
Rocky Mountains, 102, 105
Roosevelt, Franklin D., 227, 238, 241

S

Sacagawea, 100, 102-104
Salt, 76
Salvation Army, 227
Santa Fe Trail, 126-127
Schools, 154, 193, 214, 227, 243
Scott, Dred, 174
Scott, Harriet, 174
Sedalia, 205, 246, 279
Senate, U.S., 253, 254-255
September 11, 2001, 244
Sibley, George, 106
Sibley, Mary Easton, 106
Sikeston, 34
Silver Dollar City, 277
Slavery, 80-81, 107, 149, 160-167, 187, 188, 192
Smith, Joseph, 134
Spain/Spanish, 27, 71, 89-91, 94
Spirit of St. Louis, 225
Springfield, 33, 35, 183, 248
St. Charles, 89, 101, 111
St. Francis River, 34
St. Joseph, 30, 35, 121, 141, 155, 197
St. Louis Art Museum, 219
St. Louis Blues, 245
St. Louis Cardinals, 228-229, 245, 277
St. Louis Rams, 245
St. Louis University, 245
St. Louis World's Fair, 205, 218-219
St. Louis Zoo, 218, 219
St. Louis, 29, 30, 35, 53, 78, 81, 82, 105, 114-115, 117, 121, 138, 142, 155, 160, 174, 199, 206, 211, 237, 243
Statehood, 111
Ste. Genevieve, 76-77, 80, 81-83
Steamboats, 138-139
Stephens, Helen, 229
Streetcars, 212

T

Taum Sauk Mountain, 33
Taxes, 260-261, 262, 264
Telegraph, 186
Telephone, 211
Tolton, Augustine, 183
Tolton, Martha Jane, 183
Tourism, 277
Trade, 56, 70, 72, 77-79, 106 *See also* fur traders
Truman State University, 30
Truman, Bess Wallace, 222, 238
Truman, Harry S., 30, 222, 238, 241, 243
Tuskegee Institute, 214
Twain, Mark, 30, 163, 202-203

U-V

U.S. Supreme Court, 174, 243
Underground Railroad, 165
Valle family, 77
Van Arsdale, Sam, 232
Van Meter State Park, 58
Vernon County, 167
Vietnam War, 244
Voting, 8, 225, 253, 262
Voyageurs, 86

W

War in Iraq, 244
Warrensburg, 201, 206
Washington, 139, 158
Washington, D.C., 103, 172, 188, 230, 241, 242, 243, 244, 254
Washington, George, 90, 91, 250
Weston, 164
Westport, 121
Whistle Stop Tour, 241
White River, 33
Whitman, Marcus, 129
Whitman, Narcissa, 129
Wilder, Laura Ingalls, 204
Wilson's Creek, 179
Woodland Indians, 52
World Series, 228
World War I, 220-221, 222
World War II, 228, 236-239, 240

X-Z

York, 100-104
Young, Brigham, 137
Zinc, 43

Credits

The following abbreviations are used for sources where several images were obtained:

LOC – Library of Congress Prints and Photographs Division
MDT – Missouri Division of Tourism
AP – AP/Wide World Photos
KC – Kansas City Convention & Visitors Association
SS – ShutterStock.com
KSHS – Kansas State Historical Society, Topeka
GR – Gary Rasmussen
CMSHS – Cahokia Mounds State Historic Site
GSPA – Gibbs Smith, Publisher Archive
NW – North Wind Picture Archives
GCNY – The Granger Collection, New York
SHSM – Used by permission, State Historical Society of Missouri, Columbia

Prelims: v-vi SS/Billy Lobo H., vi KC, vii-ix GR. **Chapter One:** 2-3 GR, 4 Reunion des Musees Nationaux/Art Resource, NY, 5 clipart.com, 9 WVAS Ruth Yeager Collection, 10 (top left) National Archives, 10 (bottom left) photos.com, 10 (center) Photos.com, (top right) John Alley, (bottom right) Photo by Jean Crossman, Courtesy of the Amherst History Museum. **Chapter Two:** 14-15 NASA, 17 ShutterPoint.com/Shelly Long, 25 (right) MDT, 26 photos.com, 27 MDT, 28 (top) photos.com, (bottom) MDT, 30 dreamstime.com/Colin Stitt, 31 MDT, 32 MDT, 33 MDT, 34 AP, 35 (top) SS/Jose Gil, (bottom) KC, 36 PhotosToGo.com/Jim Wark, 38 GR, 40 GR, 41 MDT, (bottom) LaVonda Walton/U.S. Fish & Wildlife Service, 44 SS/Terry Alexander. **Chapter Three:** 46-47 Illinois Historic Preservation Agency, 48 GR, 49 GR, 51 (clockwise, top left) photos.com, KSHS, KSHS, KSHS, KSHS, photos.com, 52 GR, 53 Hopewell Culture National Historical Park NPS, 54 CMSHS/William R. Iseminger, 55 CMSHS/L.K. Townsend, 56-57 CMSHS/Michael Hampshire, 57 CMSHS, 59 Smithsonian American Art Museum, Washington, DC/Art Resource, NY, 60 photos.com, 61 GSPA, 62 Nebraska State Historical Society, Museum of Nebraska History Collections, 63 GR, 64 GR, 65 photos.com, 66 AP. **Chapter Four:** 68-69 Reunion des Musees Nationaux/Art Resource, NY, 71 Architect of the Capitol, 72 GR, 73 SS/Robert Mizerek, 74 GSPA, 75 clipart.com, 76 MDT, 77 MDT, 79 GCNY, 80 (top) photos.com (bottom) NW, 81 GSPA, 82 NW, 83 MDT, 85 MDT, 86-87 Corel Professional Photos, National Archive of Canada, 87 GR, 88 GSPA, 90 LOC, 93 GCNY. **Chapter Five:** 96-97 Painting "Lewis and Clark: The Departure from St. Charles, May 21, 1804" by Gary R. Lucy. Courtesy of the Gary R. Lucy Gallery, Inc., Washington, MO – www.garylucy,com, 99 GCNY, 100 (top) Montana Historical Society, "Lewis and Clark at Three Forks," by Edgar S. Paxon, Don Beatty, photographer, (bottom) LOC, 101 (top) LOC, (bottom) GR, 102 GSPA, 103 GCNY, 104 photos.com, 105 SS/Mark Hayes, 106 Missouri Valley Special Collections, Kansas City Public Library, Kansas City Missouri, 107 Missouri Valley Special Collections Kansas City Public Library, Kansas City Missouri, 109 LOC, 111 MDT/Greater Saint Charles Convention and Visitors Bureau. **Chapter Six:** 114-115 GCNY, 116 SS/Jose Gil, 117 SHSM, 118 (left) GSPA, (top) SHSM, 119 (top) SHSM, (bottom) LOC, 120 SHSM, 121 GSPA, 122 KC, 123 GCNY, 124-125 Glen S. Hopkinson, 125 Susan Myers, 127 KSHS, 129 (top) Oregon Historical Society, (bottom) LOC, 130-131 Scottsbluff National Monument, painting by William Henry Jackson, 132 GSPA, 133 GSPA, 134 "Saints Driven from Jackson County, Missouri" C.C.A. Christensen. Courtesy of Brigham Young University Museum of Art. All Rights Reserved, 135 Painting "Court Martial of Joseph Smith" by Robert T. Barrett, 136 William Henry Jackson, 138 Jon Burton, 139 (top) LOC, (right) Arabia Steamboat Museum, 140 SHSM, 141 (top) Nevada Historical Society, (bottom) LOC, 142 GSPA. **Chapter Seven:** 144-145 GCNY, 146 GR, 147 GR, 148 NW, 149 (top) SHSM, (bottom) GSPA, 150 (top) Nebraska State Historical Society, Museum of Nebraska History Collections, 150 (left) Pocumtuck Valley Memorial Association, Memorial Hall Museum, Deerfield, Massachusetts, 151 Kindra Clineff, 152 (top) SHSM, (left) GR, 153 iStockPhoto.com/Jeff Kroph, 154 SHSM, 155 (center) photos.com, (right) clipart.com, 156 NW, 157 (top) NW, (bottom) Jeffrey Gall Collection, 158 SHSM, 159 NW, 160 GSPA, 161 SHSM, 163 LOC, 164 GCNY, 165 NW, 166 (left) Western Historical Manuscript Collection, University of Missouri – St. Louis, (right) LOC, 167 West Virginia State Archives. **Chapter Eight:** 170-171 GCNY, 172 KSHS, 173 KSHS, 174 (both) LOC, 175 LOC, 176 GCNY, 177 (top) LOC, (bottom) clipart.com, 178 SHSM, 179 GSPA, 181 (top) SHSM, (bottom) KSHS, 182 KSHS, 183 GCNY, 184-185 SHSM, 187 GSPA, 188 (top) LOC, (left) clipart.com, 189 photos.com. **Chapter Nine:** 190-191 Painting "The Eads Bridge Under Construction, 1873" by Gary R. Lucy. Courtsey of the Gary R. Lucy Gallery, Inc. Washington, MO – www.garylucy,com, 192 GCNY, 193 (left) LOC, (right) SHSM, 194 SHSM, 195 SS/Joy Fera, 196 NW, 197 GSPA, 198 SHSM, 199 Audrain County Historical Society, 200 (both) SHSM, 201 MDT, 202 LOC, 204 SHSM, 205 (both) GSPA, 206 SHSM. **Chapter Ten:** 208-209 SHSM, 211 (top) photos.com, (bottom) LOC, 212 SHSM, 213 WSVA Howard Hiner Collection, 214 Iowa State University Library / Special Collections Department, 215 (top) GCNY, (right) SHSM, 216 National Archives, 217 (left) Wyoming State Archives, Department of State Parks and Cultural Resources, (right) SHSM, 218 SHSM, 219 (top) Chicago Daily News Negatives Collection, SDN-002639, Courtesy of the Chicago Historical Society, (bottom) SHSM, 220-221 (all) LOC, 222 LOC, 223 (top) National Archieves, (right) photos.com, 224 Corbis, 225 LOC, 227 Franklin D. Roosevelt Library & Museum, 228 (both) AP, 229 (top) LOC, (bottom) SHSM, 230-231 Hirshhorn Museum and Sculpture Garden, Smithsonian Institution, Gift of Joseph H. Hirshhorn, 1966. Photographer, Lee Stalsworth, 232 MDT. **Chapter Eleven:** 234-234 KC, 236 National Archives, 237 (top) LOC, (bottom) Susan Myers, 238 LOC, 239 LOC, 240 GSPA, 241 AP, 242 LOC, 243 GSPA, 244 (top) The Herald Dispatch, (bottom) GSPA, 245 (both) MDT, 246 MDT. **Chapter Twelve:** 248-248 PhotosToGo.com/Anel Vohra, 251 iStockPhoto.com / Andre Nantel, 252-253 Jon Burton, 255 GSPA, 256 GSPA, 258 MDT, 260-262 Jon Burton. **Chapter Thirteen:** 266-267 KRT Photo Archives/Jerry Naunheim Jr., 268 SS/GeoM, 269 SS/Erik Lam, 270-271 Jon Burton, 272 GSPA, 273 photos.com, 275 SS/David William Taylor, 276 MDT, 277 SS/Ann Rex, 278 (top) KC, (middle) KC, (bottom) Hallmark Cards, Inc., 279 (top) Fitz's Root beer, (bottom) MDT, 281 Sarah Hatch.